Laotse, James Legge and others

The Original Chinese Texts of the Work of Laou-tsze

,the Great Learning, the Doctrine of the Mean

Laotse, James Legge and others

The Original Chinese Texts of the Work of Laou-tsze
, the Great Learning, the Doctrine of the Mean

ISBN/EAN: 9783743660991

Printed in Europe, USA, Canada, Australia, Japan

Cover: Foto ©Lupo / pixelio.de

More available books at **www.hansebooks.com**

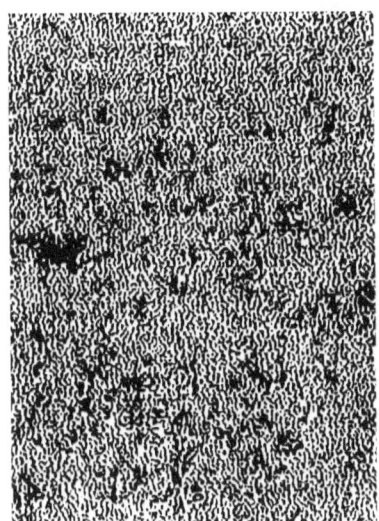

THE LIBRARY
of
VICTORIA UNIVERSITY
Toronto

譯双和英全集編
英和支那古典全集
第三編

雙英
譯和

中　大　老
庸　學　子
　　全

東日本毎社賓
貴族院議員
德富蘇峰先生推獎（廣瀬又二

神學博士
オックスフォード大學教授
ジェームズ、レッグ先生英譯（清水起正）編註

東京神田

一二三子堂書店發行

はしがき

　『三十の輻は一つ轂を共にす、其の無きに當つて車の用あり、埴を埏して以て器を爲る、其の無きに當つて器の用あり、戸牖を鑿つて以て室を爲る、其の無きに當つて室の用あり。故に有るを以て利を爲し、無きを以て用を爲す』（老子第十一章）と無の用を説いて二千年前能く虛無主義の濫觴をなした老子、『國を治むるは赤子を保んずるが如し、心誠に之れを求むれば中らずと雖も遠からず』と云ひ政治と道德の相對性的原理を提唱した大學、『知者は之に過ぎ愚者は及ばず、賢者は之に過ぎ不肖者は及ばず』と理想に馳せず現實に墮せざる中道の至德を高調した中庸、斯の世界的三大文獻に邦語の嚴正無比なる譯文と懇切無二なる註解とを施して猶ほ足れりとせず、更に之れにレッグ博士の英文譯註を對列せしめ、以て現代人が久しく待望して已まさる所を充たさんとするもの、これ卽ち本書である。

　抑も本書の英譯者たるレッグ博士は何人ぞと云へば、博士は實に今を去ること七十餘年の昔一宣教師として香港に來たり、爾後三十餘年の久しきに亙る在職中殆んど寢食を廢して支那語の研究に精進し出來英米人には到底不可解英譯など思ひも寄らずとされたる東洋民族の聖典論語、大學、中庸、孟子、書經、詩經、春秋、老子、莊子等を矢繼ぎ早に譯了し而も之を英譯支

那古典全集と題して任地香港に於いて私費刊行を了せる恐くは空前また絶後の篤學者である。されば博士の支那語の世界最高權威たる名聲は漸く天下に周ねく、英國牛津大學は支那語學の教授として博士を招聘し、佛蘭西學士院は最高賞を贈つて博士の功を永久に宣揚した。想ふに斯かる曠世的大譯文は、常に東洋哲學に關心を持つ、または東洋人固有の思想を認識せんとする歐米人のみならず、英語若くは漢文の研究に努力を惜しまぬ我々日本國民にも一石二鳥的の最良研究書として必讀を値すべきものとして毫も疑を容る可からざるものであらねばならぬ。然るに何故か我が邦に於いては、孔孟の學を國民道德の基調とし英語漢文を準國語の如く尊重するに拘らず、可惜斯の金字塔的文獻のみは日を追ふて益々その眞價を認められつゝありと謂ふを得べき所か、今は却つて或は漸く世上に散佚湮滅せんとするの虞、否その存在をすら全く忘却せられんとするの憾さへ無きにしも非らざる實狀をなしてゐる。さればにや、レツグ博士の英譯漢文叢書とし云へば香港譯者私費刊行版牛津大學復興版いづれも今は三百金を投ずるも尚ほその入手を至難とする文字通り門外不出の稀覯書たらしめて何人も之れを怪まぬ。況んや從來一部好學家の需用を充たしつゝあつた彼の上海商務印書館發行の複寫本華英四書さへ、一昨春勃發の上海事變に際し該書館が我が空軍の爆擊に遇ひ忽ち烏有に歸して、全く絕版の已む

なきに陷りしが如きは世人の全く風馬牛とする所である。此に於いて乎我等は淺學菲才敢てその任に非ざるを顧みるの暇だになく本全集の大衆版化刊行を思ひ立ち、昨春先づ第一卷として論語を發行し、昨秋次いでまた孟子を發行したるに幸にも江湖博雅の驩迎を辱ふし、今更に本書を我等の敬愛惜かざる天下同學諸賢の座右に薦むることを得たるは我等の眞に幸榮とし且つ感謝して已まぬ所である。

昭和八年二月建國紀念の佳日

廣 瀬 又 一
清 水 起 正

內 容 目 次

老 子
THE WORK OF LAO-TSZE

	頁
上編	2— 70
PART I	3— 71
下編	72—162
PART II	73—163

大 學
THE GREAT LEARNING

第一章——第十章 . . . . . . 164—202
CHAPTER I—CHAPTER X . . . . . 165—203

中 庸
THE DOCTRINE OF THE MEAN

第一章——第三十三章 . . . . . 204—278
CHAPTER I—CHAPTER XXXIII . . . 205—279

THE ORIGINAL CHINESE TEXTS

OF

THE WORK OF LAOU=TSZE, THE GREAT LEARNING, THE DOCTRINE OF THE MEAN

WITH

THEIR JAPANESE TRANSLATIONS & NOTES

BY

O. SHIMIZU & M. HIROSE

AND

THEIR ENGLISH TRANSLATIONS & NOTES

BY

JAMES LEGGE, D. D.,

Professor in the Oxford University,
Published in 1861,
At the Author's in Hongkong, China.

老子

（道德經）

上　篇

　　第一章　一　道可道、非常道。名可名、非常名。――道の道とすべきは常の道に非らず。名の名とすべきは常の名に非らず。

　　二　無名天地之始[1]。有名[2]萬物之母。――無名は天地の始にして、有名は萬物の母なり。

　　三　故常無欲[3]以觀其妙[4]。常有欲[5]以觀其徼[6]。――故に常に欲無ければ以て其の妙を觀、常に欲有れば以て其の徼(けう)を觀る。

　　四　此兩者同出而異名[7]。同[8]謂之玄。玄之又玄。衆妙之門。――此の兩者は出を同ふして名を異にす。同じくする之を玄と謂ふ、玄の又玄なるは衆妙の門なり。

　　註　此の第一節は老子がその理想とする眞の道即ち宇宙の大本、自然の原理、萬物の根本は絕對普遍永恒不易のものであつて、我々が此の道又は彼の道と稱する又は名づくる相對界の變化消滅する道ではないと、開卷先づ世人の所謂道を味噌の味噌臭きは眞の味噌に非らずと喝破したもの。
　　1. 無名の道即ち曰く言ひ難き眞の道は天地發生の源泉也。 2. 有名の德即ち無名の道の具體化したもの。手取り早く云へば茲の無名は道、有名は德。 3. 常無欲とは要するに體道者の心境。 4. 道の神秘。

THE WORK OF LÂO=TSZE.
(THE TÂO TEH KING.)

PART I.

CHAPTER I. 1. The Tâo that can be trodden is not the enduring and unchanging Tâo. The name that can be named is not the enduring and unchanging name.

2. *Conceived of as* having no name, it is the Originator of heaven and earth; *conceived of as* having a name, it is the Mother of all things.

3. Always without desire we must be found,
If its deep mystery we would sound;
But if desire always within us be,
Its outer fringe is all that we shall see.

4. Under these two aspects, it is really the same; but as development takes place, it receives the different names. Together we call them the Mystery. Where the Mystery is the deepest is the gate of all that is subtle and wonderful.

體道, 'Embodying the Tâo.' The author sets forth, as well as the difficulty of his subject would allow him, the nature of the Tâo in itself, and its manifestation. To understand the Tâo one must be partaker of its nature.

Par. 3 suggests the words of the apostle John, 'He that loveth not knoweth not God; for God is love.' Both the Tâo, Lâo-ʒze's ideal in the absolute, and its Teh, or operation, are comprehended

5. 常有欲は要するに有徳者のことを云ふ。 6. 道の徼即ち道の外廓、因に云ふ、従来十数種に上る老子の解説書はいづれもレッグ博士と異なり常無欲以観其妙を常無(じやうむ)以て其妙を観んと欲すと訓むである。同様に常有欲以観其徼も常有(じやういう)以て其徼を観んと欲すと訓むである。 7. 道は斯く妙徼両様に現示するもその実は一元なれば、其の進展発達の過程に於いて其の名を異するのみ。 8. 妙徼の自徳介同抱一するを云ふ。因に云ふ、此の一節に於ても本書の英訳者レッグ博士は従来の解説者と大いに其の訓み下し方を異にしてゐる、即ち従来の学者は拊この一節を「此の両者は同じく出でヽ名を異にす。同じく之を玄と謂ふ。玄の又玄。衆妙の門。」と訓むである。

〔老子の特色は支那古典中最も哲理幽玄文体難解の点に在ることは天下周知の事実であるが、全篇中に些末も歴史的記述の無いこと固有名詞を一つも含まぬこと等も亦見逃すべからざる特徴である。〕

第二章　一　天下皆知美之爲美、斯惡已[1]、皆知善之爲善、斯不善已。——天下皆美の美たるを知らば、斯に惡あるのみ。皆善の善たるを知らば、斯に不善あるのみ。

二　故有無相生、難易相成、長短相形、高下相傾、音聲相和、前後相隨。——故に有無相生じ、難易相成り、長短相形はれ、高下相傾き、音聲相和し、前後相隨ふ。

三　是以聖人處無爲之事、行不言之敎[2]。——是を以て聖人は無爲の事に處り、不言の敎を行ふ。

四　萬物作焉而不辭[3]、生而不有[4]、爲而不恃、功成而不居、夫唯不居是以不去[5]。——萬物作りて辭せず、生じて有せず、爲して恃まず、功成りて居らず、夫れ唯居らず是を以て去らず。

註　1. 斯惡已を普通は斯れ惡なるのみと訓むに反し、レッグ博士は上の如く訓み、天地間の事物は凡て相對的にのみ存在する、そして其の價値も單に比較的に定まつてゐるに過ぎぬの意に解してゐる。 2. 世

in this chapter, the latter being the Tâo with the name, the Mother of all things.

CHAPTER II. 1. All in the world know the beauty of the beautiful, and in doing this they have *the idea of* what ugliness is; they all know the skill of the skilful, and in doing this they have *the idea of* what the want of skill is.

2. So it is that existence and non-existence give birth the one to *the idea of* the other; that difficulty and ease produce the one *the idea of* the other; that length and shortness fashion out the one the figure of the other; that *the idea of* height and lowness arise from the contrast of the one with the other; that the musical notes and tones become harmonious through the relation of one with another; and that being before and behind give the idea of one following another.

3. Therefore the sage manages affairs without doing anything, and conveys his instructions without the use of speech.

4. All things spring up, and there is not one which declines to show itself; they grow, and there is no claim made for their ownership; they go through their processes, and there is no expectation *of a reward for the results.* The work is accomplished, and there is no resting in it *as an achievement.*

The work is done, but how no one can see;
'Tis this that makes the power not cease to be.

養身, 'The Nourishment of the Person.' But many of Ho-shang Kung's titles are more appropriate than this.

The chapter starts with instances of the antinomies, which

の眞善美なるものはより眞善美ならぬものより見てこそ左樣であるが、より眞善美なるものから見れば僞惡醜である、それ故聖人は絶對的の立場に在つて無爲の事を行ひ不言の敎を說く。 3. 道は萬物を發生せしめて然するを辭せしめぬ。 4. 生育の後も我が有とはせぬ。 5. 道はその功德を自己のものとして威張らないからその功德は却つて永く道に附隨して去らぬ。

第三章 一　不尙賢[1]、使民不爭、不貴難得之貨、使民不爲盜、不見可欲[2]、使心不亂。――賢を尙（たつと）ばされば民をして爭はさらしむ。得難きの貨（たから）を貴ばされば民をして盜むことを爲さゞらしむ。欲す可きを見（あらは）さゞれば心をして亂れさらしむ。

二　是以聖人之治、虛其心[3]、實其腹、弱其志、强其骨。――是を以て聖人の治むるや、其の心を虛（むなし）ふし、其の腹を實（み）たし、其の志を弱ふし、其の骨を强ふす。

三　常使[4]民無知無欲、使夫知者不敢爲也、爲無爲則無不治。――常に民をして知無く欲無からしむ。夫（か）の知者をして敢て爲さゞらしむ。無爲を爲せば治まらずといふことなし。

註　1. 賢人を尊重しなければ人民は賢を競ふて相爭ふやうなことはない。賢にほこらずんばと訓むが在來の訓み方。　2. 要するに人民の欲する所を現はさなければ人民は心を亂さぬ。欲す可きを顯みずんばと訓むが在來の訓み方。　3. 民の心。　4. 使の主語は聖人。

suggest to the mind each of them the existence of its corresponding opposite; and the author finds in them an analogy to the 'contraries' which characterize the operation of the Tâo, as stated in chapter 40. He then proceeds to describe the action of the sage in par. 3 as in accordance with this law of contraries; and, in par. 4, that of heaven and earth, or what we may call nature, in the processes of the vegetable world.

Par. 2 should be rhymed, but I could not succeed to my satisfaction in the endeavour to rhyme it. Every one who can read Chinese will see that the first four members rhyme. The last two rhyme also, the concluding 盈 being pronounced so;—see the Khang-hsî dictionary in voc.

CHAPTER III. 1. Not to value and employ men of superior ability is the way to keep the people from rivalry among themselves; not to prize articles which are difficult to procure is the way to keep them from becoming thieves; not to show them what is likely to excite their desires is the way to keep their minds from disorder.

2. Therefore the sage, in the exercise of his government, empties their minds, fills their bellies, weakens their wills, and strengthens their bones.

3. He constantly *tries to* keep them without knowledge and without desire, and where there are those who have knowledge, to keep them from presuming to act *on it*. When there is this abstinence from action, good order is universal.

安民, 'Keeping the People at Rest.' The object of the chapter is to show that government according to the Tâo is unfavourable to the spread of knowledge among the people, and would keep them rather in the state of primitive simplicity and ignorance, thereby securing their restfulness and universal good order. Such is the uniform teaching of Lâo-ȝze and his great follower Kwang-ȝze, and of all Tâoist writers.

第四章　一　道冲、而用之或不盈[1]、淵乎[2]似萬物之宗[3]。──道は冲にして之を用ひ或は盈たさず、淵として萬物の宗に似たれり。

二　挫其銳[4]、解其紛、和其光、同其塵[5]。湛兮似若存[6]。──其の銳きを挫き、其の紛たるを解き、其の光を和げ、其塵を同ふせよ。湛として存するが若きに似たれり。

三　吾不知誰之子、象帝之先[7]。──吾誰が子たるを知らず、帝の先に象たり。

註　1. 之を用ひるに盈たさず、況んや溢れしむるをや、これ道の用法也。　2. 深くして測り知る可からざる貌。　3. 宗家、元祖。　4. 我々は宜しく我々の圭角を斂むべしの意。　5. 我々は宜しく他人と昏冥を一にすべしの意。　6. それ道は猶ほ谿間の湛水の如くうらゝかに澄みて清く長へに存するに似たりの意。　7. 此の一節は道は誰の子たるか、神より先にありたるらしの意。

第五章　一　天地不仁、以萬物爲芻狗[1]、聖人不仁、以百姓爲芻狗。──天地は仁ならず、萬物を以て芻狗と爲す、聖人は仁ならず、百姓を以て芻狗と爲す。

二　天地之間、其猶橐籥[1]乎、虛而不屈、動而愈出[2]。多言數窮、不如守中[3]。──天地の間は其れ猶ほ橐籥（ふいご）のごとき乎、虛にして屈せず、動いて愈々出づ。多く言へば數々窮まる、中を守るに如かず。

註　1. 天萬物を生じ地之を養ふも萬物に對して何等恩仇の行も仁不

CHAPTER IV. 1. The Tâo is *like* the emptiness of a vessel; and in our employment of it we must be on our guard against all fulness. How deep and unfathomable it is, as if it were the Honoured Ancestor of all things!

2. We should blunt our sharp points, and unravel the complications of things; we should attemper our brightness, and bring ourselves into agreement with the obscurity of others. How pure and still the Tâo is, as if it would ever so continue!

3. I do not know whose son it is. It might appear to have been before God.

無源, 'The Fountainless.' There is nothing before the Tâo; it might seem to have been before God. And yet there is no demonstration by it of its presence and operation. It is like the emptiness of a vessel. The second character = 沖 = 盅; — see Khang-hsî on the latter. The practical lesson is, that in following the Tâo we must try to be like it.

CHAPTER V. 1. Heaven and earth do not act from *the impulse of* any wish to be benevolent; they deal with all things as the dogs of grass are dealt with. The sages do not act from *any wish to be* benevolent; they deal with the people as the dogs of grass are dealt with.

2. May not the space between heaven and earth be compared to a bellows?

'Tis emptied, yet it loses not its power;
'Tis moved again, and sends forth air the more.
Much speech to swift exhaustion lead we see;
Your inner being guard, and keep it free.

虛用, 'The Use of Emptiness.' Quiet and unceasing is the

仁の念もない、萬物を觀ること芻狗の如しである。 芻狗は草を以て狗に形どり犠牲に代用するものなれども祭畢れば人之を恣樂して顧みぬ。 2. 宇宙は譬へばふいどのやうなものでその本體を求むれば空虛靜寂無きが如くであるが、その作用は愈よ動いて愈よ出でこれを盡さんとして盡すことが出來ぬ活動振りを續けてゐる。 3. 我々の心の中をいふ。

第六章　谷神[1]不死、是謂玄牝[2]、玄牝之門、是謂天地根、綿綿若存、用之不勤[3]。——谷神は死せず、是を玄牝(げんぴ)と謂ふ。玄牝の門、是を天地の根と謂ふ、綿綿として存する若(ごと)し、之を用ひて勤(いたは)らず。

註　1. 谷神は第一章第二節の萬物の母たる有名の道即ち德と同一物を喩へたる名（谷は空虛靜寂ゆへ不滅の表徵）。 2. 萬物を無限に産み出す神秘的なものゝ意。 3. 綿綿若存用之不勤は徐ろに用ひ勞役せしめぬ故天地の根即ち德は永久に存續すべしの意。 因に云ふ此の一章は全部押韻譯文亦然り。

operation of the Tâo, and effective is the rule of the sage in accordance with it.

The grass-dogs in par. 1 were made of straw tied up in the shape of dogs, and used in praying for rain; and afterwards, when the sacrifice was over, were thrown aside and left uncared for. Heaven and earth and the sages dealt so with all things and with the people; but the illustration does not seem a happy one. Both *K*wang-ǵze and Hwâinan mention the grass-dogs. See especially the former, XIV, 25 a, b. In that Book there is fully developed the meaning of this chapter. The illustration in par. 2 is better. The Chinese bellows is different to look at from ours, but the principle is the same in the construction of both. The par. concludes in a way that lends some countenance to the later Tâoism's dealing with the breath.

CHAPTER VI. The valley spirit dies not, aye the same;
The female mystery thus do we name.
Its gate, from which at first they issued forth,
Is called the root from which grew heaven and earth.
Long and unbroken does its power remain,
Used gently, and without the touch of pain.

成象, 'The Completion of Material Forms.' This title rightly expresses the import of this enigmatical chapter; but there is a foundation laid in it for the development of the later Tâoism, which occupies itself with the prolongation of life by the management of the breath (氣) or vital force.

'The valley' is used metaphorically as a symbol of 'emptiness' or 'vacancy;' and 'the spirit of the valley' is the something invisible, yet almost personal, belonging to the Tâo, which constitutes the Teh (德) in the name of our *K*ing. 'The spirit of the valley' has come to be a name for the activity of the Tâo in all the realm of its operation. 'The female mystery' is the Tâo with a name of chapter 1, which is 'the Mother of all things.' All living beings have a father and mother. The pro-

第七章　一　天地長久、天地所以能長且久者、以其不自生[1]、故能長生。――天は長く地は久し、天地の能く長く且つ久しき所以のものは其の自ら生きざるを以てなり、故に能く長生す。

二　是以聖人後其身而身先[2]、外其身而身存[3]、非以無私邪、故能成其私[4]。――是を以て聖人は其の身を後にして身先だつ、其の身を外にして身存す。私無きを以てに非ずや、故に能く其の私を成すは。

註　1. 天地は人間のやうに自己の生存のために私意私慾を逞ふし齷々として自ら生を僞ふことをしないからであるの意。　2. 後其身而身先とはその身を人の爲に後にする故人に推されて人の上に立つ意。　3. 外其身而身存とは我身を視ること他人の如く餘所々々しき故却つてその身を全ふするの意。　4. 成其私とは自分の目的を成就するを云ふ。

第八章　一　上善[1]若水、水善利萬物而不爭、處衆人所惡[2]、故幾於道矣。――上善は水の若し。水は善く萬物を利して爭はず、衆人の惡む所に處る、故に道に幾し。

二　居善地[3]、心善淵[4]、與善仁[5]、言善信、政善治、事善能、動善時。――居の善は地なり、心の善は淵なり、與みすること

cesses of generation and production can hardly be imaged by us but by a recognition of this fact; and so Lâo-3ze thought of the existing realm of nature—of life—as coming through an evolution *not a creation* from the primal air or breath, dividing into two, and thence appearing in the forms of things, material and immaterial. The chapter is found in Lieh-3ze (I, 1 b) quoted by him from a book of Hwang-Tî; and here Lâo-3ze has appropriated it, and made it his own.

CHAPTER VII. 1. Heaven is long-enduring and earth continues long. The reason why heaven and earth are able to endure and continue thus long is because they do not live of, or for, themselves. This is how they are able to continue and endure.

2. Therefore the sage puts his own person last, and yet it is found in the foremost place; he treats his person as if it were foreign to him, and yet that person is preserved. Is it not because he has no personal and private ends, that therefore such ends are realised?

韜光, 'Sheathing the Light.' The chapter teaches that one's best good is realised by not thinikng of it, or seeking for it. Heaven and earth afford a pattern to the sage, and the sage affords a pattern to all men.

CHAPTER VIII. 1. The highest excellence is like *that of* water. The excellence of water appears in its benefiting all things, and in its occupying, without striving *to the contrary,* the low place which all men dislike. Hence *its way* is near to *that of* the Tâo.

2. The excellence of a residence is in *the suitability of* the place; that of the mind is in abysmal

の善は仁なり、言の善は信なり、政の善は治なり、事の善は能なり、動の善は時なり。

三　夫惟不爭[6]、故無尤矣。――夫れ惟だ爭はず、故に尤(とが)無し。

註　1. 絕對の善又は惡はないが强いて之を臨別しその上善なるもの。2. ＝下位。3. 居の善は安住の地に悠々自適することであるの意。4. 心の善は虛靜淵默である。5. 與の善は仁者と與に在ること。6. 自然に從つて爭はぬ意。

第九章　一　持而盈之不如其已[1]、揣而銳之[2]不可長保。――持つて之を盈(み)たすは其の已むに如かず、揣(た)でて之を銳(するど)くするは長保つ可からず。

二　金玉滿堂莫之能守、富貴而驕自遺其咎[3]。功成名遂身退天之道。――金玉堂に滿つれば之を能く守ること莫く、富貴にして驕(おご)れば自ら其の咎(とが)を遺(のこ)す。功成り名遂げて身退くは天の道なり。

註　1. 水を一杯盛つた器を手に持つて盜す心配をする位なら初から手に持たぬが增し。持而盈之は盈而持之を倒にしたもので、彼の枕流漱石が枕石漱流即ち石に枕し流に口そゝぐの倒なると同じく、古文に往々見る所謂倒語法又は錯綜法の一例。2. 揣而銳之も同巧異曲。因に云ふ、漢籍國字解は揣の字ををさむと訓む。3. 所謂驕る平家は久しからず、實家と今樣で書く三代目等の類。

stillness; that of associations is in their being with the virtuous; that of government is in its securing good order; that of *the conduct of* affairs is in its ability; and that of *the initiation of* any movement is in its timeliness.

3. And when *one with the highest excellence* does not wrangle *about his low position,* no one finds fault with him.

易性, 'The Placid and Contented Nature.' Water, as an illustration of the way of the Tâo, is repeatedly employed by Lâo-3ze.

The various forms of what is excellent in par. 2 are brought forward to set forth the more, by contrast, the excellence of the humility indicated in the acceptance of the lower place without striving to the contrary.

CHAPTER IX.

1. It is better to leave a vessel unfilled, than to attempt to carry it when it is full. If you keep feeling a point that has been sharpened, the point cannot long preserve its sharpness.

2. When gold and jade fill the hall, their possessor cannot keep them safe. When wealth and honours lead to arrogancy, this brings its evil on itself. When the work is done, and one's name is becoming distinguished, to withdraw into obscurity is the way of Heaven.

運夷; but I cannot give a satisfactory rendering of this title. The teaching of the chapter is, that fulness and complacency in success are contrary to the Tâo.

The first clauses of the two sentences in par. 1, 持而盈之, 揣而銳之=盈而持之, 銳而揣之, are instances of the 'inverted' style not uncommon in the oldest composition. 'The way of Heaven' ='the Heavenly Tâo' exemplified by man.

老子上篇

第十章　一　載￼¹營魄抱一能無離乎。專氣致柔能如嬰兒乎。滌除玄覽能無疵乎。――營魄を載せ抱一せば能く離るゝこと無からん。氣を專らにし柔を致せば能く嬰兒の如くならん。玄覽を滌除せば能く疵無からん。

二　愛民治國、能無爲乎。天門開闔、能無雌乎。明白四達、能無知乎²。――民を愛し國を治めて、能く無爲ならん乎。天門を開闔して、能く雌たる無からん乎。明白四に達して、能く知る無からん乎。

三　生之畜之³、生而不有⁴、爲而不恃、長而不宰。是謂玄德。――之を生み之を畜ひ、生じて有せず、爲して恃まず、長めて宰らず。是を玄德と謂ふ。

註　1. 魂と魄とを一緒に抱きかゝへてゐれば離れ離れにならぬだらう。滿腔の氣を傾け全身を柔弱にしてゐれば嬰兒のやうになるだらう。心の幻像を洗ひ去つたら心は淸淨無垢になるだらう。營＝魂＝神明の官。魄＝耳目の官。氣＝血氣。玄覽＝心眼に映つる奇々怪々な幻像。　2. 無爲にして民を愛し國を治むることは出來まいか。牝鷺のやうに謙讓謙退で鼻息荒く振舞ふことは出來まいか。無智蒙昧の如く見えて直感智を天下四方に達せしむることは出來まいか。天門＝鼻孔。闔＝閉。明白＝聰明。　3. 道は萬物を生み萬物をやしなふ。　4. 生育しても我物にしない。

CHAPTER X. 1. When the intelligent and animal souls are held together in one embrace, they can be kept from separating. When one gives undivided attention to the *vital* breath, and brings it to the utmost degree of pliancy, he can become as a *tender* babe. When he has cleansed away the most mysterious sights *of his imagination*, he can become without a flaw.

2. In loving the people and ruling the state, cannot he proceed without any *purpose of* action? In the opening and shutting of his gates of heaven, cannot he do so as a female bird? While his intelligence reaches in every direction, cannot he *appear to* be without knowledge?

3. *The Tâo* produces *all things* and nourishes them; it produces them and does not claim them as its own; it does all, and yet does not boast of it; it presides over all, and yet does not control them. This is what is called 'The mysterious Quality' *of the Tâo*.

能氐. 'Possibilities.' This chapter is one of the most difficult to understand and translate in the whole work. Even Kû Hsî was not able to explain the first member satisfactorily. The text of that member seems well supported; but I am persuaded the first clause of it is somehow corrupt.

The whole seems to tell what can be accomplished by one who is possessed of the Tâo. In par. 3 he appears free from all self-consciousness in what he does, and of all self-satisfaction in the results of his doing. The other two paragraphs seem to speak of what he can do under the guidance of the Tâo for himself and for others. He can by his management of his vital breath bring his body to the state of Tâoistic perfection, and

第十一章 三十輻¹共一轂²、當其無³有車之用、埏⁴埴以爲器、當其無⁶有器之用、鑿戸牖⁵以爲室、當其無⁶有室之用、故有之以爲利無之以爲用⁷。──三十の輻は一つ轂を共にし、其の無きに當つて車の用あり、埴を埏して以て器を爲る、其の無きに當つて器の用あり、戸牖を鑿つて以て室を爲り、其の無きに當つて室の用あり。故に之れ有るは以て利を爲し之れ無きは以て用を爲す。

註 1. 車の矢。 2. 車の矢の集る所。 3. 心棒の通る空虛。 4. でつちこねる。 5. 戸と窓に同じ。 6. 室の中虛なる所。某書には壁の空虛なる窓に解してある。 7. この處を普通は故に有の利を爲すは無の用を爲せばなりと訓む。

第十二章 一 五色¹令人目盲²、五音³令人耳聾、五味⁴令人口爽、馳騁田獵⁵令人心發狂、難得之貨令人行妨⁶。──五色は人をして目を盲せしめ、五音は人をして耳を聾せしめ、五味は人をして口を爽れしめ、馳騁田獵は人をして心に狂を發せしめ、得難きの貨は人をして行ひを妨げしむ。

二 是以聖人爲腹⁷不爲目⁸、故去彼⁹取此¹⁰。──是を以て聖人は腹を爲して目を爲さず、故に彼を去つて此を取る。

keep his intelligent and animal souls from being separated, and he can rule men without purpose and effort. 'The gates of heaven' in par. 2 is a Tâoistic phrase for the nostrils as the organ of the breath;—see the commentary of Ho-shang Kung.

CHAPTER XI. The thirty spokes unite in the one nave; but it is on the empty space *for the axle*, that the use of the wheel depends. Clay is fashioned into vessels; but it is on their empty hollowness, that their use depends. The door and windows are cut out *from the walls* to form an apartment; but it is on the empty space *within*, that its use depends. Therefore, what has a *positive* existence serves for profitable adaptation, and what has not that for *actual* usefulness.

無用, 'The Use of what has no Substantive Existence.' The three illustratinos serve to set forth the freedom of the Tâo from all pre-occupation and purpose, and the use of what seems useless.

CHAPTER XII. 1. Colour's five hues from th' eyes their sight will take;
Music's five notes the ears as deaf can make;
The flavours five deprive the mouth of taste;
The chariot course, and the wild hunting waste
Make mad the mind; and objects rare and strange,
Sought for, men's conduct will to evil change.
2. Therefore the sage seeks to satisfy *the craving of* the belly, and not the *insatiable longing of the* eyes. He puts from him the latter, and prefers to seek the former.

檢欲, 'The Repression of the Desires.' Government in accordance

註　1. ＝青赤白黑黃。2. 盲目とせざりしは押韻のため、以下同斷。3. ＝宮商角徵羽（宮は土、商は金、角は木、徵は火、羽は水の聲）。4. ＝鹹酸甘苦辛。　5. 馬を馳せ車を騎つて禽を田（か）り獸を獵る遊樂。6. 德行を妨げる。　7. 腹慾を滿たせば自己を修養する。　8. 目慾を滿たせば自己の奴隸となる。　9. ＝目。　10. ＝腹。

第十三章　一　寵辱若驚¹、貴大患若身²。――寵と辱とは驚くが若くし、貴と大患とは身の若くす。

二　何謂寵辱、辱爲下³、得之若驚、失之若驚⁴。何謂貴大患若身、吾所以有大患者爲吾有身、及吾無身、吾有何患――何をか寵と辱と謂ふ、辱は下を爲す。之を得るも驚くが若く、之を失ふも驚くが若し。何をか貴と大患とは身の若くすと謂ふ。吾に大患有る所以は吾に身有るが爲めなり。吾身無きに及ばゞ、吾何の患か有らん。

三　故貴以身爲天下則可寄⁵於天下、愛以身爲天下乃可以託⁶於天下。――故に貴ぶに身を以て天下を爲むるときは則ち天下

with the Tâo seeks to withdraw men from the attractions of what is external and pleasant to the senses and imagination, and to maintain the primitive simplicity of men's ways and manners. Compare chapter 2. The five colours are Black, Red, Green or Blue, White, and Yellow; the five notes are those of the imperfect Chinese musical scale, our G. A, B, D, E; the five tastes are Salt, Bitter, Sour, Acrid, and Sweet.

I am not sure that Wang Pî has caught exactly the author's idea in the contrast between satisfying the belly and satisfying the eyes; but what he says is ingenious: 'In satisfying the belly one nourishes himself; in gratifying the eyes he makes a a slave of himself.'

CHAPTER XIII. 1. Favour and disgrace would seem equally to be feared; honour and great calamity, to be regarded as personal conditions *of the same kind.*

2. What is meant by speaking thus of favour and disgrace? Disgrace is being in a low position *after the enjoyment of favour.* The getting that *favour* leads to the apprehension *of losing it,* and the losing it leads to the fear of *still greater calamity* :—this is what is meant by saying that favour and disgrace would seem equally to be feared.

And what is meant by saying that honour and great calamity are to be *similarly* regarded as personal conditions? What makes me liable to great calamity is my having the body *which I call myself*; if I had not the body, what great calamity could come to me?

3. Therefore he who would administer the kingdom, honouring it as he honours his own person, may be employed to govern it, and he who would

に寄る可し、愛するに身を以て天下を爲るときは乃ち以て天下に託す可し。

註 1. 俗人は辱められる時にのみ驚くが達人は寵辱孰れの場合にも驚くが如し。 2. 達人には貴賤即ち榮達も大患も同じく一身上の大事件の如し。 3. 得寵の境遇より失寵の境遇に下るをいふ。 4. 寵を得ては之を失はんことを怖れて驚き、之を失つては更に大なる辱を受けんことを怖れて驚く。 5. 寄らると同義。 6. 託されると同義。 本節は前節の寵（＝愛）と貴に關する問の答辯である。

第十四章 一 視之不見、名曰夷。聽之不聞、名曰希。搏之不得、名曰微。此三者不可致詰、故混而爲一[1]。――之を視れども見ず、名けて夷と曰ふ。之を聽けども聞かず、名けて希と曰ふ。之を搏(と)れども得ず、名けて微と曰ふ。此の三者は致(きは)め詰(なじ)む可からず、故に混じて一と爲す。

二 其上[2]不皦、其下[3]不昧、繩繩兮[4]不可名、復歸於無物、是謂無狀[5]之狀無象[6]之象、是謂恍惚。――其の上にして明(あきら)かならず、其の下にして昧(くら)からず。繩繩として名づく可からず、無物に復歸す。是を無狀の狀無象の象と謂ふ。是を恍惚と謂ふ。

三 迎之不見其首[7]、隨之不見其後。執古之道以御今之有、能

administer it with the love which he bears to his own person may be entrusted with it.

厭恥, 'Loathing Shame.' The chapter is difficult to construe, and some disciples of Kû Hsî had to ask him to explain it as in the case of chapter 10. His remarks on it are not to my mind satisfactory. Its object seems to be to show that the cultivation of the person according to the Tâo, is the best qualification for the highest offices, even for the government of the world. Par. 3 is found in *K*wang-ჳze (XI, 18 b) in a connexion which suggests this view of the chapter. It may be observed, however, that in him the position of the verbal characters in the two clauses of the paragraph is the reverse of that in the text of Hoshang Kung, so that we can hardly accept the distinction of meaning of the two characters given in his commentary, but must take them as synonyms. Professor Gabelentz gives the following version of *K*wang-ჳze: 'Darum, gebraucht er seine Person achtsam in der Verwaltung des Reiches, so mag man ihm die Reichsgewalt anvertrauen; ... liebend (schonend) ... übertragen.'

CHAPTER XIV. 1. We look at it, and we do not see it, and we name it 'the Equable.' We listen to it, and we do not hear it, and we name it 'the Inaudible.' We try to grasp it, and do not get hold of it, and we name it 'the Subtle.' With these three qualities, it cannot be made the subject of description; and hence we blend them together and obtain The One.

2. Its upper part is not bright, and its lower part is not obscure. Ceaseless in its action, it yet cannot be named, and then it again returns and becomes nothing. This is called the Form of the Formless, and the Semblance of the Invisible; this is called the Fleeting and Indeterminable.

3. We meet it and do not see its Front; we

知古始、是謂道紀[8]。――之を迎へて其の首を見ず、之に隨つて其の後を見ず。古の道を執つて以て今の有を御し能く古の始を知る、是を道紀と謂ふ。

註　1. 道は到底五官の作用では致詰することの出來ぬ、別言すれば認識することの不可能な存在であるから之を所謂夷希微三者を打つて一丸としたものだと形容した。　2. 仰いで見るをいふ。　3. 俯してうかぶふをいふ。　4. 活動の古今に亙つてかはらぬ貌。　5. 目に見え手に取れる形。　6. 目には見えるが手に取れぬ形。　7. ＝前面。　8. 古の道を體得し今の萬有を統御し道は今も猶昔ながらの道として萬有界を支配し毫もその始と異らぬことを知る、これを道紀即ち道を解くといふ。

第十五章　一　古之善爲士[1]者微妙玄通、深不可識。夫惟不可識、故强爲之容[2]。――古の善く士たる者は微妙玄通、深くして識る可からず。夫れ惟だ識る可からず、故に强いて之が容を爲す。

二　豫兮若冬涉川[3]、猶兮若畏四鄰[4]、儼若客[5]、渙若氷將釋[6]、敦兮其若樸[7]、曠兮其若谷[8]、渾兮其若濁[9]。――豫として冬川を

follow it, and do not see its Back. When we can lay hold of the Tâo of old to direct the things of the present day, and are able to know it as it was of old in the beginning, this is called *unwinding* the clue of Tâo.

妙玄, 'The Manifestation of the Mystery.' The subject of par. 1 is the Tâo, but the Tâo in its operation, and not the primal conception of it, as entirely distinct from things, which rises before the mind in the second paragraph. The Chinese characters which I have translated ' the Equable,' ' the Inaudible,' and ' the Subtle,' are now pronounced Î, Hî, and Wei, and in 1823 Rémusat fancied that they were intended to give the Hebrew tetragrammaton which he thought had come to Lâo-ȝze somehow from the West, or been found by him there. It was a mere fancy or dream ; and still more so is the recent attempt to revive the notion by Victor von Strauss in 1870, and Dr. Edkins in 1884 The idea of the latter is specially strange, maintaining, as he does, that we should read the characters according to their old sounds. Lâo-ȝze has not in the chapter a personal Being before his mind, but the procedure of his mysterious Tâo, the course according to which the visible phenomena in the universe take place, incognisable by human sense and capable of only approximate description by terms appropriate to what is within the domain of sense.

CHAPTER XV. 1. The skilful masters *of the Tâo* in old times, with a subtle and exquisite penetration, comprehended its mysteries, and were deep *also* so as to elude men's knowledge. As they were thus beyond men's knowledge, I will make an effort to describe of what sort they appeared to be.

2. Shrinking looked they like those who wade through a stream in winter; irresolute like those

渉るが若く、猶として四鄰を畏るゝが若く、儼として客の若く、渙として氷の將に釋けんとするが若く、敦として其れ樸の若く、曠として其れ谷の若く、渾として其れ濁れるが若し。

三　孰能濁、以靜之¹⁰徐清、孰能安、以久之¹¹徐生¹²。——孰か能く濁をきよめん、以て之を靜にせば徐ろに清まらん。孰か能く安んぜん、以て之を久ふせば徐ろに生ぜん。

四　保此道者不欲盈、夫惟不盈、是以能敝不新成。——此の道を保つ者は盈つることを欲せず、夫れ惟だ盈ちず、是を以て能く敝ぶれ新ならずして成る。

註　1. ＝得道の士。　2. 無謀な試みだが強いて之を形容して見るの意。　3. 殷冬川を渉るに躊躇する如し。　4. 四鄰を畏れて進退遲疑猶豫する如し。　5. 客として他家へ行き堅くなつて挫へる如し。　6. 打寬いで氷水の將にとけんとする如し。　7. 質實なること山から切り出したての材木の如し。　8. 内を虚にして容れざるなく應ぜざるなき谷の如し。9. 世の衆愚俗惡と混つて擇ぶなき濁るが如し。　10. 滔々として流るゝ濁水。　11. 滔々として流れて久しきに耳らしむ。　12. 安靜生ぜん。

第十六章　一　致虛極、守靜篤¹。萬物竝²作吾以觀其復³。夫物芸芸⁴各歸其根。歸根曰靜。靜曰復命⁵。——虛を致すことは極

who are afraid of all around them; grave like a guest *in awe of his host*; evanescent like ice that is melting away; unpretentious like wood that has not been fashioned into anything; vacant like a valley, and dull like muddy water.

3. Who can *make* the muddy water *clear*? Let it be still, and it will gradually become clear. Who can secure the condition of rest? Let movement go on, and the condition of rest will gradually arise.

4. They who preserve this method of the Tâo do not wish to be full *of themselves*. It is through their not being full of themselves that they can afford to seem worn and not appear new and complete.

顯德, 'The Exhibition of the Quality,' that is, of the Tâo, which has been set forth in the preceding chapter. Its practical outcome is here described in the masters of it of old, who in their own weakness were yet strong in it, and in their humility were mighty to be co-workers with it for the good of the world.

The variety of the readings in par. 4 is considerable, but not so as to affect the meaning. This par. is found in Hwâinan (XII, 23 a) with an unimportant variation. From the illustration to which it is subjoined he understood the fulness, evidently as in chapter 9, as being that of a vessel filled to overflowing. Both here and there such fulness is used metaphorically of a man overfull of himself; and then Lâo-ʒze slides into another metaphor, that of a worn-out garment. The text of par. 3 has been variously tampered with. I omit the 久 of the current copies, after the example of the editors of the great recension of the Yung-lo period (A. D. 1403—1424) of the Ming dynasty.

CHAPTER XVI. 1. The *state of* vacancy should be brought to the utmost degree, and

めよ、靜を守ることは篤かれ。萬物並び作り吾以て其の復るを觀る。夫れ物は芸芸(うんうん)として各々其の根に歸す。根に歸するを靜と曰ふ。靜を復命と曰ふ。

二　復命曰常[6]、知常曰明[7]。不知常妄作[8]凶。知常容[9]。容乃公[10]。公乃王[11]。王乃天。天乃道。道[12]乃久、沒身不殆、──復命を常と曰ひ、常を知るを明と曰ふ。常を知らざれば妄作りて凶なり。常を知れば容る。容れゝば乃ち公なり。公なれば乃ち王なり。王は乃ち天なり。天は乃ち道なり。道は乃ち久しく、身を沒ふるまで殆(あやふ)からず。

註　1. 極めて心を虚にし固く心の靜を守れ。　2. 等しくの意。　3. 本源に歸へる。　4. 萬物の盛んに成長する貌を形容する語。　5. 使命を果せることを報ずること。　6. 復命は萬物不易の常則。　7. 常則を知るは明智。　8. ＝起。　9. ＝寛容。　10. 萬物に胸襟を公開すること。　11. 王者の性格。　12. 道を體する人、得道の人。

that of stillness guarded with unwearying vigour. All things alike go through their processes of activity, and *then* we see them return *to their original state*. When things *in the vegetable world* have displayed their luxuriant growth, we see each of them return to its root. This returning to their root is what we call the state of stillness; and that stillness may be called a reporting that they have fulfilled their appointed end.

2. The report of that fulfilment is the regular, unchanging rule. To know that unchanging rule is to be intelligent; not to know it leads to wild movements and evil issues. The knowledge of that unchanging rule produces a *grand* capacity and forbearance, and that capacity and forbearance lead to a community *of feeling with all things*. From this community of feeling comes a kingliness of character; and he who is king-like goes on to be heaven-like. In that likeness to heaven he possesses the Tâo. Possessed of the Tâo, he endures long; and to the end of his bodily life, is exempt from all danger of decay.

歸根, 'Returning to the Root.' The chapter exhibits the operation of the Tâo in nature, in man, and in government; an operation silent, but all-powerful; unaccompanied with any demonstration of its presence, but great in its results.

An officer receives a charge or commission from his superior (受命); when he reports the execution of it he is said 復命. So all animate things, including men, receive their charge from the Tâo as to their life, and when they have fulfilled it they are represented as reporting that fulfilment; and the fulfilment and

第十七章 一　太上¹不知有之²、其次親之³譽之、其次畏之⁴、其次侮之⁵。故信不足焉有不信。——太上は之れ有るを知らず。其の次ぎは之に親み之を譽む。其の次ぎは之を畏る。其の次ぎは之を侮る。故に信足らざれば不信有り。

二　猶分其貴言、功成事遂⁶、百姓皆曰我自然⁷。——猶として其れ言を貴び、功成り事遂げて、百姓皆曰ふ、我自ら然りと。

註　1. ＝大昔。 2. 民國君有るを知らず。或は不を下と見て民國君有るを知る(のみにしてその政の良否を知らず無意識的に太平を享樂する)と訓む、兩者同巧異曲。 3. 聖王の政。 4. 刑戮を以て治むる政。 5. 兵馬の實權足らず民の侮を招ぐ政。 6. 太上の國君は不言無爲の政を以て國を治む。 7. 無爲而化せる太上の民はその安眠高枕を誰のお蔭でもなく自ら然りと曰ふ。

report are described as their unchanging rule, so that they are the Tâo's impassive instruments, having no will or purpose of their own,—according to Lâo-ȝze's formula of 'doing nothing and yet doing all things (無爲而無不爲).'

The getting to possess the Tâo, or to be an embodiment of it, follows the becoming Heaven or Heaven-like; and this is in accordance with the saying in the fourth chapter that 'the Tâo might seem to have been before God.' But, in Kwang-ȝze especially, we often find the full possessor and displayer of the Tâo spoken of as 'Heaven.' The last sentence, that he who has come to the full possession of the Tâo is exempt from all danger of decay, is generally illustrated by a reference to the utterances in chapter 50; as if Lâo-ȝze did indeed see in the Tâo a preservative against death.

CHAPTER XVII.

1. In the highest antiquity, *the people* did not know that there were *their rulers*. In the next age they loved them and praised them. In the next they feared them; in the next they despised them. Thus it was that when faith *in the Tâo* was deficient *in the rulers* a want of faith in them ensued *in the people.*

2. How irresolute did those *earliest rulers* appear, showing *by their reticence* the importance which they set upon their words! Their work was done and their undertakings were successful, while the people all said, 'We are as we are, of ourselves!'

淳風, 'The Unadulterated Influence.' The influence is that of the Tâo, as seen in the earliest and paradisiacal times. The two chapters that follow are closely connected with this, showing how the silent, passionless influence of the Tâo was gradually and injuriously superseded by 'the wisdom of the world,' in the conduct of government. In the first sentence there is a small various reading of 不 for 下, but it does not affect the meaning

第十八章 一　大道廢有仁義、智慧出有大僞。[1]——大道廢れて仁義有り、智慧出でゝ大僞有り。

二　六親[2]不和有孝慈[3]、國家昏亂有忠臣。——六親和せずして孝慈有り、國家昏亂して忠臣有り。

註　1. 天地自然の大道が行はれなくなつて仁義の說が起つた、人間に智慧が出るやうになつて社會に詐欺奸曲が起つた。　2. ＝父子兄弟夫婦。　3. 孝子慈孫。

第十九章 一　絕聖棄智民利百倍、絕仁棄義民復孝慈、絕巧棄利盜賊無有[1]。——聖を絕ち智を棄つるときは民の利百倍なり、仁を絕ち義を棄つるときは民孝慈に復る、巧を絕ち利を棄るときは盜賊有ること無し。

二　此三者以爲文不足、故令有所屬[2]。見素抱樸少私寡欲。——此の三者は以て文足らずと爲す、故に屬する所有らしむ。見ること素に抱くこと樸ならば私を少ふし欲を寡ふす。

of the passage. The first clause of par. 2 gives some difficulty; 其貴言, 'they made their words valuable or precious,' i.e. 'they seldom spake;' chapter 1 Sam. iii. 1.

CHAPTER XVIII. 1. When the Great Tâo *Way or Method* ceased to be observed, benevolence and righteousness came into vogue. *Then* appeared wisdom and shrewdness, and there ensued great hypocrisy.

2. When harmony no longer prevailed throughout the six kinships, filial sons found their manifestation; when the states and clans fell into disorder, loyal ministers appeared.

俗海, 'The Decay of Manners.' A sequel to the preceding chapter, and showing also how the general decay of manners afforded opportunity for the display of certain virtues by individuals. Observe 'the Great Tâo,' occurring here for the first time as the designation of 'the Tâo.'

CHAPTER XIX. 1. If we could renounce our sageness and discard our wisdom, it would be better for the people a hundredfold. If we could renounce our benevolence and discard our righteousness, the people would again become filial and kindly. If we could renounce our artful contrivance and discard our *scheming for* gain, there would be no thieves nor robbers.

2. Those three methods *of government*
Thought olden ways in elegance did fail
And made these names their want of worth to veil;
But simple views, and courses plain and true
Would selfish ends and many lusts eschew.

註　1.　絶聖棄智絶仁棄義絶巧棄利は莊子の中にも反覆高唱されてゐる。　2.　聖智、仁義、巧利の三者はその價値無きを蔽はんためにその聖智云々の美名を借りた。此の一句の訓み方も從來の解釋書とは同じでない。

第二十章　一　絶學無憂、唯之與阿相去幾何、善之與惡相去何若、人之所畏不可不畏,荒兮其未央哉[1]。──學を絶つときは憂無し。唯と阿と相去る幾何、善と惡と相去る何若。人の畏るゝ所は畏れずんばある可からず。荒として其れ未だ央らず。

二　衆人熙熙如享大牢如春登臺、我獨泊兮其未兆、若嬰兒之未孩、乘乘兮若無所歸、衆人皆有餘、我獨若遺、我愚人之心也哉沌沌兮。──衆人は熙熙として大牢を享るが如く春臺に登るが如し。我獨り泊として其れ未だ兆さず、嬰兒の未だ孩らざるが若く、乘乘として歸する所無きが若し。衆人は皆餘り有り、我獨り遺れたるが若し。我は愚たる人の心なれや沌沌たり。

俗人昭昭、我獨若昏、俗人察察、我獨悶悶、澹兮其若海、飂兮似無所止、衆人皆有以、我獨頑且鄙、我獨異於人、而貴求食於母[3]。──俗人は昭昭たり、我獨り昏きが若し。俗人は察察たり、我獨り悶悶たり、澹として其れ海の若し、飂として止ま

返淳, 'Returning to the Unadulterated Influence.' The chapter desires a return to the simplicity of the Tâo, and shows how superior the result would be to that of Ihe more developed systems of morals and government which had superseded it. It is closely connected with the two chapters that precede. Lâo-ʒze's call for the renunciation of the methods of the sages and rulers in lieu of his fancied paradisiacal state is repeated ad nauseam by Kwang-ʒze.

CHAPTER XX. 1. When we renounce learning we have no troubles.

The *ready* 'yes,' and *flattering* 'yea;'—
Small is the difference they display.
But mark their issues, good and ill;—
What space the gulf between shall fill?
What all men fear is indeed to be feared; but how wide and without end is the range of questions *asking to be discussed*!

2. The multitude of men look satisfied and pleased; as if enjoying a full banquet, as if mounted on a tower in spring. I alone seem listless and still, my desires having as yet given no indication of their presence. I am like an infant which has not yet smiled. I look dejected and forlorn, as if I had no home to go to. The multitude of men all have enough and to spare. I alone seem to have lost everything. My mind is that of a stupid man; I am in a state of chaos.

Ordinary men look bright and intelligent, while I alone seem to be benighted. They look full of discrimination, while I alone am dull and confused. I seem to be carried about as on the sea, drifting

る所無きに似たり。衆人は皆以すること有り、我獨り頑として且鄙し。我獨り人に異なり母(道)に食を求むることを貴ぶ。

註 1. 學問を絕てば心の憂は全く無くなる。即座にはいと答へるのと、阿諛的にへいと答へるのとは答へ方に於いては何程の相違も無からう、しかし好感を與へるのと惡感を催させるのとの其の結果には雲泥の差異が有らうと學者は言ふだらう。勿論人の畏れることは畏れなければならぬが、しかし斯うした學者の攻究を待つ問題は際限なくある。 2. 世間の人は學問に滿足して大盤振舞をうけたやうに、吸日臺に登つたやうに嬉しがつてゐるが、絕對の學に志す自分のみは身も心も靜まりかへつて何等の欲望も兆してゐない、まるでまだ笑ふことの出來ぬ嬰兒のやうである、歸るに家のない人のやうである。衆人は金に有り餘つてゐるやうである、自分のみはすべてを失つたものヽやうである。愚物の心を持つものとは自分のことだらう、沌々として物の分別がつかぬ。熙々は樂しい貌。大牢は大饗應。泊は靜まりかへつた貌。乘々は怏々として樂まぬ貌。 3. 此の一節も俗學の徒と老子の學を修むる士の區別を誇張的に形容したもの。察々は分別心に富む形容。澹兮は淡々たる貌。飂は風のまにまに吹かれゆく貌。求食於母は母(みち)を味ふことを求むとも訓む。

第二十一章 孔德之容、唯道是從。道之爲物、唯恍唯惚。惚兮恍、其中有象。恍兮惚、其中有物。窈兮冥兮、其中有精[1]。其精甚眞、其中有信。自古及今其名不去[2]、以閱[3]衆甫[4]。吾何以知衆甫之然哉、以此[5]。——孔德の容は唯だ道に是れ從ふ。道の物たる唯だ恍唯だ惚。惚たり恍たり、其の中象有り。恍たり惚た

as if I had nowhere to rest. All men have their spheres of action, while I alone seem dull and incapable, like a rude borderer. *Thus* I alone am different from other men, but I value the nursing mother *the Tâo*.

異俗, 'Being Different from Ordinary Men.' The chapter sets forth the difference to external appearance which the pursuit and observance of the Tâo produces between its votaries and others; and Lâo-ʒze speaks in it as himself an example of the former. In the last three chapters he has been advocating the cause of the Tâo against the learning and philosophy of the other school of thinkers in the country. Here he appears as having renounced learning, and found an end to the troubles and anxieties of his own mind; but at the expense of being misconceived and misrepresented by others. Hence the chapter has an autobiographical character.

Having stated the fact following the renunciation of learning, he proceeds to dwell upon the troubles of learning in the rest of par. 1. Until the votary of learning knows everything, he has no rest. But the instances which he adduces of this are not striking nor easily understood. I cannot throw any light on the four lines about the 'yes' and the 'yea.'

Confucius (Ana. XVI, viii) specifies three things of which the superior man stands in awe; and these and others of a similar nature may have been the things which Lâo-ʒze had in his mind. The nursing-mother at the end is, no doubt, the Tâo in operation, 'with a name,' as in chapter 1; 'the mysterious virtue' of chapters 51 and 52.

CHAPTER XXI. The grandest forms of active force
From Tâo come, their only source.
Who can of Tâo the nature tell?
Our sight it flies, our touch as well.
Eluding sight, eluding touch,

り、其の中物有り。窈たり冥たり、其の中精有り。其の精甚だ眞なり、其の中信有り。古より今に及ぶまで其の名は去らず、以て衆甫を閲ぶ。吾何を以て衆甫の然ることを知らんや、此を以てなり。

註　1. 萬物の發生する根本原理たる道は元來は絶對に靜的のものであるが、萬物に發現するに方つては先づ動的に變じなければならぬ。道が斯く動的の狀態に變つた處を孔德と名づけるのであるが、この孔德を充分に形容することは頗る困難で、一言して云へば道に準ずるものといふ外はない。然らば道とは如何なるものかと云はば固より形無く目以て見るべからざるも唯恍惚として捕捉すべからざる中に何等か象有り……の意。　2. 道てふ名は一日も天下を去らず。　3. ＝梳。　4. ＝萬彙＝萬有。　5. 道の斯の性質を指す。

第二十二章　一　曲則全[1]、枉則直[2]、窪則盈[3]、弊則新[4]、少則得、多則惑。――曲るときは則ち全し、枉るときは則ち直し、窪なるときは則ち盈つ、弊るときは則ち新し、少きときは則ち得、多きときは則ち惑ふ。

The forms of things all in it crouch;
Eluding touch, eluding sight,
There are their semblances, all right.
Profound it is, dark and obscure;
Things' essences all there endure.
Those essences the truth enfold
Of what, when seen, shall then be told.
Now it is so; 'twas so of old.
Its name—what passes not away;
So, in their beautiful array,
Things form and never know decay.

How know I that it is so with all the beauties of existing things? By this *nature of the Tâo.*

虛心. 'The Empty Heart.' But I fail to see the applicability of the title. The subject of the chapter is the Tâo in its operation. This is the significance of the 德 in the first clause or line, and to render it by 'virtue,' as Julien and Chalmers do, only serves to hide the meaning. Julien, however, says that 'the virtue', is that of the Tâo; and he is right in taking 從, the last character of the second line, as having the sense of 'from,' 'the source from,' and not, as Chalmers does, in the sense of 'following.'

Lâo-ʒze's mind is occupied with a very difficult subject—to describe the production of material forms by the Tâo; how or from what, he does not say. What I have rendered 'semblances,' Jullen 'les images,' and Chalmers 'forms,' seems, as the latter says, in some way to correspond to the 'Eternal Ideas' of Plato in the Divine Mind. But Lâo-ʒze had no idea of 'personality' in the Tâo.

CHAPTER XXII. 1. The partial becomes complete; the crooked, straight; the empty, full; the worn out, new. He whose *desires* are few gets them; he whose *desires* are many goes astray.

二　是以聖人抱一⁵爲天下式、不自見故明、不自是故彰、不自伐故有功、不自矜故長、夫唯不爭故天下莫能與之爭。——是を以て聖人は一を抱いて天下の式と爲り、自ら見(あらは)れず故に明なり、自ら是とせず故に彰はる、自ら伐らず故に功有り、自ら矜らず故に長たり。夫れ唯だ爭はず故に天下能く之と爭ふこと莫し。

三　古之所謂曲則全者豈虛言哉、誠全而歸之⁶。——古の所謂曲れば則ち全しといふもの豈虛言ならん哉、誠は全くして之に歸す。

註　1. 柔いものは曲るがそのために己を全うす。 2. 弱いものはたわむから眞直にもなる。 3. くぼめばこそ水もたまる。 4. 古くなつて始めて新しくなる。 5. 謙抑一點張りで萬天下の儀表となる。 6. 天下の誠に全きものは皆曲りたるものである。

第二十三章　一　希言自然、故飄風不終朝¹、驟雨不終日、孰爲此者天地、天地尚不能久而況於人乎。——言ふこと希(すくな)きは自然なり、故に飄風朝(あした)を終へず、驟雨日を終へず、孰れか此を爲す者ぞ、天地なり。天地尚ほ久ふすること能はず、而るを況んや人に於てをや。

2. Therefore the sage holds in his embrace the one thing *of humility*, and manifests it to all the world. He is free from self-display, and therefore he shines; from self-assertion, and therefore he is distinguished; from self-boasting, and therefore his merit is acknowledged; from self-complacency, and therefore he acquires superiority. It is because he is thus free from striving that therefore no one in the world is able to strive with him.

3. That saying of the ancients that 'the partial becomes complete' was not vainly spoken:—all real completion is comprehended under it.

益謙, 'The Increase granted to Humility.' This title rightly expresses the subject-matter of the chapter. I cannot translate the first clause otherwise than I have done. It was an old saying, which Lâo-ʓze found and adopted. Whether it was intended to embrace all the cases which are mentioned may be questioned, but he employs it so as to make it do so.

'The emptiness' which becomes full is literally the hollowness of a cavity in the gronnd which is sure to be filled by overflowing water;—see Mencius, IV, ii, 18. 'The worn out' is explained by the withered foliage of a tree, which comes out new and fresh in the next spring. I have taken the first sentence of par. 2 as Wû *Khäng* does;—see his commentary in loc.

CHAPTER XXIII. 1. Abstaining from speech marks him who is obeying the spontaneity of his nature. A violent wind does not last for a whole morning; a sudden rain does not last for the whole day. To whom is it that these *two* things are owing? To Heaven and Earth. If Heaven and Earth cannot make such *spasmodic* actings last long, how much less can man!

二　故從事於道者、道者同於道[2]、德者同於德、失者同於失[3]。――故に道に從事すれば道をおこなふものは道に同じく、德をうる者は德に同じく、失ふ者は失ふに同じ。

三　同於道者道亦樂得之、同於德者德亦樂得之、同於失者失亦樂得之[4]、信不足有不信[5]。――道をおこなふに同じき者は道をおこなふて亦之を得ることを樂み、德をうるに同じき者は德をえて亦之を得ることを樂む。失ふに同じき者は失ふて亦之を得ることを樂む。信足らざれば信ならざること有り。

註　1. 自然の常態ならざる故長續きせぬ。　2. 人道に從へば、他の道に從ふ者等も道に從ふことに於て彼に一致する。　3. 道や德を失ふ者も失ふことに於いて彼に一致する。（有道の者は有道有德の者に遇はゞ其の道德を以て彼等に一致するのみならず、之を失つた者に遇つても其の失を以て彼等に一致する。）　4. 道德に缺け之に缺けることに於いて之を全ふする者に一致する者も之に缺けて亦之を全ふすることを學ぶことが出來る。　5. 此方が充分信を盡して居らねば彼方もまた信に缺ける。　第十七章第一節の末文參照。

第二十四章　跂者不立、跨者[1]不行、自見者不明[2]、自是者不彰、自伐者無功、自矜者不長、其在道[3]也曰餘食贅行[4]、物[5]或惡之、故有道者不處[6]也。――跂（つまだ）つ者は立たず、跨（またが）る者は行かず、自ら見（あらは）るゝ者は明ならず、自ら是とする者は彰れず、自ら伐（ほこ）る

2. Therefore when one is making the Tâo his business, those who are also pursuing it, agree with him in it, and those who are making the manifestation of its course their object agree with him in that; while even those who are failing in both these things gree with him where they fail.

3. Hence, those with whom he agrees as to the Tâo have the happiness of attaining to it; those with whom he agrees as to its manifestation have the happiness of attaining to it; and those with whom he agrees in their failure have also the happiness of attaining *to the Tâo. But* when there is not faith sufficient *on his part*, a want of faith *in him* ensues *on the part of the others.*

虛無, 'Absolute Vacancy.' This, I think, is the meaning of the title, 'Emptiness and Nothingness,' an entire conformity to the Tâo in him who professes to be directed by it. Such an one will be omnipotent in his influence in all others. The Tâo in him will restrain all (spasmodic) loquacity. Those who are described in par. 2 as 'failing' are not to be thought of as bad men, men given up, as Julien has it, au crime. They are simply ordinary men, who have failed in their study of the Tâo and practice of it, but are won to truth and virtue by the man whom the author has in mind. As we might expect, however, the mention of such men has much embarrassed the commentators.

Compare the concluding sentence with the one at the end of par. 1 in chapter 17.

CHAPTER XXIV. He who stands on his tiptoes does not stand firm; he who stretches his legs does not walk *easily*. So, he who displays himself does not shine; he who asserts his own views is not distinguished; he who vaunts himself does not find

者は功無く、自ら矜る者は長たらず、其の道に在けるや餘食贅行と曰ふ、物或は之を惡む。故に有道の者は處らず。

註 1. またを擴げて進む者。 2. 自盞自讃する者は赫々の名なし。 3. 道を修むる者に云はせると。 4. ＝食ひ殘りの御馳走と人體に出來る疣（いぼ）。贅＝疣。行＝形。 5. ＝自然界の物、實は人間の全般。 6. 避けて之に居らぬ即ち之を行はぬ。

第二十五章 一 有物混成、先天地生[1]。寂兮寥兮、獨立而不改、周行而不殆、可以爲天下母。――物有り混成、天地に先つて生ず。寂たり寥たり、獨立して改めず、周行して殆からず、以て天下の母たるべし。

二 吾不知其名、字之曰道[2]、強爲之名曰大。――吾其の名を知らず、之を字して道と曰ふ、強ひて之が名を爲つて大と曰ふ。

三 大曰逝[3]、逝曰遠[4]、遠曰反[5]。故道大、天大、地大、王[6]亦大。域中[7]有四大、而王處一焉。――大を逝と曰ふ、逝を遠と曰ふ、遠を反と曰ふ。故に道は大なり、天は大なり、地は大なり、

his merit acknowledged; he who is self-conceited has no superiority allowed to him. Such conditions, viewed from the standpoint of the Tâo, are like remnants of food, or a tumour on the body, which all dislike. Hence those who pursue *the course* of the Tâo do not adopt and allow them.

苦恩, 'Painful Graciousness.' The chapter should be so designated. This concludes the subject of the two previous chapters, —pursuing the course, the course of the unemotional Tâo without vain effort or display.

The remnants of food were not used as sacrificial offering;— see the Lî Kî (vol. xxvii, p. 82). In what I have rendered by 'a tumour attached to the body,' the 行 is probably, by a mistake, for 形;—see a quotation by Wû Khăng from Sze-mâ Khien. 'Which all dislike' is, literally, 'Things are likely to dislike them,' the 'things' being 'spirits and men,' as Wû explains the term.

CHAPTER XXV.
1. There was something undefined and complete, coming into existence before Heaven and Earth. How still it was and formless, standing alone, and undergoing no change, reaching everywhere and in no danger *of being exhausted!* It may be regarded as the Mother of all things.

2. I do not know its name, and I give it the designation of the Tâo *the Way or Course.* Making an effort *further* to give it a name I call it The Great.

3. Great, it passes on *in constant flow.* Passing on, it becomes remote. Having become remote, it returns. Therefore the Tâo is great; Heaven is great; Earth is great; and the *sage* king is also

王も亦大なり。域中四大有り、而して王一に處(を)る。

四　人法地、地法天、天法道、道法自然[8]。——人は地に法(のっと)り、地は天に法り、天は道に法り、道は自然に法る。

註　1. 天地創造以前に渾然たる或物が存在してゐた。　2. これとそ老子の所謂道即ち宇宙萬物の根元である。　3. 大なるが故に悠々流水の如く逝く。　4. 逝くものは遠きに到る。　5. 遠きに到れば循環作用に由つて再び元へ反へる。　6. ＝聖王。　7. ＝宇宙間。　8. 道は道それ自體の由つて然る所に則る。　即ち次に本章の說く所を最も平易に書き直して見る。——天地開闢に先だつて、渾然たる或る物が存在してゐた。此の物は六合の間に獨立自存し、寂寥として或は聲なく或は形なく、隨處に遍在して窮まる所がない。是れが乃ち森羅萬象の根本萬物の根元たる宇宙の原理であらうが、自分にはその正體が果して何物であるか解らない。そこで假に字をつければ道とでも云はうが、强いて名前をつけたら、其の無限に大なる意味で大とでもいはう。又無限大即ち悠々流水の如き意味で逝ともいふべく、周行遂々到らざる所なき意味で遠ともいふべく、其の無窮に循環する作用から反ともいふべきである。是に由つて之を觀れば道は勿論大であるが、天も大であり、地も大であり、王も亦大である。宇宙間に此の四大があり而も王がその一に居るのは、萬物の靈長たる我々の主たる王は聖者でなければならず、それ故其の聖者は道を體する者であるからである。乃ち之を要するに天地聖王は皆道に則り、道はまた自然に則つて初めて大を得るものである。

great. In the universe there are four that are great, and the *sage* king is one of them.

4. Man takes his law from the Earth; the Earth takes its law from Heaven; Heaven takes its law from the Tâo. The law of the Tâo is its being what it is.

象玄, 'Representations of the Mystery.' In this chapter Lâo approaches very near to give an answer to the question as to what the Tâo is, and yet leaves the reader disappointed. He commences by calling it 'a thing (物);' but that term does not necessitate our regarding it as 'material.' We have seen in the preceding chapter that it is used to signify 'spirits and men.' Nor does his going on to speak of it as 'chaotic (混成)' necessarily lead us to conceive it as made up of the 'material elements of things;' we have the same term applied in chapter 14 to the three immaterial constituents there said to be blended in the idea of it.

'He does not know its name,' and he designates it by the term denoting a course or way (Tâo, 道), and indicating the phenomenal attribute, the method in which all phenomena come before our observation, in their development or evolution. And to distinguish it from all other methods of evolution, he would call it 'the Great Method,' and so he employs that combination as its name in chapter 18 and elsewhere; but it cannot be said that this name has fully maintained itself in the writings of his followers. But understood thus, he here says, as in chapter 1, that it is 'the Mother of all things.' And yet, when he says that 'it was before Heaven and Earth were produced,' he comes very near his affirmations in chapters 1 and 4, that 'the nameless Tâo was the beginning (or originating cause) of Heaven and Earth,' and 'might seem to have been before God.' Was he groping after God if haply he might find Him? I think he was, and he gets so far as to conceive of Him as 'the Uncaused Cause,' but comes short of the idea of His personality. The other subordinate causes which he mentions all get their force or power from the Tâo, but after all the Tâo is simply a

第二十六章 一　重爲輕根、靜爲躁君[1]。——重きは輕きが根たり、靜かなるは躁きが君たり。

二　是以君子終日行不離輜重[2]、雖有榮觀燕處超然[3]。如何萬乘之主而以身輕天下。輕則失臣[4]、躁則失君[5]。——是を以て君子は終日行いて輜重を離れず。榮觀有りと雖も燕處して超然たり。如何ぞ萬乘の主にして身を以て天下を輕んずる。輕んずるときは則ち臣を失ふ、躁ぐときは則ち君を失ふ。

註　1. 重いものは輕いものゝ根、靜なものは躁しいものゝ本である。 2. 君子は終日後方の輜重を離れぬように前方の輕車に任せて疾行はしない。 3. 家の中に燕居してゐる時には立派な見物があつてもそれから超然として心を動かさない。 4. 國民を臣從せしむる重き信望。 5. ＝王位。

第二十七章 一　善行無轍迹、善言無瑕謫[1]、善計不用籌策[2]、善閉無關楗[3]、而不可開、善結無繩約[4]、而不可解、是以聖人常善救人、故無棄人、常善救物、故無棄物[5]、是謂襲明[6]。——善く行くものは轍迹無く、善く言ふものは瑕謫無く、善く計るものは

spontaneity, evolving from itself, and not acting from a personal will, consciously in the direction of its own wisdom and love. 'Who can by searching find out God? Who can find out the Almighty to perfection?'

The predicate of the Tâo in the chapter, most perplexing to myself, is 'It returns,' in par. 3. 'It flows away, far away, and comes back;'—are not the three statements together equal to 'It is everywhere?'

CHAPTER XXVI. 1. Gravity is the root of lightness; stillness, the ruler of movement.

2. Therefore a wise prince, marching the whole day, does not go far from his baggage waggons. Although he may have brilliant prospects to look at, he quietly remains *in his proper place*, indifferent to them. How should the lord of a myriad chariots carry himself lightly before the kingdom? If he do act lightly, he has lost his root *of gravity*; if he proceed to active movement, he will lose his throne.

重德, 'The Quality of Gravity.' Gravity and stillness are both attributes of the Tâo; and he who cultivates it must not give way to lightness of mind, or hasty action.

The rule for a leader not to separate from his baggage waggons is simply the necessity of adhering to gravity. I have adopted from Han Fei the reading of 'the wise prince' for 'the sage,' which is found in Ho-shang Kung; and later on the reading of 'has lost his root' for his 'loses his ministers,' though the latter is found also in Han Fei.

CHAPTER XXVII. 1. The skilful traveller leaves no traces of his wheels or footsteps; the skilful speaker says nothing that can be found fault with or blamed; the skilful reckoner uses

籌策を用ひず、善く閉づるものは關楗無くして而も開く可からず、善く結ぶものは繩約無くして而も解く可からず。是を以て聖人は常に善く人を救ふ、故に人を棄る無し、常に善く物を救ふ、故に物を棄る無し。是を襲明と謂ふ。

　二　故善人不善人之師、不善人善人之資[7]、不貴其師、不愛其資、雖知大迷[8]、是謂要妙[9]。――故に善人は不善人の師、不善人は善人の資なり。其の師を貴ばず、其の資を愛せずんば、知ありと雖も大いに迷ふ。是れを要妙と謂ふ。

　　註　1. 行くに巧みなものは車を驅つた後に轍（わだち）の迹を殘さぬ。瑕は玉のきず疵は言のそれ、謫は言の責即ちとが。　2. 算數に用ひる竹具。　3. 關は門を防ぐ横木楗は豎木。　4. ＝窔。　5. 同樣に聖人は自己を棄て人僞を爲さず唯人と物の自然を助けて爲はざるを以て人と物とを救ふ、隨つて自己の聰明を恃んで外物を是非輕重しないから人や物を棄てぬ。　6. 德の明光を掩ひ藏（かく）すこと。襲は掩襲の襲。　7. 善くする者は善くせざる者の仰いで師とすべきものである。善くせざる者は善くする者の引き立て役として貢獻するものでゐる。　8. 之を觀る人知あるも大いに迷ふ（その人々を如何に判斷すべきかに就いて）。　9. この至極不可解の理を要妙と謂ふ。

no tallies; the skilful closer needs no bolts or bars, while to open what he has shut will be impossible; the skilful binder uses no strings or knots, while to unloose what he has bound will be impossible. In the same way the sage is always skilful at saving men, and so he does not cast away any man; he is always skilful at saving things, and so he does not cast away anything. This is called 'Hiding the light of his procedure.'

2. Therefore the man of skill is a master *to be looked up to* by him who has not the skill; and he who has not the skill is the helper of *the reputation of* him who has the skill. If the one did not honour his master, and the other did not rejoice in his helper, an *observer*, though intelligent, might greatly err about them. This is called 'The utmost degree of mystery.'

巧用, 'Dexterity in Using,' that is, in the application of the Tâo. This is the substance of the chapter, celebrating the effective but invisible operation of the Tâo, and the impartial exercise of it for the benefit of all men and all things.

I have given the most natural construction of the two characters at the end of par. 1, the only possible construction of them, so far as I can see, suitable to the context. The action of the Tâo (non-acting and yet all-efficient) and that of the sage in accordance with it, are veiled by their nature from the sight of ordinary men.

It is more difficult to catch the scope and point of par. 2. If there were not the conditions described in it, it would be hard for even an intelligent onlooker to distinguish between the man who had the skill and the man without it, between him who possessed the Tâo, and him who had it not, which would be strange indeed.

第二十八章 ― 知其雄守其雌[1]、爲天下谿[2]。爲天下谿、常德不離、復歸於嬰兒。知其白、守其黑[3]、爲天下式。爲天下式、常德不忒[4]、復歸於無極。知其榮、守其辱、爲天下谷。爲天下谷、常德乃足、復歸於樸[5]。――其の雄を知つて其の雌を守るときは天下の谿と爲る。天下の谿と爲るときは常の德離れず嬰兒に復歸す。其の白きを知つて其の黑きを守るときは天下の式と爲る。天下の式と爲るときは常の德忒はず無極に復歸す。其の榮を知つて其の辱を守るときは天下の谷と爲る。天下の谷と爲るときは常の德乃ち足り樸に復歸す。

二 樸[6]散則爲器、聖人用之[7]、則爲官長、故大制不割[8]。――樸散するときは則ち器と爲る。聖人用ひらるるときは則ち官の長と爲る。故に大制は割れず。

註 1. 强きを知つて弱きを守る。 2. 百流の谿谷に宗注する如く萬民の復歸する處となる。 3. 欲智明白にして暗愚昧味を守る。 4＝變。 5.＝太初素樸。 6. 工作の材。 7. 用之は用ひらるればと同義。 8. 大道を以て天下を制御し萬民を傷殺するの橫政に出でぬ。

第二十九章 ― 將欲取天下而爲之者、吾見其不得已、天下

CHAPTER XXVIII. 1. Who knows his manhood's strength,
Yet still his female feebleness maintains;
As to one channel flow the many drains,
All come to him, yea, all beneath the sky.
Thus he the constant excellence retains;—
The simple child again, free from all stains.

Who knows how white attracts,
Yet always keeps himself within black's shade,
The pattern of humility displayed,
Displayed in view of all beneath the sky;
He in the unchanging excellence arrayed,
Endless return to man's first state has made.

Who knows how glory shines,
Yet loves disgrace, nor e'er for it is pale;
Behold his presence in a spacious vale,
To which men come from all beneath the sky.
The unchanging excellence completes its tale;
The simple infant man in him we hail.

2. The unwrought material, when divided and distributed, forms vessels. The sage, when employed, becomes the Head of all the Officers *of government*; and in his greatest regulations he employs no violent measures.

_{反樸, 'Returning to Simplicity.' The chapter sets forth humility and simplicity, an artless freedom from all purpose, as characteristic of the man of Tâo, such as he was in the primeval time. 'The sage' in par. 2 may be 'the Son of Heaven,'—the Head of all rule in the kingdom, or the feudal lord in a state.}

CHAPTER XXIX. 1. If any one should wish

神器、不可爲[1]也、爲者敗之、執者失之。──將に天下を取らん と欲して之を爲る者は吾其の得ざるを見るのみ。天下は神器な り、爲可からず。爲る者は敗れ、執る者は失ふ。

二　凡物或行、或隨[2]。或歔、或吹[3]。或強、或羸。或载[4]、或 隳[5]。是以聖人去甚[6]、去奢、去泰[7]。──凡そ物或は行き、或は 隨ふ。或は歔し、或は吹く。或は強く、或は羸し。或は载し、 或は隳る。是を以て聖人は甚しきを去り、奢りを去り、泰を去 る。

註　1. 人爲を以て左右す可からず。　2. 前に行くかと見れば忽ち後 に隨ふ、即ち榮枯盛衰は掌を反すが如し。　3. 春の氣の如く温又秋の 氣の如く寒（ひや）す。　4. ＝貯。　5. ＝毀。　6. ＝過大の努力。　7. ＝安逸。

第三十章　一　以道佐人主者、不以兵強天下[1]、其事好還[2]。 ──道を以て人主を佐くる者は兵を以て天下に強からず。其れ 事は還ることを好む。

to get the kingdom for himself, and to effect this by what he does, I see that he will not succeed. The kingdom is a spirit-like thing, and cannot be got by active doing. He who would so win it destroys it; he who would hold it in his grasp loses it.

2. The course and nature of things is such that
What was in front is now behind;
What warmed anon we freezing find.
Strength is of weakness oft the spoil;
The store in ruins mocks our toil.

Hence the sage puts away excessive effort, extravagance, and easy indulgence.

無爲, 'Taking no Action.' All efforts made with a purpose are sure to fail. The nature of the Tâo necessitates their doing so, and the uncertainty of things and events teaches the same lesson.

That the kingdom or throne is a 'spirit-like vessel' has become a common enough saying among the Chinese. Julien has, 'L'Empire est comme un vase divin;' but I always shrink from translating 神 by 'divine.' Its English analogue is 'spirit,' and the idea in the text is based on the immunity of spirit from all material law, and the uncertain issue of attempts to deal with it according to ordinary methods. Wû *Khăng* takes the phrase as equivalent to 'superintended by spirits,' which is as inadmissible as Julien's 'divin.' The Tâo forbids action with a personal purpose, and all such action is sure to fail in the greatest things as well as in the least.

CHAPTER XXX. 1. He who would assist a lord of men in harmony with the Tâo will not assert his mastery in the kingdom by force of arms. Such a course is sure to meet with its proper return.

二　師之所處荊棘生焉³、大軍之後必有凶年⁴。――師の處る所には荊棘生ず。大軍の後には必ず凶年有り。

三　故善者果而已矣、不敢以取強焉⁵、果而勿矜、果而勿伐、果而勿驕、果而不得已⁶、果而勿強⁷。――故に善き者は果ならくのみ、敢て以て強を取らず、果して矜る勿し、果して伐る勿し、果して驕る勿し、果して已むを得ず、果して強き勿し。

四　物壯則老、是謂非道⁸。非道早已。――物壯んなれば則ち老ゆ。是を道に非らずと謂ふ。道に非らざるものは早く已む。

註　1. 武力を示して天下に強がらぬ。　2. 已に出づるものは已に還る、我兵を以て人を害せば人亦兵を以て我を害す。　3. 大軍の屯する處住民逃散して田園に荊棘生ず、人と爭はゞ心田に荊棘生ず。　4. 大戰爭の後には饑饉が起る。前句と同巧異曲也。　5. 良將は戰爭を果決斷行するのみにして敢て強がらぬ、有道者の道を決行するも亦然り。　6. 已むを得ず戰爭を果決する。　7. 果決して強がらぬ。老子の道の本體も強に非らず弱なり。

第三十一章　一　夫佳兵者¹不祥之器、物或惡之²、故有道者不處³。――夫れ佳きも兵は不祥の器なり、物或は之を惡む。故に有道者は處らず。

2. Wherever a host is stationed, briars and thorns spring up. In the sequence of great armies there are sure to be bad years.

3. A skilful *commander* strikes a decisive blow, and stops. He does not dare *by continuing his operations* to assert and complete his mastery. He will strike the blow, but will be on his guard against being vain or boastful or arrogant in consequence of it. He strikes it as a matter of necessity; he strikes it, but not from a wish for mastery.

4. When things have attained their strong maturity they become old. This may be said to be not in accordance with the Tâo: and what is not in accordance with it soon comes to an end.

<small>俭武, 'A Caveat against War.' War is contrary to the spirit of the Tâo, and, as being so, is productive of misery, and leads to early ruin. It is only permissible in a case of necessity, and even then its spirit and tendencies must be guarded against.

In translating 果 by 'striking a decisive blow,' I have, no doubt, followed Julien's 'frapper un coup décisif.' The same 果 occurs six times in par. 3, followed by 而, and 8iâo Hung says that in all but the first instance the 而 should be taken as equivalent to 於, so that we should have to translate, 'He is determined against being vain,' &c. But there is no necessity for such a construction of 而.

'Weakness' and not 'strength' is the character of the Tâo; hence the lesson in par. 4.</small>

CHAPTER XXXI. 1. Now arms, however beautiful, are instruments of evil omen, hateful, it may be said, to all creatures. Therefore they who have the Tâo do not like to employ them.

二　是以君子居則貴左[4]、用兵則貴右、兵者不祥之器、非君子之器、不得已而用之、恬淡爲上、故不美也[5]、若美必樂之、樂之者是樂殺人也。夫樂殺人者不可得志於天下矣。——是を以て君子居るには則ち左を貴び、兵を用ひるときは則ち右を貴ぶ。兵は不祥の器なり、君子の器に非らず。已むを得ずして之を用ふ。恬淡（てんたん）を上と爲す。故に美（よみ）せず、若し美せば必ず之を樂まん。之を樂む者は是れ人を殺すことを樂むなり。夫れ人を殺すことを樂む者は志を天下に得可からず。

三　故吉事尚左、凶事尚右。是以偏將軍處左[6]、上將軍處右。言居上勢、則以喪禮處之[7]。殺人衆多、以悲哀泣之[8]、戰勝以喪禮處之[9]。——故に吉事には左を尚び、凶事には右を尚ぶ。是を以て偏將軍は左に處（を）り、上將軍は右に處る。上に居るの勢を言ふとき則ち喪の禮を以て之に處す。人を殺すこと衆多なれば悲哀を以て之を泣く。戰勝てば喪の禮を以て之に處（を）る。

註　1. 在來の訓み方は兵を佳くする者。　2. 世人恐くは之を惡む。　3. 之を用ひず。　4. 君子は平生居るには左を上席とする。　5. 君子は恬淡（＝靜謐）を尚び兵を用ひて勝つを美（よみ）せず。　6. 凶事には左は下位故偏（＝副）將軍之に居る。　7. 上將軍の席次を定めるに喪の禮を以てする。　8. 有道の士は人を殺すこと多ければ戰に勝つも悲泣する。　9. 凱旋將軍が喪の禮を以て席に着くは當然。

2. The superior man ordinarily considers the left hand the most honourable place, but in time of war the right hand. Those sharp weapons are instruments of evil omen, and not the instruments of the superior man;—he uses them only on the compulsion of necessity. Calm and repose are what he prizes; victory *by force of arms* is to him undesirable. To consider this desirable would be to delight in the slaughter of men; and he who delights in the slaughter of men cannot get his will in the kingdom.

3. On occasions of festivity to be on the left hand is the prized position; on occasions of mourning, the right hand. The second in command of the army has his place on the left; the general commanding in chief has his on the right;—his place, that is, is assigned to him as in the rites of mourning. He who has killed multitudes of men should weep for them with the bitterest grief; and the victor in battle has his place *rightly* according to those rites.

偃武, 'Stilling War.' The chapter continues the subject of the preceding. The imperially-appointed editors of Wang Pî's Text and Commentary (1765) say that from the beginning of par. 2 to the end, there is the appearance of text and commentary being mixed together; but they make no alteration in the text as it is found in Ho-shang Kung, and in all other ancient copies.

The concluding sentence will suggest to some readers the words of the Duke of Wellington, that to gain a battle was the saddest thing next to losing it.

第三十二章

一　道常無名[1]。――道の常なるは名無し。

二　樸雖小天下不敢臣[2]、侯王若能守[3]、萬物將自賓[4]。――樸として小なりと雖も天下敢て臣とせず、侯王若し能く守らば萬物將に自ら賓(おのづか)せんとす。

三　天地相合以降甘露[5]、人莫之令而自均[6]。――天地相合はど以て甘露を降し、人之を令すること莫くして自ら均し。

四　始制有名[7]、名亦既有、夫亦將知止[8]、知止所以不殆[9]。――始めて制して名有り、名亦既に有り、夫れ亦將に止まることを知らんとす。止まることを知るは殆(あやふ)からざる所以なり。

五　譬道之在天下由川谷之於江海也[10]。――譬へば道の天下に在けるは由ほ川谷の江海に於けるがごとし。

註　1. 永劫不易の道は之を名づくることが出來ぬ。　2. 樸小な道でも之を體得する者を天下の人は臣隷視しない。　3. 侯王若し道を能く持すれば。　4. 賓從と同義。　5. 道の統率の下に於ては天地相合して甘露を降す。　6. 人の命令を待たず六合を均霑す。　7. 道は活動を始制するや否や名を得た。　8. 道と名さへ附きさへすれば人はそれに安んずることが出來る。　9. 道に安んずることが出來れば最早過誤失敗を招く危險はない。　10. 萬物は幾千萬の川谷、道は江海である。

CHAPTER XXXII. 1. The Tâo, considered as unchanging, has no name.

2. Though in its primordial simplicity it may be small, the whole world dares not deal with *one embodying* it as a minister. If a feudal prince or the king could guard and hold it, all would spontaneously submit themselves to him.

3. Heaven and Earth *under its guidance* unite together and send down the sweet dew, which, without the directions of men, reaches equally everywhere as of its own accord.

4. As soon as it proceeds to action, it has a name. When it once has that name, *men* can know to rest in it. When they know to rest in it, they can be free from all risk of failure and error.

5. The relation of the Tâo to all the world is like that of the great rivers and seas to the streams from the valleys.

聖德. Chalmers translates this by 'sagely virtue.' But I cannot adopt that rendering, and find it difficult to supply a better. The 'virtue' is evidently the Attribute of the Tâo come out from the condition of the Absolute, and capable of being named. In the former state it has no name; in the latter, it has. Par. 1 and the commencement of par. 4 must both be explained from ch. 1.

The 'primordial simplicity' in par. 2 is the Tâo in its simplest conception, alone, and by itself, and the 始制 in par. 4 is that Tâo come forth into operation and become Teh, the Teh which affords a law for men. From this to the end of the paragraph is very obscure. I have translated from the text of Wang Pî. The text of Ho-shang Kung is different, and he comments upon it as it stands, but to me it is inexplicable.

第三十三章　一　知人者智、自知者明。勝人者有力、自勝者強。知足者富、强行者有志[1]。――人を知る者は智なり、自ら知る者は明なり。人に勝つ者は力有り、自ら勝つ者は強し。足ることを知る者は富めり、強(つと)め行ふ者は志有り。

二　不失其所[2]者久、死而不亡者[3]壽。――其の所を失はざる者は久し、死して亡(ほろ)びざる者は壽(なが)し。

註　1. 智、明、有力、強、富、鐵石心等は客觀的に見たる體道者の性質にして、主觀的に見たる彼の愚、弱等々の性質に對するもの。　2. 自然に隨つて其所を失はぬ者。　3. 幻滅界に在つて生死の外に超然たる者。此の一句より觀れば老子も靈魂不滅論者、來世存在信者たることを推知することが出來る。

第三十四章　一　大道汎兮其可左右[1]。――大道は汎(はん)として其れ左右しつ可し。

CHAPTER XXXIII. 1. He who knows other men is discerning; he who knows himself is intelligent. He who overcomes others is strong; he who overcomes himself is mighty. He who is satisfied with his lot is rich; he who goes on acting with energy has a *firm* will.

2. He who does not fail in the requirements of his position, continues long; he who dies and yet does not perish, has longevity.

辨德, 'Discriminating between (different) Attributes.' The teaching of the chapter is that the possession of the Tâo confers the various attributes which are here most distinguished. It has been objected to it that elsewhere the Tâo is represented as associated with dulness and not intelligence, and with weakness and not with strength. But these seem to be qualities viewed from without, and acting on what is beyond itself. Inwardly, its qualities are the very opposite, and its action has the effect of enlightening what is dark, and overcoming what is strong.

More interesting are the predicates in par. 2. Ṣiâo Hung gives the comment on it of the Indian monk, Kumâragîva, 'one of the four suns of Buddhism,' and who went to China in A.D. 401: 'To be alive and yet not alive may well be called long; to die and yet not be dead may well be called longevity.' He also gives the views of Lû Năngshih (A.D. 1042-1120) that the freedom from change of Lieh-ʒze, from death of *K*wang-ʒze, and from extinction of the Buddhists, have all the same meaning as the concluding saying of Lâo-ʒze here; that the human body is like the covering of the caterpillar or the skin of the snake; that we occupy it but for a passing sojourn. No doubt, Lâo-ʒze believed in another life for the individual after the present. Many passages in *K*wang-ʒze indicate the same faith.

CHAPTER XXXIV. 1. All-pervading is the Great Tâo! It may be found on the left hand and on the right.

二　萬物恃之以生、而不辭[2]。功成不居、衣被萬物、而不爲主、故常無欲、可名於小矣[3]。萬物歸焉[4]、而不知主、可名於大矣。――萬物之を恃(たの)んで以て生ず、而して辭せず。功成りて居らず、萬物を衣被して主たらず、故に常に欲すること無し、小と名づく可し。萬物焉(これ)に歸し、而も主たることを知らず、大と名づく可し。

三　是以[5]聖人能成其大也、以其不自大故能成其大。――是を以て聖人は能く其の大を成す、其の自ら大なりとせざるを以ての故に能く其の大を成す。

註　1. 道は瀰漫自由で我々の前後に見左右に執ることが出來る。 2. 道は萬物を生ぜしむるものであるから萬物は道に臣從して生ずることを辭せぬ。　3. 道は萬物の主宰者とならず德を隱くし用を微にして常に欲する所なく小と謂ふべし。 4. 萬物は道に歸宗する。　5. 道と同じ方法を以つて。

第三十五章　一　執大象天下往[1]、往而不害、安平泰。――大象を執れば天下往く、往いて害せず、安平泰。

二　樂與餌、過客止、道之出言、淡乎其無味、視之不足見、聽之不足聞、用之不可旣[2]。――樂と餌とは過客を止む。道の言に出づる淡乎として其れ味無く、之を視れども見るに足らず、之

2. All things depend on it for their production, which it gives to them, not one refusing obedience to it. When its work is accomplished, it does not claim the name of having done it. It clothes all things as with a garment, and makes no assumption of being their lord;—it may be named in the smallest things. All things return *to their root and disappear*, and do not know that it is it which presides over their doing so;—it may be named in the greatest things.

3. Hence the sage is able *in the same way* to accomplish his great achievements. It is through his not making himself great that he can accomplish them.

任成, 'The Task of Achievement.' The subject is the greatness of what the Tâo, called here by Lâo's own name for it in ch. 25, does; and the unconscious simplicity with which it does it; and then the achievements of the sage who is permeated by the Tâo. Par. 2 is descriptive of the influence of the Tâo in the vegetable world. The statements and expressions are much akin to those in parts of chapters 2, 10, and 51, and for Ho-shang Kung's difficult reading of 不名有 some copies give 而不居, as in chapter 2.

CHAPTER XXXV. 1. To him who holds in his hands the Great Image *of the invisible Tâo*, the whole world repairs. Men resort to him, and receive no hurt, but *find* rest, peace, and the feeling of ease.

2. Music and dainties will make the passing guest stop *for a time*. But though the Tâo as it comes from the mouth, seems insipid and has

を聽けども聞くに足らざるも、之を用ひれば既す可からず。

註　1. 大象を執つて天下に往くと訓むも可。大象は無象の象即ち大道。天下往は天下之に歸すの意。　2. 歌樂盛饌の與ふる樂は一時的、道の齎す樂は永久的なるを述ぶ。

第三十六章　一　將欲噏之[1]、必固張之[2]、將欲弱之、必固强之、將欲廢之、必固興之、將欲奪之、必固與之、是謂微明[3]──將に之を噏めんと欲すれば必ず固に之を張く。將に之を弱めんと欲すれば必ず固に之を强うす。將に之を廢んと欲すれば必ず固に之を興す。將に之を奪はんと欲すれば必ず固に之を與ふ。是を微明と謂ふ。

二　柔之勝剛、弱之勝强。──柔は剛に勝ち、弱は强に勝つ。

三　魚不可脫於淵[4]、國之利器不可以示人[5]。──魚は淵より脫る可からず、國の利器は以て人に示す可からず。

註　1. 息を吸ふ。　2. 息を吐く。　3. 德行の光明を微にすること（第二十七章の襲明と同義）。　4. 魚は深淵より淺瀬に移れば容易に捕られてしまふ。　5. 貨殖政富の術は民に示す可からず、民は素樸無智なるを宜しとす。

no flavour, though it seems not worth being looked at or listened to, the use of it is inexhaustible.

仁德, 'The Attribute of Benevolence.' But there seems little appropriateness in this title. The subject of the chapter is the inexhaustible efficacy of the Tâo for the good of the world.

The Great Image (of the invisible Tâo) is a name for the Tâo in its operation; as in chapters 14 and 41. He who embodies this in his government will be a centre of attraction for all the world. Or the 天下往 may be taken as a predicate of the holder of the Great Image:—'If he go all under heaven teaching the Tâo.' Both constructions are maintained by commentators of note. In par. 2 the attraction of the Tâo is contrasted with that of ordinary pleasures and gratifications.

CHAPTER XXXVI. 1. When one is about to take an inspiration, he is sure to make a *previous* expiration; when he is going to weaken another, he will first strengthen him; when he is going to overthrow another, he will first have raised him up; when he is going to despoil another, he will first have made gifts to him:—this is called 'Hiding the light *of his procedure.*'

2. The soft overcomes the hard; and the weak the strong.

3. Fishes should not be taken from the deep; instruments for the profit of a state should not be shown to the people.

微明, 'Minimising the Light;' equivalent, as Wû *Khăng* has pointed out, to the 襲明 of ch. 27.

The gist of the chapter is to be sought in the second paragraph, where we have two instances of the action of the Tâo by contraries, supposed always to be for good.

But there is a difficulty in seeing the applicability to this of the cases mentioned in par. 1. The first case, indeed, is merely

第三十七章　一　道常無爲而無不爲。──道の常は爲ること無くして爲ずといふこと無し。

二　侯王若能守[1]、萬物將自化。──侯王若し能く守るときは萬物將た自ら化せん。

三　化而欲作、吾將鎭以無名之樸[2]。無名之樸、亦將不欲。不欲以靜、天下將自正。──化せん而して作らんと欲せば、吾將た鎭むるに無名の樸を以てせん。無名の樸は、亦將た不欲なり。不欲にして以て靜なれば、天下將た自ら正し。

a natural phenomenon, having no moral character; but the others, as they have been illustrated from historical incidents, by Han Fei and others at least, belong to schemes of selfish and unprincipled ambitious strategy, which it would be injurious to Lâo-ʒze to suppose that he intended.

Par. 3 is the most frequently quoted of all the passages in our *King*, unless it be the first part of ch. 1. Fishes taken from the deep, and brought into shallow water, can be easily taken or killed; that is plain enough. 'The sharp instruments of a state' are not its 'weapons of war,' nor its 'treasures,' nor its 'instruments of government,' that is, its rewards and punishments, though this last is the interpretation often put on them, and sustained by a foolish reference to an incident, real or coined, in the history of the dukedom of Sung. The lî khî are 'contrivances for gain,' machines, and other methods to increase the wealth of a state, but, according to the principles of Lâo-ʒze, really injurious to it. These should not be shown to the people, whom the Tâoistic system would keep in a state of primitive simplicity and ignorance. This interpretation is in accordance with the meaning of the characters, and with the general teaching of Tâoism. In no other way can I explain the paragraph so as to justify the place undoubtedly belonging to it in the system.

CHAPTER XXXVII. 1. Tâo in its regular course does nothing *for the sake of doing it*, and so there is nothing which it does not do.

2. If princes and kings were able to maintain it, all things would of themselves be transformed by them.

3. If this transformation became to me an object of desire, I would express the desire by the nameless simplicity.

> Simplicity without a name
> Is free from all external aim.

註 1. 道を守る。 2. 萬物の自ら化せんことを起さしめんとの希望の如きは無名の樸を以て之を打ち鎭めよう。主語の侯王を表はすべき第三人稱を第一人稱にしたるは叙述を活躍せしむるためか、左なくば老子侯王に代つて曰ふためならん。

> With no desire, at rest and still,
> All things go right as of their will.

為政, 'The Exercise of Government.' This exercise should be according to the Tâo, doing without doing, governing without government.

The subject of the third paragraph is a feudal prince or the king, and he is spoken of in the first person, to give more vividness to the style, unless the 吾, 'I,' may, possibly, be understood of Lâo-ʒze himself personating one of them.

下　篇

第三十八章　一　上德不德、是以有德。下德不失德、是以無德[1]。――上德は德とせず、是を以て德有り。下德は德を失はず、是を以て德無し。

二　上德無爲而無以爲[2]、下德爲之而有以爲[3]。――上德は無爲にして以て爲すこと無し、下德は之を爲して以て爲すこと有り。

三　上仁爲之而無以爲[4]、上義爲之而有以爲[5]。――上仁は之を爲して以て爲すこと無し、上義は之を爲して以て爲すこと有り。

四　上禮爲之而莫之應、則攘臂而仍之[6]。――上禮は之を爲して之に應ふること莫きときは、則ち臂を攘げて之を仍く。

五　故失道而後德、失德而後仁、失仁而後義、失義而後禮。――故に道を失つて後德あり、德を失つて後仁あり、仁を失つて後義あり、義を失つて後禮あり。

PART II.

CHAPTER XXXVIII. 1. *Those who* possessed in highest degree the attributes *of the Tâo* did not *seek* to show them, and therefore they possessed them *in fullest measure*. *Those who* possessed in a lower degree those attributes *sought how* not to lose them, and therefore they did not possess them *in fullest measure*.

2. *Those who* possessed in the highest degree those attributes did nothing *with a purpose*, and had no need to do anything. *Those who* possessed them in a lower degree were *always* doing, and had need to be so doing.

3. *Those who* possessed the highest benevolence were *always seeking* to carry it out, and had no need to be doing so. *Those who* possessed the highest righteousness were *always seeking* to carry it out, and had need to be so doing.

4. *Those who* possessed the highest *sense of* propriety were *always seeking* to show it, and when men did not respond to it, they bared the arm and marched up to them.

5. Thus it was that when the Tâo was lost, its attributes appeared; when its attributes were lost, benevolence appeared; when benevolence was lost, righteousness appeared; and when righteousness was lost, the proprieties appeared.

六　夫禮者忠信之薄而亂之首也、前識⁷者道之華⁸而愚之始也。——夫れ禮は忠信の薄きにして亂の首なり、前識は道の華にして愚の始なり。

七　是以大丈夫處其⁹厚不取其薄、居其實不居其華。故去彼¹⁰取此¹¹。——是を以て大丈夫は其の厚きに處り其の薄きを取らず、其の實に居つて其の華に居らず。故に彼を去り此を取る。

註　1. 充分に德を具へてゐぬ者は德を失ふまいとするから充分に德を具へることが出來ぬ。　2. 何事をも爲すべき必要なし。　3. 之を爲す必要あり。　4. 常に仁を爲さんとして仁を爲すを要せず。　5. 常に義を無さんとして而も義を爲すを要す。　6. 禮は上なるものすら腕力に訴へても答禮を迫まる、また言ふに足らず。　7. ＝智。　8. 實の反。　9. 道。　10. 薄と華。　11 厚と實。要するに此の一章は仁義禮智信の有爲の餘にして無爲の大道に比し取るに足らざるを說く。

6. Now propriety is the attenuated form of leal-heartedness and good faith, and is also the commencement of disorder; swift apprehension is *only* a flower of the Tâo, and is the beginning of stupidity.

7. Thus it is that the Great man abides by what is solid, and eschews what is flimsy; dwells with the fruit and not with the flower. It is thus that he puts away the one and makes choice of the other.

論德, 'About the Attributes;' of Tâo, that is. It is not easy to render teh here by any other English term than 'virtue,' and yet there would be a danger of its thus misleading us in the interpretation of the chapter.

The 'virtue' is the activity or operation of the Tâo, which is supposed to have come out of its absoluteness. Even Han Fei so defines it here,—'Teh is the meritorious work of the Tâo.'

In par. 5 we evidnetly have a résumé of the preceding paragraphs, and, as it is historical, I translate them in the past tense; though what took place on the early stage of the world may also be said to go on taking place in the experience of every individual. With some considerable hesitation I have given the subjects in those paragraphs in the concrete, in deference to the authority of Ho-shang Kung and most other commentators. The former says, 'By "the highest teh" is to be understood the the rulers of the greatest antiquity, without name or designation, whose virtue was great, and could not be surpassed.' Most ingenious, and in accordance with the Tâoistic system, is the manuer in which Wû *Khǎng* construes the passage, and I am surprised that it has not been generally accepted. By 'the higher teh' he understands 'the Tâo,' that which is prior to and above the Teh (上德者, 在德之上, 道也); by 'the lower teh,' benevolence, that which is after and below the Teh; by 'the higher benevolence,' the Teh which is above benevolence; by 'the higher righteousness,' the benevolence which is above righteous-

第三十九章　一　昔之得一者[1]、天得一以淸、地得一以寧、神得一以靈、谷得一以盈、萬物得一以生、王侯得一以爲天下貞[2]、其致之一也[3]。――昔より一を得たる者あり、天は一を得て以て淸し、地は一を得て以て寧し、神は一を得て以て靈なり、谷は一を得て以て盈つ、萬物は一を得て以て生ず、王侯は一を得て以て天下の貞と爲る、其の之を致すは一也。

二　天無以淸將恐裂、地無以寧將恐發、神無以靈將恐歇、谷無以盈將恐竭、萬物無以生將恐滅、侯王無以貞而貴高將恐蹶。――天以て淸きこと無くんば將に恐くは裂けんとす。地以て寧きこと無くんば將に恐くは發かんとす。神以て靈なること無くんば將に恐くは歇まんとす。谷以て盈つること無くんば將に恐くは竭きんとす。萬物以て生ずること無くんば將に恐くは滅びんとす。侯王以て貞なること無くして貴高なれば將に恐くは蹶(くつがへ)らんとす。

三　故貴以賤爲本、高以下爲基。是以侯王自稱孤寡不穀[4]。此其以賤爲本邪非乎。故致數車無車[5]、不欲琭々[6]如玉、落々如石[7]。――

ness; and by 'the higher propriety,' the righteousness which is above propriety. Certainly in the summation of these four paragraphs which we have in the fifth, the subjects of them would appear to have been in the mind of Lâo-ʒze as thus defined by Wû.

In the remainder of the chapter he goes on to speak depreciatingly of ceremonies and knowledge, so that the whole chapter must be understood as descriptive of the process of decay and deterioration from the early time in which the Tâo and its attributes swayed the societies of men.

CHAPTER XXXIX. 1. The things which from of old have got the One *the Tâo* are—

> Heaven which by it is bright and pure;
> Earth rendered thereby firm and sure;
> Spirits with powers by it supplied;
> Valleys kept full throughout their void;
> All creatures which through it do live;
> Princes and kings who from it get
> The model which to all they give.

All these are the results of the One *Tâo*.

> 2. If heaven were not thus pure, it soon would rend;
>> If earth were not thus sure, 'twould break and bend;
>> Without these powers, the spirits soon would fail;
>> If not so filled, the drought would parch each vale;
>> Without that life, creatures would pass away;
>> Princes and kings, without that moral sway,
>> However grand and high, would all decay.

3. Thus it is that dignity finds its *firm* root in its *previous* meanness, and what is lofty finds its

故に貴は賤を以て本と爲し、高は下を以て基と爲す。是を以て侯王は自ら孤寡不穀と稱す。此れ其の賤を以て本と爲るか非か。故に車を數ることを致せば車無く、琭々として玉の如くなるを欲せず、落々として石の如し。

註 1. 他書は「昔の一を得たる者は」と訓む。一は道を指す。 2. 正即ち龜鑑の意。 3. 此等の結果を牧めたるは等しく皆道を得たるに依る。 4. 孤は遺孤、寡は寡德、不穀はこしきなき車の略。 5. 車の部分々々を輪、輻(や)、轂(こしき)と數へ上げても車の車たる目的を現はすものを認めることは出來ぬ。虛にしてよく化するをいふ、詳言すれば王侯も有司百官も個々別々に観れば政府の政府たる何んでもない意。 6. 玉の美を形容する辭。 7. 他書玆を琭々玉の如く落々石の如くなるを欲せずと訓む。

第四十章 一 反者道之動[1]、弱者道之用[2]。——反は道の動、

stability in the lowness *from which it rises*. Hence princes and kings call themselves 'Orphans,' 'Men of small virtue,' and as 'Carriages without a nave. Is not this an acknowledgment that in their considering themselves mean they see the foundation of their dignity? So it is that in the enumeration of the different parts of a carriage we do not come on what makes it answer the ends of a carriage. They do not wish to show themselves elegant-looking as jade, but *prefer* to be coarse-looking as an *ordinary* stone.

法本, 'The Origin of the Law.' In this title there is a reference to the Law given to all things by the Tâo, as described in the conclusion of chapter 25. And the Tâo affords that law by its passionless, undemonstrative nature, through which in its spontaneity, doing nothing for the sake of doing, it yet does all things.

The difficulty of translation is the third paragraph. The way in which princes and kings speak depreciatingly of themselves is adduced as illustrating how they have indeed got the spirit of the Tâo; and I accept the last epithet as given by Ho-shang Kung, 'naveless' (毂), instead of 毂 (='the unworthy'), which is found in Wang Pî, and has been adopted by nearly all subsequent editors. To see its appropriateness here, we have only to refer back to chapter 11, where the thirty spokes, and the nave, empty to receive the axle, are spoken of, and it is shown how the usefulness of the carriage is derived from that emptiness of the nave. This also enables us to give a fair and consistent explanation of the difficult clause which follows, in which also I have followed the text of Ho-shang Kung. For his 车, Wang Pî has 舆, which also is found in a quotation of it by Hwâi-nan 3ze; but this need not affect the meaning. In the translation of the clause we are assisted by a somewhat similar illustration about a horse in the twenty-fifth of *K*wang-3ze's Books, par. 10.

CHAPTER XL. 1. The movement of the Tâo

弱は道の用。

二　天下之物生於有、有生於無³。――天下の物は有に生り、有は無に生る。

註　1. 反動あればこそ道は原動する。　2. 強は弱弱は強、故に道の功用は弱に存す。　3. 萬有は有形に生じ、有形は無形に生ずる。上篇第一章の無名は天地の始有名は萬物の母參看。

第四十一章　一　上士聞道勤而行之¹、中士聞道若存若亡²、下士聞道大笑之、不笑不足以爲道³。――上士は道を聞いて勤めて之を行ふ。中士は道を聞いて存するが若く亡するが若し。下士は道を聞いて大に之を笑ふ、笑はずんば以て道と爲るに足らず。

二　故建言有之⁴、明道若昧、夷道⁵若纇、進道若退、上德若谷、大白⁶若辱、廣德若不足、建德⁷若偸、質眞⁸若渝、大方⁹無隅、大器晚成¹⁰、大音希聲¹¹、大象無形¹²。――故に言を建つるに之れ有り、明道は昧きが若し、夷道は纇が若し、進道は退くが若し、上德は谷の若し、大白は辱たるが若し、廣道は足らざるが若し、建德

> By contraries proceeds;
> And weakness marks the course
> Of Tâo's mighty deeds.

2. All things under heaven sprang from It as existing *and named*; that existence sprang from It as non-existent *and not named*.

去用, 'Dispensing with the Use (of Means);'—with their use, that is, as it appears to us. The subject of the brief chapter is the action of the Tâo by contraries, leading to a result the opposite of what existed previously, and by means which might seem calculated to produce a contrary result.

In translating par. 2 I have followed Ȝiâo Hung, who finds the key to it in ch. 1. Having a name, the Tâo is 'the Mother of all things;' having no name, it is 'the Originator of Heaven and Earth.' But here is the teaching of Lâo-ȝze:—'If Tâo seems to be before God,' Tâo itself sprang from nothing.

CHAPTER XLI. 1. Scholars of the highest class, when they hear about the Tâo, earnestly carry it into practice. Scholars of the middle class, when they have heard about it, seem now to keep it and now to lose it. Scholars of the lowest class, when they have heard about it, laugh greatly at it. If it were not *thus* laughed at, it would not be fit to be the Tâo.

2. Therefore the sentence-makers have thus expressed themselves:—

> 'The Tâo, when brightest seen, seems light to lack;
>
> Who progress in it makes, seems drawing back;
> Its even way is like a rugged track.
> Its highest virtue from the vale doth rise;
> Its greatest beauty seems to offend the eyes;

は偸なるが若し、質眞は渝るが若し、大方は隅無し、大器は晩く成る、大音は聲希なり、大象は形無しと。

三　道隱無名。夫惟道。善貸且成[13]。——道は隱れて名無し。夫れ惟だ道は善く貸して且成す。

註　1. 無爲にして能く道を行ふ者は聖人に限る。2. 心に道を保存するが如く或は亡失するが如く半聖半俗の境に在る。3. 下士即ち無識の士に聊けり笑はるゝやうな道でなければ以て道とするに足らぬ。4. 故に道は自然の裏に隱れて形容を絶してゐることを悟らぬ俗人原に古人は斯う云ふてゐる。5. ＝平道。6. 德の淸澄純白なるもの。7. 堅固な德。8. 質實な德。9. 大方形の德。10. 道や德は大器故一朝にして成らず。11. 德は大音にして而も聲を出すことは稀。12. 道や德は大象故形無きが如し。13. 道は善く萬物に其の力を貸して各自の德を大成させる。

第四十二章　一　道生一、一生二、二生三、三生萬物[1]。萬物負陰而抱陽[2]。沖氣以爲和[3]。——道は一を生じ、一は二を生じ、二は三を生じ、三は萬物を生ず。萬物は陰を負ふて陽を抱く。沖氣は以て和することを爲す。

二　人之所惡唯孤寡不穀[4]、而王公以爲稱[5]、故物或損之而益、益之而損。——人の惡む所は唯孤寡不穀なり、而して王公以て稱と爲す。故に物或は之を損して益し、之を益して損す。

And he has most whose lot the least supplies.
Its firmest virtue seems but poor and low;
Its soiid truth seems change to undergo;
Its largest square doth yet no corner show;
A vessel great, it is the slowest made;
Loud is its sound, but never word it said;
A semblance great, the shadow of a shade.'

3. The Tâo is hidden, and has no name; but it is the Tâo which is skilful at imparting *to all things what they need* and making them complete.

同異, 'Sameness and Difference.' The chapter is a sequel of the preceding, and may be taken as an illustration of the Tâo's proceeding by contraries.

Who the sentence-makers were whose sayings are quoted we cannot tell, but it would have been strange if Lâo-ʓze had not had a large store of such sentences at his command. The fifth and sixth of those employed by him here are found in Lieh-ʓze (II, 15 a), spoken by Lâo in reproving Yang Kû, and in VII, 3 a, that heretic appears quoting an utterance of the same kind, with the words, 'according to an old saying (古語有之).'

CHAPTER XLII.
1. The Tâo produced One; One produced Two; Two produced Three; Three produced All things. All things leave behind them the Obscurity *out of which they have come*, and go forward to embrace the Brightness *into which they have emerged*, while they are harmonised by the Breath of Vacancy.

2. What men dislike is to be orphans, to have little virtue, to be as carriages without naves; and yet these are the designations which kings and princes use for themselves. So it is that

三　人之所教亦我義教之[6]、強梁者不得其死[7]、吾將以爲教父[8]。――人の教ゆる所亦我義として之を教ふ。強梁なる者は其の死を得ず、吾將に以て教の父と爲さんとす。

註　1. 一と一と二となり、二と一と三となり是より以往萬物生ず。一は太極、二は陰陽、三は天地人三才に當る。　2. 萬物は陰より出でゝ陰を負ひ陽に入つて陽を抱く。　3. 陽の氣にも非らず陰の氣にも非らざる沖氣即ち虛氣は萬物を和す。　4. 積極の陽と消極の陰とは互に相抱合し相輔成すべきものであるが何故か俗人は消極の孤寡不穀を操ふ。　5. 流石に王公のみは自らを孤とか寡とか不穀とかと称へる。　6. 益は損を招き損は益を招くてふ自然の道理は昔から人の相教へ相戒めそ所であるから自分も亦其の理を説かねば義理が惡い。　7. 強梁な者には自然的の大往生は出來ぬ。　8. 自分は強梁……其死を基礎として損の益、益の損の理を教へよう。

some things are increased by being diminished, and others are diminished by being increased.

3. What other men *thus* teach, I also teach. The violent and strong do not die their natural death. I will make this the basis of my teaching.

道化, 'The Transformations of the Tâo.' In par. 2 we have the case of the depreciating epithets given to themselves by kings and princes, which we found before in ch. 39, and a similar lesson is drawn from it. Such depreciation leads to exaltation, and the contrary course of self-exaltation leads to abasement. This latter case is stated emphatically in par. 3, and Lâo-3ze says that it was the basis of his teaching. So far therefore we have in this chapter a repetition of the lesson that 'the movement of the Tâo is by contraries,' and that its weakness is the sure precursor of strength. But the connexion between this lesson and what he says in par. 1 it is difficult to trace. Up to this time at least it has baffled myself. The passage seems to give us a cosmogony. 'The Tâo produced One.' We have already seen that the Tâo is 'The One.' Are we to understand here that the Tâo and the One were one and the same? In this case what would be the significance of the 生 ('produced')?—that the Tâo which had been previously 'non-existent' now became 'existent,' or capable of being named? This seems to be the view of Sze-mâ Kwang (A. D. 1009—1086).

The most singular form which this view assumes is in one of the treatises on our *King*, attributed to the Tâoist patriarch Lü (呂祖道德經解), that 'the One is Heaven, which was formed by the congealing of the Tâo.' According to another treatise, also assigned to the same Lü (道德眞經合解), the One was 'the primordial ether;' the Two, 'the separation of that into its Yin and Yang constituents;' and the Three, 'the production of heaven, earth, and man by these.' In quoting the paragraph Hwâi-nan 3ze omits 道生一, and commences with 一生二, and his glossarist, Kâo Yû, makes out the One to be the Tâo, the Two to be Spiritual Intelligences (神明), and the Three to be the Harmonising Breath. From the mention of the Yin and Yang

第四十三章　一　天下之至柔[1]馳騁天下之至堅、無有入於無間[2]、是以知無爲之有益也。――天下の至柔は天下の至堅を馳騁せしむ。有ること無きは無間に入る。是を以て無爲の益有ることを知る。

　　二　不言之敎、無爲之益、天下希及之矣[3]。――不言の敎無爲の益天下之に及ぶ希(すく)なし。

　　註　1. ＝水。　2. 至徹至虛有る無きの氣は無間に入つて空隙を餘さない。　3. 天下に不言の敎無爲の益に匹敵する物は鮮いは誤解謬解である。天下に不言の敎を垂れ無爲の益を收める者は鮮いの意。

第四十四章　一　名與身孰親、身與貨孰多[1]、得與亡孰病[2]。――名と身と孰が親しき、身と貨と孰が多(たから)き、得ると亡ふと孰が病(うしな)ましき。

　　二　是故甚愛[3]必大費[4]、多藏[5]必厚亡[6]。――是の故に甚だ愛す

that follows, I believe that Lâo-ʒze intended by the Two these two qualities or elements in the primordial ether, which would be 'the One.' I dare not hazard a guess as to what 'the Three' were.

CHAPTER XLIII.

1. The softest thing in the world dashes against and overcomes the hardest; that which has no *substantial* existence enters where there is no crevice. I know hereby what advantage belongs to doing nothing *with a purpose*.

2. There are few in the world who attain to the teaching without words, and the advantage arising from non-action.

徧用, 'The Universal Use (of the action in weakness of the Tâo).' The chapter takes us back to the lines of ch. 40, that

'Weakness marks the course
Of Tâo's mighty deeds.'

By 'the softest thing in the world' it is agreed that we are to understand 'water,' which will wear away the hardest rocks. 'Dashing against and overcoming' is a metaphor taken from hunting. Ho-shang Kung says that 'what has no existence' is the Tâo; it is better to understand by it the unsubstantial air (氣) which penetrates everywhere, we cannot see how.

Compare par. 2 with ch. 2, par. 3.

CHAPTER XLIV.

1. Or fame or life,
    Which do you hold more dear?
   Or life or wealth,
    To which would you adhere?
   Keep life and lose those other things;
   Keep them and lose your life :—which brings
    Sorrow and pain more near?

2. Thus we may see,

れば大いに費（つひ）え、多く蔵（をさ）むれば必ず厚く亡ぶ。

三　知足不辱、知止⁷不殆、可以長久。――足ることを知れば辱められず、止まることを知れば殆からず以て長久なるべし。

註　1. ＝重。 2. 名と貨とを得ると自己を亡ふとは何れが悲しきかと普通は解釋するが、レツグ博士は自己を保存し名と貨を亡ふと名と貨を保存し自己を亡ふと何れが悲しきの意に飜譯した。 3. 名を愛す。 4. 精力を消耗する。 5. 貨を藏む。 6. 心の平安を亡ふ。 7. 安んずに同じ。因に云ふ、本章は詩經流の古き押韻法に合ふと。

第四十五章　一　大成若缺其用不敝、大盈若冲其用不窮、大直若屈、大巧若拙、大辯若訥。――大成は缺けたるが若く其の用敝（やぶ）れず。大盈（えい）は冲（うつろ）なるが若く其の用窮まらず。大道は屈（かが）るが若く、大巧は拙なるが若く、大辯は訥（とつ）なるが若し。

二　躁勝寒、靜勝熱²、清靜爲天下正³。――躁は寒に勝つ、靜は熱に勝つ、清靜は天下の正と爲る。

註　1. 自分の大業を取るに足らずとする者の精力は永續する。 2. 躁靜即ち人爲的の動靜は一時的の寒暑を制するに過ぎぬ。 3. 動にもあらず靜にもあらざる自然的の清靜に至つては能く天下の正法となる。

>   Who cleaves to fame
>   Rejects what is more great;
>   Who loves large stores
>   Gives up the richer state.
> 3. Who is content
>   Needs fear no shame.
>   Who knows to stop
>   Incurs no blame.
>   From danger free
>   Long live shall he.

立戒, 'Cautions.' The chapter warns men to let nothing come into competition with the value which they set on the Tâo. The Tâo is not named, indeed, but the idea of it was evidently in the writer's mind.

The whole chapter rhymes after a somewhat peculiar fashion; familiar enough, however, to one who is acquainted with the old rhymes of the Book of Poetry.

CHAPTER XLV. 1. Who thinks his great achievements poor
   Shall find his vigour long endure.
   Of greatest fulness, deemed a void,
   Exhaustion ne'er shall stem the tide.
   Do thou what's straight still crooked deem;
   Thy greatest art still stupid seem,
   And eloquence a stammering scream.

2. Constant action overcomes cold; being still overcomes heat. Purity and stillness give the correct law to all under heaven.

洪德, 'Great or Overflowing Virtue.' The chapter is another illustration of the working of the Tâo by contraries.

According to Wû Khăng, the action which overcomes cold is

四十六章　一　天下有道却走馬以糞¹、天下無道戎馬生於郊²。——天下道有れば走馬を却けて以て糞る。天下道無ければ戎馬郊に生まる。

二　罪莫大於可欲³、禍莫大於不知足、咎莫大於欲得、故知足之足常足⁴。——罪は可欲より大るは莫し。禍は足ることを知らざるより大なるは莫し。咎は得ることを欲するより大なるは莫し。故に足ることを知るの足るは常に足る。

註　1. 天下に道が行はるれば人民は足ることを知つて争はぬから戦場を走る軍馬を廢して耕作に従はせることが出来る。　2. 天下に道が行はれなければ貪慾厭く無きの人民は相奪はずんば已まぬから郊野に戎馬（軍馬）が飼育されるやうになる。　3. 欲を許す即ち欲を逞うす。　4. 足ることを充分に知れば富にも足り貧にも足り貴にも足り賤にも足り行くとして足らずといふことなし。

第四十七章　一　不出戸知天下、不窺牖見天道¹。其出彌遠其知彌少²。——戸を出でずして天下を知り、牖を窺はずして天道を見る。其の出づること彌々遠ければ其の知ること彌々少し。

二　是以聖人不行而知、不見而名³、不爲而成。——是を以て聖人は行かずして知り、見ずして名づけ、爲さずして成せり。

that of the Yang element in the developing primordial ether; and the stillness which overcomes heat is that of the contrary Yin element. These may have been in Lâo-ɜze's mind, but the statements are so simple as hardly to need any comment. Wû further says that the purity and stillness are descriptive of the condition of non-action.

CHAPTER XLVI. 1. When the Tâo prevails in the world, they send back their swift horses to *draw* the dung-carts. When the Tâo is disregarded in the world, the war-horses breed in the border lands.

2. There is no guilt greater than to sanction ambition; no calamity greater than to be discontented with one's lot; no fault greater than the wish to be getting. Therefore the sufficiency of contentment is an enduring and unchanging sufficiency.

俭欲, 'The Moderating of Desire or Ambition.' The chapter shows how the practice of the Tâo must conduce to contentment and happiness.

In translating par. 1 I have, after Wû Khăng, admitted a 車 after the 糞, his chief authority for doing so being that it is so found in a poetical piece by Kang Hăng (A. D. 78—139). Kû Hsî also adopted this reading (朱子大全, XVIII, 7 a). In par. 2 Han Ying has a tempting variation of 多欲 for 可欲, but I have not adopted it because the same phrase occurs elsewhere.

CHAPTER XLVII. 1. Without going outside his door, one understands *all that takes place* under the sky; without looking out from his window, one sees the Tâo of Heaven. The farther that one goes out *from himself*, the less he knows.

2. Therefore the sages got their knowledge without travelling; gave their *right* names to things

註　1. 內省に由つて絕對の直觀知を得た聖人のことをいふ。　2. 外界に相對的の知見を求める俗人のことをいふ。出づるとは心を外にするをいふ。　3. 見(あらは)さずして名ありとも訓む。

第四十八章　一　爲學日益、爲道日損[1]。――學を爲れば日に益し、道を爲れば日に損す。

二　損之[2]又損以至於無爲、無爲而無不爲矣[3]。――之を損して又損し以て無爲に至る。無爲にして爲さずといふこと無し。

三　故取天下者常以無事、及其有事不足以取天下。――故に天下を取る者は常に事無きを以てす、其の事有るに及んでは以て天下を取るに足らず。

註　1. 外に向つて學問をすれば日々に智識を益すことを求める、內に向つて道を修めれば日々に作爲行動を減ずることを求める。　2. 作

without seeing them; and accomplished their ends without any purpose of doing so.

覽遠, 'Surveying what is Far-off.' The chapter is a lesson to men to judge of things according to their internal conviction of similar things in their own experience. Short as the chapter is, it is somewhat mystical. The phrase, 'The Tâo' or way of Heaven, occurs in it for the first time; and it is difficult to lay down its precise meaning. Lâo-3ze would seem to teach that man is a microcosm; and that, if he understand the movements of his own mind, he can understand the movements of all other minds. There are various readings, of which it is not necessary to speak.

I have translated par. 2 in the past tense, and perhaps the first should also be translated so. Most of it is found in Han Ying, preceded by 'formerly' or 'anciently.'

CHAPTER XLVIII. 1. He who devotes himself to learning *seeks* from day to day to increase *his knowledge*; he who devotes himself to the Tâo *seeks* from day to day to diminish *his doing*.

2. He diminishes it and again diminishes it, till he arrives at doing nothing *on purpose*. Having arrived at this point of non-action, there is nothing which he does not do.

3. He who gets as his own all under heaven does so by giving himself no trouble *with that end*. If one take trouble *with that end*, he is not equal to getting as his own all under heaven.

忘知, 'Forgetting Knowledge;'—the contrast between Learning and the Tâo. It is only by the Tâo that the world can be won.

3iâo Hung commences his quotations of commentary on this chapter with the following from Kumâragîva on the second par.: —'He carries on the process of diminishing till there is nothing coarse about him which is not put away. He puts it away till

爲行動。3. 無爲は自然故大用窮りなく爲さゞる所がない。4. 有事を以てするやうになれば天下を取ることは出來ぬ。

第四十九章 一 聖人無常心以百姓心爲心¹。――聖人には常の心無し、百姓の心を以て心と爲す。

二 善者吾亦善之、不善者吾亦善之²、得善矣³。信者吾亦信之、不信者吾亦信之、得信矣。――善なる者は吾亦之に善にす、不善なる者も吾亦之に善にす。善を得。信なる者は吾亦之に信にす、不信なる者も吾亦之に信にす。信を得。

三 聖人之在天下惵々爲天下渾心、百姓皆注其耳目、聖人皆孩之⁴。――聖人の天下に在るや惵々として天下の爲に心を渾(まろかし)にす。百姓皆其の耳目を注(そゝ)ぐ。聖人は皆之を孩(かい)にす。

he has forgotten all that was bad in it. He then puts away all that is fine about him. He does so till he has forgotten all that was good in it. But the bad was wrong, and the good is right. Having diminished the wrong, and also diminished the right, the process is carried on till they are both forgotten. Passion and desire are both cut off; and his virtue and the Tâo are in such union that he does nothing; but though he does nothing, he allows all things to do their own doing, and all things are done.' Such is a Buddhistic view of the passage, not very intelligible, and which I do not endorse.

In a passage in the 'Narratives of the School' (Bk. IX, Art. 2), we have a Confucian view of the passage:—'Let perspicacity, intelligence, shrewdness, and wisdom be guarded by stupidity, and the service of the possessor will affect the whole world; let them be guarded by complaisance, and his daring and strength will shake the age; let them be guarded by timidity, and his wealth will be all within the four seas; let them be guarded by humility, and there will be what we call the method of "diminishing it, and diminishing it again."' But neither do I endorse this.

My own view of the scope of the chapter has been given above in a few words. The greater part of it is found in *K*wang-*y*ze.

CHAPTER XLIX. 1. The sage has no invariable mind of his own; he makes the mind of the people his mind.

2. To those who are good *to me*, I am good; and to those who are not good *to me*, I am also good;—and thus *all* get to be good. To those who are sincere *with me*, I am sincere; and to those who are not sincere *with me*, I am also sincere;—and thus *all* get to be sincere.

3. The sage has in the world an appearance of indecision, and keeps his mind in a state of indifference to all. The people all keep their eyes

註　1．聖人には固定した心が無く能く物に應じ物を受ける。　2．善惡は固とこれ相對的のもので何れを取り何れを棄つる譯にも行かぬ。3．斯くすれば總てが善になる。斯くして吾は善不善を分たぬ至善を得とも解す。　4．聖人の天下に在るや一般民衆のために其の私を忘れ渾然として心に異を立てぬから民衆は其の耳目を聖人に注ぐこと慈父の如く、聖人も民衆を視ること孩兒の如くである。憬々は愛憎取捨等に不決斷の形容。

第五十章 ―― 出生入死[1]。――出づれば生き入れば死す。

and ears directed to him, and he deals with them all as his children.

任德, 'The Quality of Indulgence.' The chapter shows how that quality enters largely into the dealing of the sage with other men, and exercises over them a transforming influence, dominated as it is in him by the Tâo.

My version of par. 1 is taken from Dr. Chalmers. A good commentary on it was given by the last emperor but one of the earlier of the two great Sung dynasties, in the period A. D. 1111-1117:—'The mind of the sage is free from pre-occupation and able to receive; still, and able to respond.'

In par. 2 I adopt the reading of 得 ('to get') instead of the more common 德 ('virtue' or 'quality'). There is a passage in Han Ying (IX, 3b, 4a), the style of which, most readers will probably agree with me in thinking, was moulded on the text before us, though nothing is said of any connexion between it and the saying of Lâo-ȝze. I must regard it a sequel to the conversation between Confucius and some of his disciples about the principle (Lâo's principle) that 'Injury should be recompensed with Kindness,' as recorded in the Con. Ana., XIV, 36. We read:—'Ȝze-lû said, "When men are good to me, I will also be good to them; when they are not good to me, I will also be not good to them." Ȝze-kung said, "When men are good to me, I will also be good to them; when they are not good to me, I will simply lead them on, forwards it may be or backwards." Yen Hui said, "When men are good to me, I will also be good to them; when they are not good to me, I will still be good to them." The views of the three disciples being thus different, they referred the point to the Master, who said, "The words of Ȝze-lû are such as might be expected among the (wild tribes of) the Man and the Mo; those of Ȝze-kung, such as might be expected among friends; those of Hui, such as might be expected among relatives and near connexions."' This is all. The Master was still far from Lâo-ȝze's standpoint, and that of his own favourite disciple, Yen Hui.

CHAPTER L. 1. Men come forth and live; they enter *again* and die.

二　生之徒十有三、死之徒十有三[2]。――生の徒十に三有り、死の徒十に三有り。

三　民之生動之死地亦十有三、夫何故、以其生生之厚[3]。――民の生きんとして動すれば死地に之くもの亦十に三有り、夫れ何の故ぞ、其の生きることを生きるとするの厚きを以てなり。

四　蓋聞善攝生者[4]陸行不遇兕虎[5]、入軍不被甲兵[6]。兕無所投其角、虎無所措其爪、兵無所容其刃。夫何故、以其無死地焉[7]。――蓋し聞く、善く生を攝むる者は陸に行きて兕（野牛の類）虎に遇はず、軍に入つて甲兵を被らず。兕も其の角を投ずる所無く、虎も其の爪を措く所無く、兵も其の刃を容るゝ所無し。夫れ何の故ぞ、其の死地無きを以てなり。

註　1. 人間は無より有に出でては生き有より無に入つては死ぬ、即ち生は二つの無の中間物。　2. 人間生死の樣を見るに天壽を全ふするもの十に三、天壽を傷くるもの十に三なり。他書は十有三を十三に解す。　3. 延命長壽をこれ事とするを以てなり。　4. 十の九以外の者即ち十に一の體道者。　5. 襲撃に遇はぬ、遂背すれば遇ふもその襲撃を受けぬ意。　6. 甲兵の難を被らぬ意。　7. 斯かる人々は既に生死の慮に超越して全身に死地死相がないからである。

2. Of every ten three are ministers of life *to themselves*; and three are ministers of death.

3. There are also three in every ten whose aim is to live, but whose movements tend to the land *or place* of death. And for what reason? Because of their excessive endeavours to perpetuate life.

4. But I have heard that he who is skilful in managing the life entrusted to him for a time travels on the land without having to shun rhinoceros or tiger, and enters a host without having to avoid buff coat or sharp weapon. The rhinoceros finds no place in him into which to thrust its horn, nor the tiger a place in which to fix its claws, nor the weapon a place to admit its point. And for what reason? Because there is in him no place of death.

貴生, 'The Value set on Life.' The chapter sets forth the Tâo as an antidote against decay and death.

In par. 1 life is presented to us as intermediate between two non-existences. The words will suggest to many readers those in Job i. 21.

In pars. 2 and 3 I translate the characters 十有三 by 'three in ten,' instead of by 'thirteen,' as Julien and other translators have done. The characters are susceptible of either translation according to the tone in which we read the 有. They were construed as I have done by Wang Pî; and many of the best commentators have followed in his wake. 'The ministers of life to themselves' would be those who eschewed all things, both internal and external, tending to injure health; 'the ministers of death,' those who pursued courses likely to cause disease and shorten life; the third three would be those who thought that by mysterious and abnormal courses they could prolong life, but only injured it. Those three classes being thus disposed of,

第五十一章 一 道¹生之²、德³畜之、物⁴形之、勢⁵成之。是以萬物莫不尊道而貴德。——道之を生し、德之を畜ち、物之を形ちし、勢之を成す。是を以て、萬物道を尊び、德を貴はずといふこと莫し。

二 道之尊德之貴夫莫之命而常自然⁶。——道の尊德の貴夫れ之を命ずること莫し、而も常に自ら然り。

三 故道生之、畜之、長之、育之、成之、熟之、養之、覆之。——故に道之を生し、之を畜ち、之を長なし、之を育み、之を成し、之を熟し、之を養ひ、之を覆ふ。

四 生而不有、爲而不恃、長而不宰、是謂玄德⁷。——生じて有せず、爲して恃まず、長なして宰らず、是を玄德と謂ふ。

註 1. 道とは宇宙萬物を發生せしめた原勢力をいふ。 2. 森羅萬象即ち現象界のあらゆる物象。 3. その初は靜的である道が動的に變じた時に即ち作用した時に之を德と謂ふ。 4. 各物の性質。 5. 各物の情

there remains only one in ten rightly using the Tâo, and he is spoken of in the next paragraph.

This par. 4 is easy of translation, and the various readings in it are unimportant, differing in this respect from those in par. 3. But the aim of the author in it is not clear. In ascribing such effects to the possession of the Tâo, is he 'trifling,' as Dr. Chalmers thinks? or indulging the play of his poetical fancy? or simply saying that the Tâoist will keep himself out of danger?

CHAPTER LI. 1. All things are produced by the Tâo, and nourished by its outflowing operation. They receive their forms according to the nature of each, and are completed according to the circumstances of their condition. Therefore all things without exception honour the Tâo, and exalt its outflowing operation.

2. This honouring of the Tâo and exalting of its operation is not the result of any ordination, but always a spontaneous tribute.

3. Thus it is that the Tâo produces *all things*, nourishes them, brings them to their full growth, nurses them, completes them, matures them, maintains them, and overspreads them.

4. It produces them and makes no claim to the possession of them; it carries them through their processes and does not vaunt its ability in doing so; it brings them to maturity and exercises no control over them;—this is called its mysterious operation.

養德, 'The Operation (of the Tâo) in Nourishing Things.' The subject of the chapter is the quiet passionless operation of the Tâo in nature, in the production and nourishing of things

勢。　6. 道や德は王侯のやうに人に尊貴せよと命令するものではなく自ら人に尊貴されるものである。　7. 道や德が萬物を生育し長養し庇護し成熟せしめて已まず、而もこれを私有せず、その功を恃まず、育ての親としてこれを主宰せぬ所は父母の子に對する親德なぞの喩ではないから自分は之を玄德卽ち神秘な德と謂ふ。

第五十二章　一　天下有始、以爲天下母[1]。──天下始有り、以て天下の母と爲る。

二　既得其母以知其子、既知其子復守其母沒身不殆[2]。──既に其の母を得れば以て其の子を知る、既に其の子を知り復た其の母を守れば身を沒るまで殆からず。

三　塞其兌閉其門終身不勤[3]、開其兌濟其事終身不救[4]。──其の兌を塞ぎ其の門を閉づれば、身を終るまで勤らず、其の兌を開き其の事を濟ませば、身を終るまで救はれず。

四　見小曰明、守柔曰剛[5]。──小を見るを明と曰ふ、柔を守るを剛と曰ふ。

五　用其光復歸其明無遺身殃是謂襲常[6]。──其の光を用て其の明に復歸すれば身の殃を遺すこと無し。是を襲常と謂ふ。

throughout the seasons of the year;—a theme dwelt on by Lâo-ʒze, in II, 4, X, 3, and other places.

The Tâo is the subject of all the predicates in par. 1, and what seem the subjects in all but the first member should be construed adverbially,

On par. 2 Wû *Khăng* says that the honour of the Son of Heaven is derived from his appointment by God, and that then the nobility of the feudal princes is derived from him; but in the honour given to the Tâo and the nobility ascribed to its operation, we are not to think of any external ordination. There is a strange reading of two of the members of par. 3 in Wang Pî, viz. 亭之毒之 for 成之熟之. This is quoted and predicated of 'Heaven,' in the Nestorian Monument of Hsî-an in the eighth century.

CHAPTER LII. 1. *The Tâo* which originated all under the sky is to be considered as the mother of them all.

2. When the mother is found, we know what her children should be. When one knows that he is his mother's child, and proceeds to guard *the qualities of* the mother that belong to him, to the end of his life he will be free from all peril.

3. Let him keep his mouth closed, and shut up the portals *of his nostrils,* and all his life he will be exempt from laborious exertion. Let him keep his mouth open, and *spend his breath* in the promotion of his affairs, and all his life there will be no safety for him.

4. The perception of what is small is *the secret of* clear-sightedness; the guarding of what is soft and tender is *the secret of* strength.

5. Who uses well his light,
   Reverting to its *source so* bright,

註　1. 萬物養生の根本原始たる道は天下の母と云ふことが出來るの意。　2. 若しも我々が直感知を以て天下の母を知らば斯の母の子たるものは宜しく如何にあるべき乎をも知る。若しも已が斯の母の子たることを知り　更に進んで己の承け繼ぎたる母の特性を守護すれば終生世に處して危險がない。　3. 五官の知覺を抑えれば終身心勞せずに道に住することが出來る。　4. 口鼻を閉き氣息态々外物を追へば一生救はれぬ。　5. 小を見るは明を得る秘訣、柔を守れば人と爭はず即ち剛である。　6. 自然を知り自然を用ひ而も自然に滯らず自然の母體なる道に復歸して之を忘却しなければ身の禍をのこすことはない、自然の用を永恒不易に私藏するとは是を謂ふ。光＝自然。明＝道。襲＝護。常＝不易。

Will from his body ward all blight,
And hides the unchanging from men's sight.

歸元, 'Returning to the Source.' The meaning of the chapter is obscure, and the commentators give little help in determining it. As in the preceding chapter, Lâo-ʒze treats of the operation of the Tâo on material things, he seems in this to go on to the operation of it in man, or how he, with his higher nature, should ever be maintaining it in himself.

For the understanding of paragraph 1 we must refer to the first chapter of the treatise, where the Tâo, 'having no name,' appears as 'the Beginning' or 'First Cause' of the world, and then, 'having a name,' as its 'Mother.' It is the same thing or concept in both of its phases, the ideal or absolute, and the manifestation of it in its passionless doings. The old Jesuit translators render this par. by 'Mundus principium et causam suam habet in Divino 有, seu actione Divinae sapientiae quae dici potest ejus mater.' So far I may assume that they agreed with me in understanding that the subject of the par. was the Tâo.

Par. 2 lays down the law of life for man thus derived from the Tâo. The last clause of it is given by the same translators as equivalent to 'Unde fit ut post mortem nihil ei timendum sit,'—a meaning which the characters will not bear. But from that clause, and the next par., I am obliged to conclude that even in Lâo-ʒze's mind there was the germ of the sublimation of the material frame which issued in the asceticism and life-preserving arts of the later Tâoism.

Par. 3 seems to indicate the method of 'guarding the mother in man,' by watching over the breath, the protoplastic 'one' of ch. 42, the ethereal matter out of which all material things were formed. The organs of this breath in man are the mouth and nostrils (nothing else should be understood here by 兌 and 門 ;—see the explanations of the former in the last par. of the fifth of the appendixes to the Yî in vol. xvi, p. 432); and the management of the breath is the mystery of the esoteric Buddhism and Tâoism.

In par. 4 'The guarding what is soft' is derived from the

第五十三章 一　使我介然[1]有知[2]行於大道、唯施[3]是畏。――我をして介然として知る有り大道を行はしめば唯だ施すことを是れ畏る。

二　大道甚夷而民[4]好徑[5]。――大道は甚だ夷(たいらか)なり、而るを民は徑(こみち)を好む。

三　朝甚除、田甚蕪、倉甚虛、服文采、帶利劍、厭飮食、資財有餘、是謂盜誇。非道哉。――朝は甚だ除(をさま)り、田は甚だ蕪れ、倉は甚だ虛(むな)しきも、文采を服し、利劍を帶(は)し、飮食に厭き、資財餘り有る、是を盜の誇ると謂ふ。道に非る哉。

註　1. 倏然又は忽然と同義。――山徑之蹊間介然用之而成路。――孟子盡心章下。然るに漢籍國字解又は字源には介然は固く守つて化せぬ貌と解してある。　2. 有知は王侯吾を知る有りの意、論語先進章の「もし或は爾を知るあらば則ち何を以てせん哉」參照。しかし國字解は自分に小知が有る意に取る。　3. 得々として大道的即ち無爲的政治を施すこと。國字解は施を大道に反する施設の意に取る。　4. 民は玆では主に政を執る者を指す。　5. 有爲的政治を喩ふ。

use of 'the solf lips' in hiding and preserving the hard and strong teeth.

Par. 5 gives the gist of the chapter:—Man's always keeping before him the ideal of the Tâo, and, without purpose, simply doing whatever he finds to do; Tâo-like and powerful in all his sphere of action.

I have followed the reading of the last character but one, which is given by 3iâo Hung instead of that found in Ho-shang Kung and Wang Pî.

CHAPTER LIII. 1. If I were suddenly to become known, and *put into a position to* conduct *a government* according to the Great Tâo, what I should be most afraid of would be a boastful display.

2. The great Tâo *or way* is very level and easy; but people love the by-ways.

3. Their court-*yards and buildings* shall be well kept, but their fields shall be ill-cultivated, and their granaries very empty. They shall wear elegant and ornamented robes, carry a sharp sword at their girdle, pamper themselves in eating and drinking, and have a superabundance of property and wealth:—such *princes* may be called robbers and boasters. This is contrary to the Tâo surely!

益證, 'Increase of Evidence.' The chapter contrasts government by the Tâo with that conducted in a spirit of ostentation and by oppression.

In the 'I' of paragraph 1 does Lâo-3ze speak of himself? I think he does. Wû *Kh*ăng understands it of 'any man,' i.e. any one in the exercise of government;—which is possible. What is peculiar to my version is the pregnant meaning given to 有知, common enough in the mouth of Confucius. I have adopted it here because of a passage in Liû Hsiang's Shwo-wăn

第五十四章　一　善建者不拔¹、善抱者不脱、子孫以祭祀不輟²。──善く建つものは抜けず、善く抱くものは脱せず、子孫祭祀を以て輟まず。

二　修之³身其德乃眞、修之家其德乃餘、修之鄕其德乃長、修之國其德乃豐、修之天下其德乃普。──之を身に修むれば其の德乃ち眞なり、之を家に修むれば其の德乃ち餘りあり、之を鄕に修むれば其の德乃ち長し、之を國に修むれば其の德乃ち豐なり、之を天下に修むれば其の德乃ち普し。

三　故以身觀身⁴、以家觀家、以鄕觀鄕、以國觀國、以天下觀天下。──故に身を以て身を觀、家を以て家を觀、鄕を以て鄕を觀、國を以て國を觀、天下を以て天下を觀る。

(XX, 13 b), where Lâo-ɟze is made to say 'Excessive is the difficulty of practising the Tâo at the present time,' adding that the princes of his age would not receive it from him. On the 'Great Tâo,' see chapters 25, 34, et al. From the twentieth book of Han Fei (12 b and 13 a) I conclude that he had the whole of this chapter in his copy of our *King*, but he broke it up, after his fashion, into fragmentary utterances, confused and confounding. He gives also some remarkable various readings, one of which (筆, instead of Ho-shang Kung and Wang Pî's 竹, character 48) is now generally adopted. The passage is quoted in the Khang-hsî dictionary under 筆 with this reading.

CHAPTER LIV.

1. What *Tâo's* skilful planter plants
    Can never be uptorn;
 What his skilful arms enfold,
    From him can ne'er be borne.
 Sons shall bring in lengthening line,
 Sacrifices to his shrine.

2. Tâo when nursed within one's self,
    His vigour will make true;
 And where the family it rules
    What riches will accrue!
 The neighbourhood where it prevails
    In thriving will abound;
 And when 'tis seen throughout the state,
    Good fortune will be found.
 Employ it the kingdom o'er,
    And men thrive all around.

3. In this way the effect will be seen in the person, by the observation of different cases; in the family; in the neighbourhood; in the state; and in the kingdom.

四　吾何以知天下之然哉、以此[5]。――吾何を以て天下の然ることを知らんや、此を以てなり。

註　1. 善く建つものは體道者が無爲を爲し無事を事として建てたもの故拔ける筈はない。　2. 子々孫々が家の連綿として亡びぬやうに祭祀を絶やさぬ。　3. ＝道。　4. 道を修めて身を觀れば身に其の結果全たしの意、以下同巧異曲。　5. 道を修める結果が天下到る處に斯くあることを吾は如何にして知るか、今述べた斯の觀方によつて。

第五十五章　一　含德之厚比於赤子[1]。毒蟲不螫[2]、猛獸不據[3]、攫鳥不搏[4]。――含德の厚りは赤子に比ふ。毒蟲螫さず、猛獸據らず、攫鳥搏たず。

二　骨弱筋柔、而握固[5]、未知牝牡之合[6]而朘[7]作[8]精之至[9]也、終日號而嗌不嗄、和[10]之至也――骨弱く筋柔く而も握ること固し、未だ牝牡の合ふことを知らざるも朘作るは精の至り也。終日號べども而も嗌嗄れざるは和の至り也。

4. How do I know that this effect is sure to hold thus all under the sky? By this *method of observation.*

修觀, 'The Cultivation (of the Tâo), and the Observation (of its Effects).' The sentiment of the first paragraph is found in the twenty-seventh and other previous chapters,—that the noiseless and imperceptible acting of the Tâo is irresistible in its influence; and this runs through to the end of the chapter with the additional appeal to the influence of its effects. The introduction of the subject of sacrifices, a religious rite, though not presented to the Highest Object, will strike the reader as peculiar in our *K*ing.

The Teh mentioned five times in par. 2 is the 'virtue' of the Tâo embodied in the individual, and extending from him in all the spheres of his occupation, and is explained differently by Han Fei according to its application; and his example I have to some extent followed.

The force of pars. 3 and 4 is well given by Ho-shang Kung. On the first clause he says, 'Take the person of one who cultivates the Tâo, and compare it with that of one who does not cultivate it;—which is in a state of decay? and which is in a state of preservation?'

CHAPTER LV. 1. He who has in himself abundantly the attributes *of the Tâo* is like an infant. Poisonous insects will not sting him; beasts will not seize him; birds of prey will not strike him.

2. *The infant's* bones are weak and its sinews soft, but yet its grasp is firm. It knows not yet the union of male and female, and yet its virile member may be excited;—showing the perfection of its physical essence. All day long it will cry without its throat becoming hoarse;—showing the harmony *in its constitution.*

三　知和曰常[11]、知常曰明[12]、益生曰祥[13]、心使氣曰強[14]。——和を知るを常と曰ふ、常を知るを明と曰ふ、生を益すを祥(わざはひ)と曰ふ、心氣を使ふを強と曰ふ。

四　物壯則老、是謂不道、不道早已。——物壯なるときは則ち老ゆ、是を道にあらずと謂ふ。道にあらざれば早く已む。

註　1. 德を外に表はさず内に充分藏する者は赤子のやうだ。　2. 尾を以て毒を射す。　3. 爪を以て攫む。　4. 翼を以て撃つ。　5. 赤子は捉力に富む。　6. 男女の交。　7. 朘はをとこのもの。　8. 立に同じ。　9. 精力至大也。　10. 體質の調和。　11. 此の和を知るを常の道即ち永恆不易の道を知るといふの意。　12. 常の道を知るを明智といふの意。　13. 生を益すものは早死する意。故の祥は左傳の將有大祥のそれのやうに殃と同義。　14. 似而非なる強壯。

第五十六章　一　知者不言、言者不知[1]——知る者は言はず、言ふ者は知らず。

二　塞其兌[2]、閉其門[3]、挫其銳[4]、解其紛[5]、和其光[6]、同其塵[7]、是謂玄同[8]。——其の兌を塞(ふさ)ぎ、其の門を閉じ、其の銳きを挫(くだ)き、

3. To him by whom this harmony is known,
The secret of the unchanging *Tâo* is shown,
And in the knowledge wisdom finds its throne.
All life-increasing arts to evil turn;
Where the mind makes the vital breath to burn,
False is the strength, *and o'er it we should mourn.*

4. When things have become strong, they *then* become old, which may be said to be contrary to the Tâo. Whatever is contrary to the Tâo soon ends.

玄符, 'The Mysterious Charm;' meaning, apparently, the entire passivity of the Tâo.

With pars. 1 and 2, compare what is said about the infant in chapters 10 and 20, and about the immunity from dangers such as here described of the disciple of the Tâo in ch. 50. My 'evil' in the second triplet of par. 3 has been translated by 'felicity;' but a reference to the Khang-hsî dictionary will show that the meaning which I give to 祥 is well authorised. It is the only meaning allowable here. The third and fourth 曰 in this par. appear in Ho-shang Kung's text as 日, and he comments on the clauses accordingly; but 曰 is now the received reading. Some light is thrown on this paragraph and the next by an apocryphal conversation attributed to Lâo-ʒze in Liû Hsiang's Shwo-wăn, X, 4 a.

CHAPTER LVI. 1. He who knows *the Tâo* does not *care to* speak *about it;* he who is *ever ready to* speak about it does not know it.

2. He *who knows it* will keep his mouth shut and close the portals *of his nostrils.* He will blunt his sharp points and unravel the complications of things; he will attemper his brightness,

其の紛たるを解き、其の光を和らげ、其の塵に同ふす、是を玄同と謂ふ。

　三　不可得而親、不可得而疏、不可得而利、不可得而貴、不可得而賤、故爲天下貴[9]。──得て親む可からず、得て疏んず可からず、得て利す可からず、得て貴ぶ可からず、得て賤む可からず、故に天下の貴たり。

　註　1. 道を知る者は道を言はず、道を言ふ者は道を知らず。道の言説すべからざるを云ふ。　2. 道を知る者は感覺的知覺の誤謬誘惑に備へるために五官を閉塞する。兌は口。　3. 門は鼻孔。　4. 鈍感になるために敏感をくだく。　5. 虚心坦懷になるために心のもつれを解く。　6. 聰明の光。　7. 世俗に混じる。　8. 神秘的同化。　9. 達道の人に限つて斯く不凡に見えるから親しむことも疏んずることも利することも害ぶことも賤むことも出來ぬ、卽ち眞に天下の至寶である。

　第五十七章　一　以正治國、以奇用兵、以無事取天下[1]。──正を以て國を治め、奇を以て兵を用ひ、事無きを以て天下を取る。

　二　吾何以知其然哉、以此、夫天下多忌諱而民彌貧[2]、人多利器國家滋昏[3]、民多技巧奇物滋起、法令滋彰盜賊多有[4]。──吾何を以て其の然ることを知る哉、此を以てなり。夫れ天下忌み諱むこと多くして民彌よ貧し。人利器多くして國家滋す昏し。民技巧多くくて奇物滋す起る。法令滋す彰はれて盜賊多く有り。

　三　故聖人云、我無爲而民自化、我好靜而民自正、我無事而

and bring himself into agreement with the obscurity *of others*. This is called 'the Mysterious Agreement.'

3. *Such an one* cannot be treated familiarly or distantly; he is beyond all consideration of profit or injury; of nobility or meanness:—he is the noblest man under heaven.

玄德, 'The Mysterious Excellence.' The chapter gives us a picture of the man of Tâo, humble and retiring, oblivious of himself and of other men, the noblest man under heaven.

Par. 1 is found in *K*wang-3ze (XIII, 20 b), not expressly mentioned, as taken from Lâo-3ze, but at the end of a string of sentiments, ascribed to 'the Master,' some of them, like the two clauses here, no doubt belonging to him, and the others, probably *K*wang-3ze's own.

Par. 2 is all found in chapters 4 and 52, excepting the short clause in the conclusion.

CHAPTER LVII. 1. A state may be ruled by *measures of* correction; weapons of war may be used with crafty dexterity; *but* the kingdom is made one's own *only* by freedom from action and purpose.

2. How do I know that it is so? By these facts:—In the kindom the multiplication of prohibitive enactments increases the poverty of the people; the more implements to add to their profit that the people have, the greater disorder is there in the state and clan; the more acts of crafty dexterity that men possess, the more do strange contrivances appear; the more display there is of legislation, the more thieves and robbers there are.

3. Therefore a sage has said, 'I will do nothing

民自富、我無欲而民自樸。──故に聖人の云く、我無爲にして民自ら化す、我靜を好んで民自ら正し、我無事にして民自ら富む、我無欲にして民自ら樸(すなほ)なり、と。

　　註　1. 國を治むるには正を以てし一旦緊急あるの際兵を用ひるには奇を以てする。しかし斯の所謂正道奇道は政治の眞諦ではない、道の取らざる有爲である、天下を取るには無爲無作を以てすべし。　2. 世間に迷信や陋習が多ければ多い程人民は生業を妨げられて貧乏になる。3. 文明の利器が益せば益す程國家は昏亂を來たす。　4. 法律が煩瑣になれば法網をくゞる者が多くなる、法は三章を貴ぶ。

　第五十八章　一　其政悶々其民醇々[1]、其政察々其民缺々[2]、禍兮禍所倚、福兮禍所伏、孰知其極[3]。──其政悶々たるときは其の民醇々たり。其の政察々たるときは其の民缺々たり。禍は福の倚る所、福は禍の伏す所。孰か其の極を知らん。

　二　其無正邪[4]、正復爲奇、善復爲妖、民之迷其日固已久矣[5]。──其れ正無からんか、正復た奇と爲らん、善復た妖と爲らん、と。民の迷ひ其の日固(まこと)に已に久し。

of purpose, and the people will be transformed of themselves; I will be fond of keeping still, and the people will of themselves become correct. I will take no trouble about it, and the people will of themselves become rich; I will manifest no ambition, and the people will of themselves attain to the primitive simplicity.'

淳風, 'The Genuine Influence.' The chapter shows how government by the Tâo is alone effective, and of universal application; contrasting it with the failure of other methods.

After the 'weapons of war' in par. 1, one is tempted to take 'the sharp implements' in par. 2 as such weapons, but the meaning which I finally adopted, especially after studying chapters 36 and 80, seems more consonant with Lâo-ȝze's scheme of thought. In the last member of the same par., Ho-shang Kung has the strange reading of 法物, and uses it in his commentary; but the better text of 法令 is found both in Hwâi-nan and Sze-mâ *Kh*ien, and in Wáng Pî.

We do not know if the writer were quoting any particular sage in par. 3, or referring generally to the sages of the past; —men like the 'sentence-makers' of ch. 41.

CHAPTER LVIII.
1. The government that seems the most unwise,
Oft goodness to the people best supplies;
That which is meddling, touching everything,
Will work but ill, and disappointment bring.

Misery!—happiness is to be found by its side! Happiness!—misery lurks beneath it! Who knows what either will come to in the end?

2. Shall we then dispense with correction? The *method of* correction shall by a turn become distortion, and the good in it shall by a turn become

三　是以聖人方而不割[6]、廉而不劌[7]、直而不肆[8]、光而不燿[9]。——是を以て聖人は方にして割らず、廉あつて劌らず、直にして肆びず、光つて輝かず。

註　1. 政が惛愚なれば民は淳朴になる。　2. 政が苛明なれば民は輕薄になる。　3. 禍福の窮極は誰か知る。　4. 在來の訓み方は「其れ正（さだまること）無からんか」である。　5. 此の事に關する民の迷は既に久しい。　6. 已正にして人を責めず。　7. 自己の廉潔を以て人を汚れたりとして捨てず。　8. 已の直を以て肆（ほしいまゝ）に流れず。　9. 自己の光を韜晦にして其の行を外に燿かさぬ。

第五十九章

一　治人事天莫如嗇[1]。——人を治め天に事るには嗇に如くは莫し。

二　夫惟嗇、是以早復[2]。早復謂之重積德、重積德[3]則無不克[4]。無不克、則莫知其極[5]。莫知其極、可以有國。——夫れ惟だ嗇是を以て早く復へる。早く復へる之を德を重ね積むと謂ふ。德を重ね積めば則ち克たずといふこと無し。克たずといふこと無ければ則ち其の極を知ること莫し。其の極を知ること莫ければ以て國を有つ可し。

三　有國之母[6]、可以長久、是謂深根固柢[7]、長生久視之道[8]。

evil. The delusion of the people *on this point* has indeed subsisted for a long time.

3. Therefore the sage is *like* a square which cuts no one *with its angles*; *like* a corner which injures no one *with its sharpness*. He is straightforward, but allows himself no license; he is bright, but does not dazzle.

<small>順化, 'Transformation according to Circumstances;' but this title does not throw light on the meaning of the chapter; nor are we helped to an understanding of it by Han Fei, with his additions and comments (XI, 3 b, 4 b), nor by Hwâi-nan with his illustrations (XII, 21 a, b). The difficulty of it is increased by its being separated from the preceding chapter of which it is really the sequel. It contrasts still further government by the Tâo, with that by the method of correction. The sage is the same in both chapters, his character and government both marked by the opposites or contraries which distinguish the procedure of the Tâo, as stated in ch. 40.</small>

CHAPTER LIX.

1. For regulating the human *in our constitution* and rendering the *proper* service to the heavenly, there is nothing like moderation.

2. It is only by this moderation that there is effected an early return *to man's normal state*. That early return is what I call the repeated accumulation of the attributes *of the Tâo*. With that repeated accumulation of those attributes, there comes the subjugation *of every obstacle to such return*. Of this subjugation we know not what shall be the limit; and when one knows not what the limit shall be, he may be the ruler of a state.

3. He who possesses the mother of the state

――國の母を有てば以て長久なる可し。是を根を深くし柢を固くすと謂ふ、長生を久しく視るの道なり。

註 1. 自分の心の中の人間味を治めたりその天稟につかへるには控え目にするに限る。在來の解釋書は治人亦天を「人を治め天に事ふ」る所謂君主の道としレッグ博士の如く各自修養の道としなかつたのみならず、嗇の字も吝嗇の嗇即ちをしむと解しひかえめにする義には取らなかつた。 2. 早く人の人たる本體に歸へるには唯嗇にするあるのみ。 3. 謂之重積德重積德を從來は大低「之を重ねて積むと謂ふ德重ねて德を積めば」云々と訓むだ。 4. 克は早復の邪魔物に勝つ意。 5. 無限に勝つ意。 6. 國の母を有つは道を體する意、從來は國を有つの母と訓むだ。 7. 植物に譬ふ。 8. 延命長壽の道。

第六十章 一 治大國若烹小鮮[1]。――大國を治むるには小鮮を烹るが若くす。

二 以道涖天下、其鬼不神。非其鬼不神、其神不傷人。非其神不傷人、聖人亦不傷之[2]。――道を以て天下に涖めば其の鬼神ならず。其の鬼神ならざるに非らず其の神人を傷らざるなり。其の神人を傷らざるに非らず聖人も亦之を傷らざるなり。

may continue long. His case is like that *of the plant* of which we say that its roots are deep and its flower stalks firm :—this is the way to secure that its enduring life shall long be seen.

守道, 'Guarding the Tâo.' The chapter shows how it is the guarding of the Tâo that ensures a continuance of long life, with vigour and success. The abuse of it and other passages in our *King* helped on, I must believe, the later Tâoist dreams about the elixir vitae and life-preserving pills. The whole of it, with one or two various readings, is found in Han Fei (VI, 4 b-6 a), who speaks twice in his comments of 'The Book.'

Par. 1 has been translated, 'In governing men and in serving Heaven, there is nothing like moderation.' But by 'Heaven' there is not intended 'the blue sky' above us, nor any personal Power above it, but the Tâo embodied in our constitution, the Heavenly element in our nature. The 'moderation' is the opposite of what we call 'living fast,' 'burning the candle at both ends.'

In par. 2 I must read 復, instead of the more common 服. I find it in Lû Teh-ming, and that it is not a misprint in him appears from his subjoining that it is pronounced like 服. Its meaning is the same as in 復歸其明 in ch. 52, par. 5. Teh is not 'virtue' in our common meaning of the term, but 'the attributes of the Tâo,' as almost always with Lâo-ʓze.

In par. 3 'the mother of the state' is the Tâo as in ch. 1, and especially in ch. 52, par. 1.

CHAPTER LX.

1. Governing a great state is like cooking small fish.

2. Let the kingdom be governed according to the Tâo, and the manes of the departed will not manifest their spiritual energy. It is not that those manes have not that spiritual energy, but it will not be employed to hurt men. It is not

三　夫兩不相傷故德交歸焉。──夫れ兩<ruby>な<rt>ふたつ</rt></ruby>がら相傷らず、故に德<ruby>交歸<rt>ともごも</rt></ruby>す。

註　1. 小魚を煮るには鱗も引かず腸も取らずそのまゝ煮るやうに、國を治めるには人民の自然に任せて作爲を加へてはならぬ。　2. 無爲自然の道を以て國を治むれば鬼神（死者の靈）も神怪さを失ふ。否其の鬼が神怪さを失ふのではない、其の神怪さを人を傷（やぶ）るに用ひないのである。否其の神怪さを人を傷るに用ひないばかりではない、聖人も亦人を傷らないのである。　3. それ故鬼神の人を傷らぬ德と聖人の人を傷らぬ德とは相侵すことなく各々道に歸するやうになる。

第六十一章　一　大國者下流、天下之交[1]。──大國は下流なり、天下の交となる。

二　天下之牝[2]、牝常以靜勝牡[3]、以靜爲下[4]。──天下の<ruby>牝<rt>ひん</rt></ruby>、牝は常に靜を以て牡に勝つ。靜を以て下ると爲す。

三　故大國以下小國、則取小國、小國以下大國、則取大國、故或下以取[5]、或下而取[6]。──故に大國は小國に下ることを以て

that it could not hurt men, but neither does the ruling sage hurt them.

3. When these two do not injuriously affect each other, their good influences converge in the virtue *of the Tâo.*

<small>居位, 'Occupying the Throne;' occupying it, that is, according to the Tâo, noiselessly and purposelessly, so that the people enjoy their lives, free from all molestation seen and unseen.

Par. 1. That is, in the most quiet and easy manner. The whole of the chapter is given and commented on by Han Fei (VI, 6 a–7 b); but very unsatisfactorily.

The more one thinks and reads about the rest of the chapter, the more does he agree with the words of Julien:—'It presents the frequent recurrence of the same characters, and appears as insignificant as it is unintelligible, if we give to the Chinese characters their ordinary meaning.'—The reader will observe that we have here the second mention of spirits (the manes; Chalmers, 'the ghosts; Julien, les démons). See ch. 39.

Whatever Lâo-ȝze meant to teach in par. 2, he laid in it a foundation for the superstition of the later and present Tâoism about the spirits of the dead;—such as appeared a few years ago in the 'tail-cutting' scare.</small>

CHAPTER LXI. 1. What makes a great state is its being *like* a low-lying, down-flowing *stream;* —it becomes the centre to which tend *all the small states* under heaven.

2. *To illustrate from* the case of all females: —the female always overcomes the male by her stillness. Stillness may be considered *a sort of* abasement.

3. Thus it is that a great state, by condescending to small states, gains them for itself; and that small states, by abasing themselves to a great

則ち小國を取り、小國は大國に下ることを以て則ち大國を取る。故に或は下つて以て取り、或は下つて而して取らる。

四　大國、不過欲兼畜人[7]、小國、不過欲入事人[8]、夫兩者各得其所欲、故大者宜爲下。――大國は人を兼ね畜(やしな)はんと欲するに過ぎず。小國は入りて人に事へんと欲するに過ぎず。夫れ兩つの者各々其の欲する所を得、故に大なる者は宜しく下ることを爲すべし。

註　1. 大國の大國たる所以は水のやうに低きに下つて天下の小國の歸宗する所となるからである。2. 天下の牝を以て例せばの意。3. 牝は靜を以て牡に下るけれども何時も靜を以て牡に勝つ。4. 世人或は靜を卑屈と思惟するならん。5. ＝大國下以取人。湯の大國を以て葛の小國を取れるなぞの類。6. ＝小國下而取于人（人に取らる）。換言すれば小國下るときは大國之を納るの意で、例へば句踐の呉に事へて越を完うせるが如きを云ふ。以取は能相動詞而取は所相動詞。7. 小國を併せて之をやしなふ。8. 大國に事へる。

第六十二章　一　道者萬物之奥、善人之寶、不善人之所保[1]。――道は萬物の奥、善人の寶とす。不善人も之に保んぜらる。

二　美言可以市、尊行可以加人[2]、人之不善、何棄之有[3]。――美言は以て尊を市る可く、美行は以て人に加ふ可し。人の不善何の棄ることか之れ有らん。

三　故立天子置三公、雖有拱璧以先駟馬[4]、不如坐進[5]此道。――故に天子として立ち三公を置き、拱璧以て駟馬に先んづること有りと雖も坐(ざ)ながら此の道を進むるに如かず。

四　古之所以貴此道者何也、不曰求以得有罪以免邪、故爲天

state, win it over to them. In the one case the abasement leads to gaining adherents, in the other case to procuring favour.

4. The great state only wishes to unite men together and nourish them; a small state only wishes to be received by, and to serve, the other. Each gets what it desires, but the great state must learn to abase itself.

謙德, 'The Attribute of Humility;'—a favourite theme with Lâo-ȝze; and the illustration of it from the low-lying stream to which smaller streams flow is also a favourite subject with him. The language can hardly but recall the words of a greater than Lâo-ȝze:—' He that humbleth himself shall be exalted.'

CHAPTER LXII. 1. Tâo has of all things the most honoured place.
No treasures give good men so rich a grace;
Bad men it guards, and doth their ill efface.

2. *Its* admirable words can purchase honour; *its* admirable deeds can raise their performer above others. Even men who are not good are not abandoned by it.

3. Therefore when the sovereign occupies his place as the Son of Heaven, and he has appointed his three ducal ministers, though *a prince* were to send in a round symbol-of-rank large enough to fill both the hands, and that as the precursor of the team of horses *in the court-yard,* such an offering would not be equal to *a lesson of* this Tâo, which one might present on his knees.

4. Why was it that the ancients prized this Tâo so much? Was it not because it could be got

下賁。――古の此の道を貴ぶ所以のものは何んぞや、求むれば以て得罪あれども以て免ると曰はずや、故に天下の貴たり。

註 1. 道は萬物中最上席に居り、善の奥座歡善人の至寶たるのみか、惡人も無意識の間に道を有つて保んぜられる。 2. 美言可以市尊、美行可以加人と書き改めて訓む。うはべばかりの美言でも世間に歡迎される、心にもない善行でも世人から尊ばれる。 3. して見ると人間は元來は道を有つてるのであるから一時の不善は何んでもない。 4. 諸侯の中に一かゝへもある寶玉を先發として四頭立ての馬車一杯の貢物を贈るものがあつてもの意。 5. 座して君主にこの道を説き進める。

第六十三章 一 爲無爲、事無事、味無味、大小、多少、報怨以德。――無爲を爲し、無事を事とし、無味を味ふ。大なれば小さくし、多ければ少くす。怨に報ゆるに德を以てす。

二 圖難於其易、爲大於其細、天下難事、必作於易、天下大事、必作於細、是以聖人終不爲大、故能成其大。――其の易きに於て難きを圖り、其の細に於て大を爲す。天下の難事は必ず易きより作り、天下の大事は必ず細より作る。是を以て聖人は終に大を爲さず、故に能く其の大を成す。

by seeking for it, and the guilty could escape *from the stain of their guilt* by it? This is the reason why all under heaven consider it the most valuable thing.

岱道, 'Practising the Tâo.' 貴道, 'The value set on the Tâo,' would have been a more appropriate title. The chapter sets forth that value in various manifestations of it.

Par. 1. For the meaning of 奥, see Confucian Analects, III, ch. 13.

Par. 2. I am obliged to adopt the reading of the first sentence of this paragraph given by Hwâi-nan, 美言可以市尊, 美行可以加人;—see especially his quotation of it in XVIII, 10 a, as from a superior man, I have not found his reading anywhere else.

Par. 3 is not easily translated, or explained. See the rules on presenting offerings at the court of a ruler or the king, in vol. xxvii of the 'Sacred Books of the East,' p. 84, note 3, and also a narrative in the 3o *K*wan under the thirty-third year of duke Hsî.

CHAPTER LXIII.

1. *It is the way of the Tâo* to act without *thinking of* acting; to conduct affairs without *feeling the* trouble of them; to taste without discerning any flavour; to consider what is small as great, and a few as many; and to recompense injury with kindness.

2. *The master of it* anticipates things that are difficult while they are easy, and does things that would become great while they are small. All difficult things in the world are sure to arise from a previous state in which they were easy, and all great things from one in which they were small. Therefore the sage, while he never does what is

三　夫輕諾、必寡信。多易必多難。是以、聖人猶難之[2]、故終無難。――夫れ輕々しく諾すれば必ず信寡し。易きこと多ければ必ず難きこと多し。是を以て聖人は猶ほ之を難んず、故に終に難きこと無し。

註　1. 大を小に考へる、これも道を治める一方法。 2. 故に聖人すら猶ほ易事を難事のやうに用心する。

第六十四章　一　其安易持[1]、其未兆易謀[2]、其脆易破[3]、其微易散。爲之於未有[4]、治之於未亂。――其の安きときは持ち易く、其の未だ兆さゞるときは謀り易く、其の脆きときは破れ易く、其の微なるときは散じ易し。之を未だ有らざるに爲し、之を未だ亂れざるに治めよ。

great, is able on that account to accomplish the greatest things.

3. He who lightly promises is sure to keep but little faith; he who is continually thinking things easy is sure to find them difficult. Therefore the sage sees difficulty even in what seems easy, and so never has any difficulties.

<small>慮始, 'Thinking in the Beginning.' The former of these two characters is commonly misprinted 具, and this has led Chalmers to mistranslate them by 'The Beginning of Grace.' The chapter sets forth the passionless method of the Tâo, and how the sage accordingly accomplishes his objects easily by forestalling in his measures all difficulties. In par. 1 the clauses are indicative, and not imperative, and therefore we have to supplement the text in translating in some such way, as I have done. They give us a cluster of aphorisms illustrating the procedure of the Tâo 'by contraries,' and conclude with one, which is the chief glory of Lâo-ʒze's teaching, though I must think that its value is somewhat diminished by the method in which he reaches it. It has not the prominence in the later teaching of Tâoist writers which we should expect, nor is it found (so far as I know) in *K*wang-ʒze, Han Fei, or Hwâi-nan. It is quoted, however, twice by Liû Hsiang;—see my note on par. 2 of ch. 49.

It follows from the whole chapter that the Tâoistic 'doing nothing' was not an absolute quiescence and inaction, but had a method in it.</small>

CHAPTER LXIV.

1. That which is at rest is easily kept hold of; before a thing has given indications of its presence, it is easy to take measures against it; that which is brittle is easily broken; that which is very small is easily dispersed. Action should be taken before a thing has made its appearance; order should be secured before disorder has begun.

二　合抱之木[5]、生於毫末、九層之臺、起於累土、千里之行、始於足下。——合抱の木も毫末より生じ、九層の臺も累土より起り、千里の行も足下より始まる。

三　爲者敗之、執者失之、聖人無爲、故無敗、無執、故無失、民之從事、常於幾成而敗之、愼終如是、則無敗事。——爲す者は敗れ、執る者は失ふ。聖人は爲すこと無し、故に敗るゝこと無し。執ること無し、故に失ふこと無し。民の事に從ふ常に幾(ほとん)んど成らんとするに於て之を敗る。終を愼む是の如くんば則ち事に敗るゝこと無し。

四　是以聖人欲不欲[6]、不貴難得之貨、學不學、復衆人之所過[7]、以輔萬物之自然、而不敢爲。——是を以て聖人は欲せざるを欲し、得難きの貨(たから)を貴ばず、學ばざるを學び、衆人の過ぐる所に復(かへ)り、以て萬物の自然を輔けて敢て爲さず。

註　1. 安定の狀態にあるものは保持し易い。　2. 事は兆さゞる前なれば對策を講じ易い。　3. 物は堅くならぬ中ならば破り易い。　4. 事は未然に處理すべし。　5. 一と抱へも有る大木。　6. 世人の欲せぬものを欲す。　7. 衆人の願みぬ所即ち自然に歸へる。

第六十五章　一　古之善爲道者、非以明民、將以愚之。——古の善く道を爲す者は以て民を明にせんとに非らず、將に以て之を愚にせんとす。

二　民之難治、以其智多、故以智治國、國之賊[1]、不以智治國、國之福。——民の治め難きは其の智の多きを以てなり、故

2. The tree which fills the arms grew from the tiniest sprout; the tower of nine storeys rose from a *small* heap of earth; the journey of a thousand lî commenced with a single step.

3. He who acts *with an ulterior purpose* does harm; he who takes hold of a thing *in the same way* loses his hold. The sage does not act *so*, and therefore does no harm; he does not lay hold *so*, and therefore does not lose his hold. *But* people in their conduct of affairs are constantly ruining them when they are on the eve of success. If they were careful at the end, as *they should be* at the beginning, they would not so ruin them.

4. Therefore the sage desires what *other men* do not desire, and does not prize things difficult to get; he learns what *other men* do not learn, and turns back to what the multitude of men have passed by. Thus he helps the natural development of all things, and does not dare to act *with an ulterior purpose of his own*.

守微, 'Guarding the Minute.' The chapter is a continuation and enlargement of the last. Wû Khăng, indeed, unites the two, blending them together with some ingenious transpositions and omissions, which it is not necessary to discuss. Compare the first part of par. 3 with the last part of par. 1, ch. 29.

CHAPTER LXV. 1. The ancients who showed their skill in practising the Tâo did so, not to enlighten the people, but rather to make them simple and ignorant.

2. The difficulty in governing the people arises from their having much knowledge. He who

に智を以て國を治むるは國の賊なり、智を以て國を治めざるは國の福なり。

三　知此兩者、亦楷式[2]、能知楷式、是謂玄德[3]、玄德深矣、遠矣、與物反矣、乃至於大順[4]。──此の兩者を知る亦楷式なり。能く楷式を知る、是を玄德と謂ふ。玄德は深し、遠し、物と反す、乃ち大順に至る。

註　1. ＝福。　2. 此の兩者を知る者は亦楷式（＝治國の規距法式）を知る。　3. 治者の神秘不可思議なる德。　4. 自然の大法即ち道。

第六十六章　一　江海所以能爲百谷王[1]者、以其善下之故、能爲百谷之王、是以、聖人欲上人以其言下之、欲先人以其身後之。──江海の能く百谷の王たる所以のものは、其の善く下る(くだ)を以ての故に、能く百谷の王たり。是を以て聖人人に上(かみ)たらんと欲して其の言(ことば)を以て之に下り、人に先たんと欲して其の身を以て之に後にす。

二　是以、處上而人不重、處前而人不能害。──是を以て上に處(を)つて人重しとせず、前に處つて人害せらるゝ能はず。

三　是以、天下樂推而不厭、以其不爭故、天下莫能與之爭。──是を以て天下樂んで推して厭はず、其の爭はざるを以ての故に、

tries to govern a state by his wisdom is a scourge to it; while he who does not *try to* do so is a blessing.

3. He who knows these two things finds in them also his model and rule. Ability to know this model and rule constitutes what we call the mysterious excellence *of a governor*. Deep and far-reaching is such mysterious excellence, showing indeed its possessor as opposite to others, but leading them to a great conformity to him.

<small>玄德, 'Pure, unmixed Excellence.' The chapter shows the powerful and beneficent influence of the Tâo in government, in contrast with the applications and contrivances of human wisdom. Compare ch. 19. My 'simple and ignorant' is taken from Julien. More literally the translation would be 'to make them stupid.' My 'scourge' in par. 2 is also after Julien's 'fléau.'</small>

CHAPTER LXVI. 1. That whereby the rivers and seas are able to receive the homage and tribute of all the valley streams, is their skill in being lower than they;—it is thus that they are the kings of them all. So it is that the sage *ruler*, wishing to be above men, puts himself by his words below them, and, wishing to be before them, places his person behind them.

2. In this way though he has his place above them, men do not feel his weight, nor though he has his place before them, do they feel it an injury to them.

3. Therefore all in the world delight to exalt him and do not weary of him. Because he does

天下能く之と争ふ莫し。

　註　1.　王は往即ち物の往いて歸するを云ふ。　因に云ふ、此の章は老子の本文に非ず誤つて註解の本文として取扱はれたるものらしと。

　第六十七章　一　天下皆謂、我大似不肖。夫唯大、故似不肖。若肖久矣、其細¹。──天下皆謂ふ、我大なるも肖ざるに似たりと。夫れ唯大なり、故に肖ざるに似たり。若し肖たらば久しからんかな、其の細なること。

　二　我有三寶、寶而持之、一曰慈、二曰儉、三曰不敢爲天下先。──我に三つの寶有り、寶として之を持つ、一に曰く慈、二に曰く儉、三に曰く敢て天下の先を爲さず。

　三　慈故能勇、儉故能廣²、不敢爲天下先故能成器長³。今捨慈且⁴勇、捨儉且廣、捨後且先、死矣⁵。──慈なるが故に能く勇なり、儉なるが故に能く廣なり、敢て天下の先をなさゞるが故に能く成器の長たり。今や慈を捨て、且に勇ならんとす、儉を

not strive, no one finds it possible to strive with him.

後已, 'Putting one's self Last.' The subject is the power of the Tâo, by its display of humility in attracting men. The subject and the way in which it is illustrated are frequent themes in the *K*ing. See chapters 8, 22, 39, 42, 61, et al.

The last sentence of par. 3 is found also in ch. 22. There seem to be no quotations from the chapter in Han Fei or Hwâi-nan; but Wû *K*hăng quotes passages from Tung *K*ung-shû (of the second century B. C.), and Yang Hsiung (B. C. 53–A. D. 18), which seem to show that the phraseology of it was familiar to them. The former says:—'When one places himself in his qualities below others, his person is above them; when he places them behind those of others, his person is before them;' the other, 'Men exalt him who humbles himself below them; and give the precedence to him who puts himself behind them.'

CHAPTER LXVII. 1. All the world says that, while my Tâo is great, it yet appears to be inferior *to other systems of teaching*. Now it is just its greatness that makes it seem to be inferior. If it were like any other *system*, for long would its smallness have been known!

2. But I have three precious things which I prize and hold fast. The first is gentleness; the second is economy; and the third is shrinking from taking precedence of others.

3. With that gentleness I can be bold; with that economy I can be liberal; shrinking from taking precedence of others, I can become a vessel of the highest honour. Now-a-days they give up gentleness and are all for being bold; economy, and are all for being liberal; the hindmost place,

捨てゝ且に廣ならんとす、後を捨てゝ且に先んぜんとす。死せんかな。

四　夫、慈以戰則勝、以守則固、天將救之、以慈衞之⁶。──夫れ慈は以て戰はゞ則ち勝ち、以て守らば則ち固（かた）からん。天將（まさ）に之を救はん、慈を以て之を衞（まも）らん。

註　1. 天下の人々は皆自分の唱道する道を大は大だが他の何ものにも似ず詰まらぬものゝやうだと云ふ。しかし大なればこそ他の何ものにも喩へやうもない劣つたものに想はれるのだ。若しも喩へられたら初から詰まらぬものであつたらう。　2. 儉約なる故廣大である。　3. 大成の器のしかも長たるもの。　4. ＝將。──戰國策「城且拔矣」。因に云ふ、漢籍國字解全書は今捨慈且勇を「今慈を捨て且つ勇あり」と訓むである。　5. 斯かる人々には活くる道はない、唯死あるのみ。　6. 天は慈者の慈を以て慈者を衞らんの意。

第六十八章　善爲士者、不武、善戰者不怒、善勝者不與¹、善用人者、爲之下、是謂不爭之德、是謂用人之力、是謂配天、古之極²。──善く士たる者は武（たけ）からず、善く戰ふ者は怒らず、

and seek only to be foremost;—*of all with the end is* death.

4. Gentleness is sure to be victorious even in battle, and firmly to maintain its ground. Heaven will save its possessor, by his *very* gentleness protecting him.

三寶. 'The Three Precious Things.' This title is taken from par. 2, and suggests to us how the early framer of these titles intended to express by them the subject-matter of their several chapters. The three things are the three distinguishing qualities of the possessor of the Tâo, the three great moral qualities appearing in its followers, the qualities, we may venture to say, of the Tâo itself. The same phrase is now the common designation of Buddhism in China,—the Tri-ratna or Ratna-traya, 'the Precious Buddha,' 'the Precious Law,' and 'the Precious Priesthood (or rather Monkhood) or Church;' appearing also in the 'Tri-sarana,' or 'formula of the Three Refuges,' what Dr. Eitel calls 'the most primitive formula fidei of the early Buddhists, introduced before Southern and Northern Buddhism separated.' I will not introduce the question of whether Buddhism borrowed this designation from Tâoism, after its entrance into China. It is in Buddhism the formula of a peculiar Church or Religion; in Tâoism a rule for the character, or the conduct which the Tâo demands from all men. 'My Tâo' in par. 1 is the reading of Wang Pî; Ho-shang Kung's text is simply 我. Wang Pî's reading is now generally adopted.

The concluding sentiment of the chapter is equivalent to the saying of Mencius (VII, ii, IV, 2), 'If the ruler of a state love benevolence, he will have no enemy under heaven.' 'Heaven' is equivalent to 'the Tâo,' the course of events,—Providence, as we should say.

CHAPTER LXVIII.

He who in *Tâo's* wars has skill
    Assumes no martial port;

善く勝つ者は與にせず、善く人を用ふる者は之が下と爲る。是を爭はざるの德と謂ふ。是を人の力を用ふと謂ふ。是を天に配すと謂ふ。古の極なり。

註 1. 善く敵に勝つ者は敵と勝負を爭ふことがないから天下に己を負かす者はない即ち善く勝つ所以である。 2. 斯かる人々こそは古の聖人の極致なりの意。

第六十九章 一 用兵有言、吾不敢爲主、而爲客[1]、不敢進寸、而退尺。是謂行無行、攘無臂、仍無敵、執無兵[2]。――兵を用ひるもの言へること有り、吾敢て主たらず客たり、敢て寸に進まず尺に退くと。是を行る無きに行り、臂無きに攘げ、敵無きに仍き、兵無きに執ると謂ふ。

二 禍莫大於輕敵。輕敵、幾喪吾寶[3]。故抗[4]兵相加[5]、哀者勝矣。――禍は敵を輕んずるより大なるは莫し。敵を輕んずれば幾んど吾が寶を喪はん。故に兵を抗げて相加はるときは哀む者勝つ。

He who fights with most good will
 To rage makes no resort.
He who vanquishes yet still
 Keeps from his foes apart;
He whose hests men most fulfil
 Yet humbly plies his art.
Thus we say, 'He ne'er contends,
 And therein is his might.'
Thus we say, 'Men's wills he bends,
 That they with him unite.'
Thus we say, 'Like Heaven's his ends,
 No sage of old more bright.'

配天, 'Matching Heaven.' The chapter describes the work of the practiser of the Tâo as accomplished like that of Heaven, without striving or crying. He appears under the figure of a mailed warrior (士) of the ancient chariot. The chapter is a sequel of the preceding, and is joined on to it by Wû *Khăng*, as is also the next.

CHAPTER LXIX. 1. A master of the art of war has said, 'I do not dare to be the host *to commence the war*; I prefer to be the guest *to act on the defensive*. I do not dare to advance an inch; I prefer to retire a foot.' This is called marshalling the ranks where there are no ranks; baring the arms *to fight* where there are no arms to bare; grasping the weapon where there is no weapon to grasp; advancing against the enemy where there is no enemy.

2. There is no calamity greater than lightly engaging in war. To do that is near losing *the gentleness* which is so precious. Thus it is that

註　1. 吾敢て攻勢に出でず守勢を執る。　2. 無い軍を進め、無い臂を突張り、無い敵に向ひ、無い武器を執る、即ち無爲を爲す。仍＝就。　3. 慈儉退の三寶（第六十七章參看）。　4. ＝擧。　5. ＝交。

第七十章　一　吾言甚易知、甚易行、天下莫能知、莫能行。──吾が言甚だ知り易く、甚だ行ひ易きも、天下能く知る莫く、能く行ふ莫し。

二　言有宗、事有君[1]。夫唯無知、是以不我知也[2]。──言宗有り、事君有り。夫れ唯だ知ること無し、是を以て我を知らず。

三　知我者希、則我貴矣、是以聖人被褐懷玉[3]。──我を知る者希なり、則ち我貴し。是を以て聖人は褐を被て玉を懷く。

註　1. 自分の言には宗として尊ぶべき獨創の根本主旨がある、自分のする事には君主と仰ぐべき法則がある。　2. これが知れないばかりに自分が知れない。　3. それ故聖人は皆うはべには毛の粗服を着てゐるが心の中には璧を懷いてゐる。

when opposing weapons are *actually* crossed, he who deplores *the situation* conquers.

玄用, 'The Use of the Mysterious *Tâo*.' Such seems to be the meaning of the title. The chapter teaches that, if war were carried on, or rather avoided, according to the Tâo, the result would be success. Lâo-ʒze's own statements appear as so many paradoxes. They are examples of the procedure of the Tâo by 'contraries,' or opposites.

We do not know who the master of the military art referred to was. Perhaps the author only adopted the style of quotation to express his own sentiments.

CHAPTER LXX.
1. My words are very easy to know, and very easy to practise; but there is no one in the world who is able to know and able to practise them.

2. There is an originating and all-comprehending *principle* in my words, and an authoritative law for the things *which I enforce*. It is because they do not know these, that men do not know me.

3. They who know me are few, and I am on that account *the more* to be prized. It is thus that the sage wears *a poor garb of* hair cloth, while he carries his *signet of* jade in his bosom.

知難, 'The Difficulty of being *rightly* Known.' The Tâo comprehends and rules all Lâo-ʒze's teaching, as the members of a clan were all in the loins of their first father (宗), and continue to look up to him; and the people of a state are all under the direction of their ruler; yet the philosopher had to complain of not being known. Lâo-ʒze's principle and rule or ruler was the Tâo. His utterance here is very important. Compare the words of Confucius in the Analects, XIV, ch. 37, et al.

Par. 2 is twice quoted by Hwâi-nan, though his text is not quite the same in both cases.

第七十一章 一 知不知上[1]、不知知病[2]。──知つて知らずとするは上みなり、知らずして知れりとするは病なり。

二 夫唯病病[3]、是以不病。聖人之不病也、以其病病、是以不病。──夫れ唯病を病む、是を以て病まず。聖人の病まざるや其の病を病むを以て、是を以て病まず。

註 1, 賢者の上智。 2. 下愚の病。 3. 知らざるを知れりとするの病を病（や）むの意。

第七十二章 一 民不畏威大威至矣[1]。──民威を畏れざれば大威至る。

二 無狹[2]其所居、無厭其所生。──其の居る所に狹（せま）ること無かれ、其生くる所を厭ふこと無かれ。

三 夫唯不厭[3]、是以不厭。──夫れ唯だ狹（せま）れず、是を以て厭はず。

四 是以聖人自知不自見、自愛不自貴、故去彼[4]取此[5]。──是を以て聖人は自ら知つて自ら見（しめ）さず、自ら愛して自ら貴ばず。故に彼を去つて此を取る。

CHAPTER LXXI. 1. To know and yet *think* we do not know is the highest *attainment*; not to know *and yet* think we do know is a disease.

2. It is simply by being pained at *the thought of* having this disease that we are preserved from it. The sage has not the disease. He knows the pain that would be inseparable from it, and therefore he does not have it.

知病, 'The Disease of Knowing.' Here, again, we have the Tâo working 'by contraries,'—in the matter of knowledge. Compare par. 1 with Confucius's accont of what knowledge is in the Analects, II, ch. 17. The par. 1 is found in one place in Hwâi-nan, lengthened out by the addition of particles; but the variation is unimportant. In another place, however, he seems to have had the correct text before him.

Par. 2 is in Han Fei also lengthened out, but with an important variation (不病 for 病病), and I cannot construe his text. His 不 is probably a transcriber's error.

CHAPTER LXXII. 1. When the people do not fear what they ought to fear, that which is their great dread will come on them.

2. Let them not thoughtlessly indulge themselves in their ordinary life; let them not act as if weary of what that life depends on.

3. It is by avoiding such indulgence that such weariness does not arise.

4. Therefore the sage knows *these things* of himself, but does not parade *his knowledge*; loves, but does not *appear to set a* value on, himself. And thus he puts the latter alternative away and makes choice of the former.

註 1. 人民が若し生に對する天の種々の脅威を畏れず慾を縱にし節を失へば大威即ち死を免れない。 2. ＝狎。 3. 厭は狹の誤。 4. ＝大威至。 5. ＝畏威。

第七十三章　一　勇於敢則殺[1]、勇於不敢則活[2]。此兩者或利或害[3]。天之所惡、孰知其故。是以聖人猶難之[4]。——敢てするに勇むときは則ち殺さる、敢てせざるに勇むときは則ち活く。此の兩者は或は利あり、或は害あり。天の惡む所孰か其の故を知らん。是を以て聖人も猶ほ之を難んず。

二　天之道、不爭而勝、不言而善應[5]、不召而自來、坦然[6]而善謀。天網恢々、疏而不失[7]。——天の道は爭はずして勝ち、言はずして善く應じ、召さずして自ら來り、坦然として善く謀る。天網恢々、疎にして失さず。

愛己, 'Loviug one's Self.' This title is taken from the expression in par. 4; and the object of the chapter seems to be to show how such loving should be manifested, and to enforce the lesson by the example of the 'sage,' the true master of the Tâo.

In par. 1 'the great dread' is death, and the things which ought to be feared and may be feared, are the indulgences of the appetites and passions, which, if not eschewed, tend to shorten life and accelerate the approach of death.

Pars. 2 and 3 are supplementary to 1. For 狎, the second character of Ho-shang Kung's text in par. 2, Wang Pî reads 狎, which has the same name as the other; and according to the Khang-hsî dictionary, the two characters are interchangeable. I have also followed Wû Khăng in adopting 狎 for the former of the two 厭 in par. 3. Wû adopted this reading from a commentator Liû of Lü-ling. It gives a good meaning, and is supported by the structure of other sentences made on similar lines.

In par. 4 'the sage' must be 'the ruler who is a sage,' a master of the Tâo, 'the king' of ch. 25. He 'loves himself,' i.e. his life, and takes the right measures to prolong his life, but without any demonstration that he is doing so.

CHAPTER LXXIII.

1. He whose boldness appears in his daring *to do wrong, in defiance of the laws,* is put to death; he whose boldness appears in his not daring *to do so* lives on. Of these two cases the one appears to be advantageous, and the other to be injurious.
But
> When Heaven's anger smites a man,
> Who the cause shall truly scan?

On this account the sage feels a difficulty *as to what to do in the former case.*

2. It is the way of Heaven not to strive, and yet it skilfully overcomes; not to speak, and yet it is skilful in *obtaining* a reply; does not call, and yet men come to it of themselves. Its demon-

註　1. 進鋭果敢に勇むときは自滅する。　2. 慈柔謙退に勇むときは生きる。　3. しかし實際について考へると前者に却つて利があり後者に却つて害があることがある。　4. 一時的には天の惡む所は果して何れにあるか聖人も惡人榮え義人亡びる耶非耶と決し兼ねる。　5. 默して言はざるも百事皆天の道に應ず。　6. ゆるやかな綱。　7. 果敢のものは必ず果敢に倒れ、慈柔のものは必ず慈柔に活きることが出來る。

第七十四章　一　民不畏死[1]、奈何以死懼之。若使民常畏死、而爲奇[2]者、吾得執而殺之、孰敢。──民死を畏れず、奈何んぞ死を以て之を懼れしめん。若し民をして常に死を畏れしめ、而も奇を爲す者は吾執へて之を殺すを得ば、孰れか敢てせん。

二　常有司殺者[3]殺。夫代司殺者殺、是謂代大匠斲。夫代大匠斲者、希有不傷手矣。──常に殺すことを司る者ありて殺す。夫の殺すことを司る者に代りて殺す、是を大匠に代つて斲ると謂ふ。夫の大匠に代つて斲る者は手を傷けずといふこと有ること希なり。

strations are quiet, and yet its plans are skilful and effective. The meshes of the net of Heaven are large; far apart, but letting nothing escape.

任殺, 'Allowing Men to take their Course.' The chapter teaches that rulers should not be hasty to punish, especially by the infliction of death. Though they may seem to err in leniency, yet Heaven does not allow offenders to escape.

While Heaven hates the ill-doer, yet we must not always conclude from Its judgments that every one who suffers from them is an ill-doer; and the two lines which rhyme, and illustrate this point, are equivalent to the sentiment in our Old Book, 'Clouds and darkness are round about Him.' They are ascribed to Lâo-ʒze by Lieh-ʒze (VI, 7 a); but, it has been said, that they are quoted by him 'in an entirely different connexion.' But the same text in two different sermons may be said to be in different connexions. In Lieh-ʒze and our *K*ing the lines have the same meaning, and substantially the same application. Indeed *K*ang *K*an, of our fourth century, the commentator of Lieh-ʒze, quotes the comment of Wang Pî on this passage, condensing it into, 'Who can know the mind of Heaven? Only the sage can do so.'

CHAPTER LXXIV. 1. The people do not fear death; to what purpose is it to *try to* frighten them with death? If the people were always in awe of death, and I could always seize those who do wrong, and put them to death, who would dare to do wrong?

2. There is always One who presides over the infliction of death. He who would inflict death in the room of him who so presides over it may be described as hewing wood instead of a great carpenter. Seldom is it that he who undertakes the hewing, instead of the great carpenter, does not cut his own hands!

註　1. 生を愛し死を畏るゝは人の本性でありながら上の苛政に苦み生活の危難を免れんとして人民が死をも畏れてゐぬ。　2. 惡事に同じ。　3. 司殺者＝天道。　4. 世の國王が絶對公平な天道に代つて生殺の權を適用するならば拙工が大匠に代つて木をけづると一般で己の未熟な技の爲めに自らを傷けぬ者は稀である。

第七十五章　一　民之飢、以其上食稅之多、是以飢。――民の飢ゆるは其の上の稅を食むの多きを以てなり、是を以て飢ゆ。

二　民之難治、以其上之有爲[1]、是以難治。――民の治め難きは其の上の爲す有るを以てなり、是を以て治め難し。

三　民之輕死、以其求生之厚[2]、是以輕死。夫唯無以生爲者是賢於貴生[3]。――民の輕々しく死するは其の生を求むるの厚きを以てなり、是を以て輕々しく死す。夫の唯生を以て爲す無きは是れ生を貴ぶに賢る。

註　1. 當路の人が人爲的の手段を用ひ過ぎる故である。　2. 生計を立てる勞苦の大なるが故である。　3. 人民の生活問題に無頓着の方が之に沒頭するには優る。此の一節を政治の要諦を説くものとせず自己保存の方法を述ぶるものとして生に執着し過ぎると兎角生を失ふ、生には無頓着の方生を貴ぶにまさると解する書物もある。

刮惑. 'Restraining Delusion.' The chapter sets forth the inefficiency of capital punishment, and warns rulers against the infliction of it. Who is it that superintends the infliction of death? The answer of Ho-shang Kung is very clear:—'It is Heaven, which, dwelling on high and ruling all beneath, takes note of the transgressions of men.' There is a slight variation in the readings of the second sentence of par. 2 in the texts of Ho-shang Kung and Wang Pî, and the reading adopted by 3iâo Hung differs a little from them both; but the meaning is the same in them all.

This chapter and the next are rightly joined on to the preceding by Wû Khăng.

CHAPTER LXXV. 1. The people suffer from famine because of the multitude of taxes consumed by their superiors. It is through this that they suffer famine.

2. The people are difficult to govern because of the *excessive* agency of their superiors *in governing them*. It is through this that they are difficult to govern.

3. The people make light of dying because of the greatness of their labours in seeking for the means of living. It is this which makes them think light of dying. Thus it is that to leave the subject of living altogether out of view is better than to set a high value on it.

貪拙. 'How Greediness Injures.' The want of the nothing-doing Tâo leads to the multiplication of exactions by the government, and to the misery of the people, so as to make them think lightly of death. The chapter is a warning for both rulers and people.

It is not easy to determine whether rulers, or people, or both, are intended in the concluding sentence of par. 2.

第七十六章　一　人之生也、柔弱、其死也、堅強、萬物草木之生也柔脆、其死也、枯槁。――人の生まるゝや柔弱なり、其の死するや堅強なり。萬物草木の生ずるや柔脆なり、其の死するや枯槁なり。

二　故堅強者死之徒、柔弱者生之徒。――故に堅強なる者は死の徒なり、柔弱なる者は生の徒なり。

三　是以兵強則不勝、木強則共[1]。――是を以て兵強ければ則ち勝たず、木強ければ則ち共す。

四　強大處下、柔弱處上。――強大なるものは下に處り、柔弱なるものは上に處る。

註　1. 共は拱に通じ幹兩手にて圍む程大にして樵夫の斧を免れざるを云ふ。

第七十七章　一　天之道、其猶張弓乎、高者抑之、下者舉之。有餘者損之[1]、不足者補之。――天の道は其れ猶ほ弓を張るごとき乎。高き者は之をおさへ、下れる者は之を舉ぐ。餘り有る者は之を損じ、足らざる者は之を補ふ。

CHAPTER LXXVI. 1. Man at his birth is supple and weak; at his dis death, firm and strong. *So it is with* all things. Trees and plants, in their early growth, are soft and brittle; at their death, dry and withered.

2. Thus it is that firmness and strength are the concomitants of death; softness, and weakness, the concomitants of life.

3. Hence he who *relies on* the strength of his forces does not conquer; and a tree which is strong will fill the out-stretched arms, *and thereby invites the feller.*

4. Therefore the place of what is firm and strong is below, and that of what is soft and weak is above.

<small>戒強, 'A Warning against (trusting in) Strength.' To trust in one's force is contrary to the Tâo, whose strength is more in weakness and humility.

In par. 1 the two characters which I have rendered by '*so it is with* all things' are found in the texts of both Ho-shang Kung and Wang Pî, but Wû Khăng and 3iâo Hung both reject them. I should also have neglected them, but they are also found in Liû Hsiang's Shwo Wăn (X, 4 a), with all the rest of pars. 1 and 2, as from Lâo-ʒze. They are an anakoluthon, such as is elsewhere found in our *King*; e. g. 天下之牝 in ch. 21, par. 2.

The 'above' and 'below' in par. 4 seem to be merely a play on the words, as capable of meaning 'more and less honourable.'</small>

CHAPTER LXXVII. 1. May not the Way *or Tâo* of Heaven be compared to the *method of* bending a bow? The *part of the bow* which was high is brought low, and what was low is raised

二　天之道、損有餘而補不足、人之道則不然、損不足以奉有餘。――天の道は餘り有るを損じて足らざるを補ふ。人の道は則ち然らず、足らざるを損じて以て餘り有るに奉す。

三　孰能有餘以奉天下、唯有道者。――孰(たれ)か能く餘り有りて以て天下に奉ぜん、唯有道者のみ。

四　是以聖人爲而不恃、功成而不處、其不欲見賢。――是を以て聖人は爲して恃まず、功成りて處らず、其の賢(けん)れるを見(あらは)すことを欲せず。

註　1. 天の道を主語として補つて解すべし。

第七十八章　一　天下柔弱、莫過於水、而攻堅強者、莫之能勝、其無以易之¹。――天下の柔弱なるもの水に過ぎたるは莫し、而も堅強なるものを攻むるに之に能く勝(か)つものなし。其れ以て之を易ふるもの無し。

二　弱之勝強、柔之勝剛、天下莫不知、莫能行²。――弱の強

up. *So Heaven* diminishes where there is superabundance, and supplements where there is deficiency.

2. It is the Way of Heaven to diminish superabundance, and to supplement deficiency. It is not so with the way of man. He takes away from those who have not enough to add to his own superabundance.

3. Who can take his own superabundance and therewith serve all under heaven? Only he who is in possession of the Tâo!

4. Therefore the *ruling* sage acts without claiming the results as his; he achieves his merit and does uot rest *arrogantly* in it:—he does not wish to display his superiority.

<small>天道, 'The Way of Heaven;' but the chapter contrasts that way, unselfish and magnanimous, with the way of man, selfish and contracted, and illustrates the point by the method of stringing a bow. This must be seen as it is done in China fully to understand the illustration. I have known great athletes in this country tasked to the utmost of their strength to adjust and bend a large Chinese bow from Peking.

The 'sage' of par. 4 is the 'King' of ch. 25. Compare what is said of him with ch. 2, par. 4, et al.</small>

CHAPTER LXXVIII. 1. There is nothing in the world more soft and weak than water, and yet for attacking things that are firm and strong there is nothing that can take precedence of it; —for there is nothing *so effectual* for which it can be changed.

2. Every one in the world knows that the soft

に勝ち、柔の剛に勝つは、天下知らざること莫く、能く行ふこと莫し。

三　故聖人云、受國之垢、是謂社稷主³、受國之不祥是謂天下王。——故に聖人の云く、國の垢を受くる、是を社稷の主と謂ひ、國の不祥を受くる、是を天下の王と謂ふと。

四　正言若反⁴。——正言は反するが若し。

註　1. 水の此の勢力を變化し得る程に有力なものはない。　2. 知つてゐるだけで實行しない。　3. 一國の恥辱を一身に蒙る弱い者は諸侯といふ強い者になつて宗廟社稷の主となることが出來る。　4. 正言は道理に反するやうに見える。

第七十九章　一　和大怨必有餘怨、安可以爲善¹。——大怨を和げて必ず餘怨あらば、安んぞ以て善と爲す可けん。

二　是以、聖人執左契²而不責³於人、有德司契⁴、無德司徹⁵。——是を以て、聖人は左契を執つて人に責めず。德有れば契を司り、德無ければ徹を司る。

overcomes the hard, and the weak the strong, but no one is able to carry it out in practice.

3. Therefore a sage has said,
    'He who accepts his state's reproach,
      Is hailed therefore its altars' lord;
    To him who bears men's direful woes
      They all the name of King accord.'

4. Words that are strictly true seem to be paradoxical.

任信, 'Things to be Believed.' It is difficult to give a short and appropriate translation of this title. The chapter shows how the most unlikely results follow from action according to the Tâo.

Par. 1. Water was Lâo-ʒze's favourite emblem of the Tâo. Compare chapters 8, 66, et al.

Par. 2. Compare ch. 36, par, 2.

Par. 3. Of course we do not know who the sage was from whom Lâo-ʒze got the lines of this paragraph. They may suggest to some readers the lines of Burns, as they have done to me :—

    'The honest man, though e'er so poor,
      Is king o' men for a' that.'

But the Tâoist of Lâo-ʒze is a higher ideal than Burn's honest man.

Par. 4 is separated from this chapter, and made to begin the next by Wû *Kh*ăng.

CHAPTER LXXIX.

1. When a reconciliation is effected *between two parties* after a great animosity, there is sure to be a grudge remaining *in the mind of the one who was wrong*. And how can this be beneficial *to the other?*

2. Therefore *to guard against this*, the sage keeps the left-hand portion of the record of the engagement, and does not insist on the *speedy* fulfilment of it by the other party. So, he who

三　天道無親、常與善人。――天道は親無く常に善人に與みす。

註　1. 大いに爭つた二人が和解した後惡かつた方が猶ほ怨恨を殘してゐたら和解した甲斐がない。　2. 契とは木を刻して劵をつくり之を中分して各其の一を執り之を合して以て信を表するもの。契に左右あり、左契は財物を貸す者の所に在り、右契は來つて財物を借りる人に付す。　3. 財物の返濟を促す責むといふ。　4. 左契を司る者は人の來つて返へすに任せ其の人を計較する心無し、故に有德と曰ふ。　5. 徹法を司る者は其の均しからざるを患ひ計較する心有り、故に無德と曰ふ。徹は通と同義にして古の助法を周の時改めて徹之法となす。八家私田を力を通じ合せ作つて均く之を歛む。八家の所得均平にして多寡無し。此の一節の大意は聖人は貸借關係で云へば債權者でありながら債務者に返金を要求しないが、無德者は利己主義一點張りであるからそれを善い事にして中々返さうとしないの意。　6. 親疎の分け隔てをしない。

第八十章　一　小國寡民、使有什佰人之器而不用、使民重死而不遠徙[1]。――小國寡民には什佰人の器有るも而も用ひざらしめん、民をして死を重んずるも而も遠く徙らざらしめん。

has the attributes *of the Tâo* regards only the conditions of the engagement, while he who has not those attributes regards only the conditions favourable to himself.

3. In the Way of Heaven, there is no partiality of love; it is always on the side of the good man.

任契, 'Adherence to Bond or Covenant.' The chapter shows, but by no means clearly, how he who holds fast to the Tâo will be better off in the end than he who will rather try to secure his own interests.

Par. 1 presents us with a case which the statements of the chapter are intended to meet:—two disputants, one good, and the other bad; the latter, though apparently reconciled, still retaining a grudge, and ready to wreak his dissatisfaction, when he has an opportunity. The 與='for,' 'for the good of.'

Par. 2 is intended to solve the question. The terms of a contract or agreement were inscribed on a slip of wood, which was then divided into two; each party having one half of it. At the settlement, if the halves perfectly fitted to each other, it was carried through. The one who had the right in the dispute has his part of the agreement, but does not insist on it, and is forbearing; the other insists on the conditions being even now altered in his favour. The characters by which this last case is expressed, are very enigmatical, having reference to the satisfaction of the government dues of Lâo-'ze's time,—a subject into which it would take much space to go.

Par. 3 decides the question by the action of Heaven, which is only another name for the course of the Tâo.

CHAPTER LXXX. 1. In a little state with a small population, I would so order it, that, though there were individuals with the abilities of ten or a hundred men, there should be no employment of them; I would make the people, while looking on death as a grievous thing, yet not remove elsewhere *to avoid it.*

二　雖有舟輿無所乘之、雖有甲兵無所陳之。——舟輿有りと雖も之に乘る所無からしめん、甲兵有りと雖も之を陳ぬる所無からしめん。

三　使民復結繩²而用之。——民をして結繩に復して之を用ひしめん。

四　甘其食³、美其服、安其居、樂其俗。——其の食を甘とし、其の服を美とし、其居に安んじ、其の俗を樂ましめん。

五　隣國相望、雞狗之聲相聞、民至老死不相往來。——隣國相望み、雞狗の聲相聞ゆるも、民老死に至るまで相往來せざらしめん。

註　1.　若し自分が寡民の一小國を得ることがあるならば之を自分の理想鄕たらしむるために人民の中に十人前百人前の器量人が有つても擧用しない、そして人民が死を畏れる本性から之を避けるために遠く他國へ移住なぞせぬように人爲的政治の代りに天の道を以て治めよう。2. 民をして文字の代りに繩を結んだ太古の時代に歸へらせよう。3. 太古人の粗食。

2. Though they had boats and carriages, they should have no occasion to ride in them; though they had buff coats and sharp weapons, they should have no occasion to don or use them.

3. I would make the people return to the use of knotted cords *instead of the written characters*.

4. They should think their *coarse* food sweet; their *plain* clothes beautiful; their *poor* dwellings places of rest; and their common *simple* ways sources of enjoyment.

5. There should be a neighbouring state within sight, and the voices of the fowls and dogs should be heard all the way from it to us, but I would make the people to old age, even to death, not have any intercourse with it.

獨立, 'Standing Alone.' The chapter sets forth what Lâo-jze conceived the ancient government of simplicity was, and what he would have government in all time to be. He does not use the personal pronoun 'I' as the subject of the thrice-recurring 使, but it is most natural to suppose that he is himself that subject; and he modestly supposes himself in charge of a little state and a small population. The reader can judge for himself of the consummation that would be arrived at;—a people rude and uninstructed, using quippos, abstaining from war and all travelling, kept aloof from intercourse even with their neighbours, and without the appliances of what we call civilisation.

The text is nearly all found in Sze-mâ *Kh*ien and *K*wang-jze. The first member of par. 1, however, is very puzzling. The old Jesuit translators, Julien, Chalmers, and V. von Strauss, all differ in their views of it. Wû *Kh*ăng and 8iâo Hung take what I have now rendered by 'abilities,' as meaning 'implements of agriculture,' but their view is based on a custom of the Han dynasty, which is not remote enough for the purpose, and on the suppression, after Wang Pî, of a 人 in Ho-shang Kung's text.

第八十一章 一 信言不美[1]、美言不信、善者不辨、辨者不善、知者不博、博者不知。——信言は美ならず、美言は信ならず、善なる者は辨ぜず、辨する者は善ならず、知る者は博からず、博き者は知らず。

二 聖人不積、既以爲人、己愈有、既以與人、己愈多。——聖人は積まず、既に以て人の爲めにして己愈々有り、既に以て人に與へて己愈々多し。

三 天之道、利而不害[2]、聖人之道、爲而不爭[3]。——天の道は利にして害せず、聖人の道は爲して爭はず。

註 1. 信實の有る人の言は飾りがないから美でない。 2. 銳利であるが我々を害さぬ。 3. 活動するが我々と爭はぬ。

CHAPTER LXXXI. 1. Sincere words are not fine; fine words are not sincere. Those who are skilled *in the Tâo* do not dispute *about it;* the disputatious are not skilled in it. Those who know *the Tâo* are not extensively learned; the extensively learned do not know it.

2. The sage does not accumulate *for himself*. The more that he expends for others, the more does he possess of his own; the more that he gives to others, the more does he have himself.

3. With all the sharpness of the Way of Heaven, it injures not; with all the doing in the way of the sage he does not strive.

顯質, 'The Manifestation of Simplicity.' The chapter shows how quietly and effectively the Tâo proceeds, and by contraries in a way that only the master of it can understand. The author, says Wû Khăng, 'sums up in this the subject-matter of the two Parts of his Treatise, showing that in all its five thousand characters, there is nothing beyond what is here said.'

Par. 2 suggests to Dr. Chalmers the well-known lines of Bunyan as an analogue of it:—

'A man there was, though some did count him mad,
The more he gave away, the more he had'

Wû Khăng brings together two sentences from *K*wang-jze (XXXIII, 21 b, 22 a), written evidently with the characters of this text in mind, which, as from a Tâoist mint, are a still better analogue, and I venture to put them into rhyme:—

'Amassing but to him a sense of need betrays;
He hoards not, and thereby his affluence displays.'

I have paused long over the first pair of contraries in par. 3 (利 and 害). Those two characters primarily mean 'sharpness' and 'wounding by cutting;' they are also often used in the sense of 'being beneficial,' and 'being injurious;'—'contraries,' both of them. Which 'contrary' had Lâo-jze in mind? I must

think the former, though differing in this from all previous translators. The Jesuit version is, 'Celestis Tâo natura ditat omnes, nemini nocet;' Julien's, 'Il est utile aux êtres, et ne leur nuit point;' Chalmers's, 'Benefits and does not injure;' and V. von Strauss's, 'Des Himmels Weise ist wolthun und nicht beschädigen.'

大　學

子程子曰。大學、孔子之遺書、而初學入德之門也。於今可見古人爲學次第者。獨賴此篇之存、而論孟次之。學者、必由是而學焉。則庶乎其不差矣。——子程子の曰く、大學は孔子の遺書にして初學德に入るの門なり。今に於いて古の人の學を爲(をさ)めし次第を見るべきもの獨り此の篇の存するに賴る。而して論孟之に次ぐ。學者必ず是に由つて學ばゞ則ち其の差(たが)はざるに庶(ちか)からんか。

一　大學[1]之道。在明明德[2]。在親民[3]。在止於至善。——大學の道は明德を明かにするに在り、民を親(あらた)にするに在り、至善に止まるに在り。

註　1. 大人の學。　2. 明德＝天性として、天性を其の本體たる明に復歸せしむるとも解く。　3. 親は新の誤記。

二　知止、而后有定[1]。定而后能靜。靜而后能安。安而后能慮。慮而后能得[2]。——止まるを知りて后定まる有り、定まりて后能く靜なり、靜にして后能く安し、安くして后能く慮(おもんぱか)る、慮

THE GREAT LEARNING.[1]

My master, the philosopher Ch'ing, says:—"The Great Learning is a book left by Confucius, and forms the gate by which first learners enter into virtue. That we can now perceive the order in which the ancients pursued their learning, is solely owing to the preservation of of this work, the Analects and Mencius coming after it. Learners must commence their course with this, and then it may be hoped they will be kept from error."

THE TEXT OF CONFUCIUS.

1. What the Great Learning teaches, is—to illustrate illustrious virtue; to renovate the people; and to rest in the highest excellence.

2. The point where to rest being known, the object of pursuit is then determined; and, that being determined, a calm unperturbedness may be attained. To that calmness there will succeed a tranquil repose. In that repose there may be careful deliberation, and that deliberation

---

[1]. The name is the adoption of the two commencing characters of the treatise, as it is similar to the customs of many books in the Bible.

りて后能く得。
　註　1. 安んずる所を知れば目的定まる。　2. 目的を遂す。

　三　物有本末。事有終始。知所先後。則近道矣。——物に本末あり、事に終始有り、先後する所を知れば則ち道に近し。

　四　古之欲明明德於天下者。先治其國。欲治其國者。先齊其家。欲齊其家者。先修其身。欲修其身者。先正其心。欲正其心者。先誠其意。欲誠其意者。先致[1]其知。致知在格[2]物。——古の明德を天下に明にせんと欲する者は先づ其國を治む。其國を治めんと欲する者は、先づ其家を齊ふ。其家を齊へんと欲する者は、先づ其身を修む。其身を修めんと欲する者は、先づ其心を正しくす。其心を正しくせんと欲する者は、先づ其意を誠にす。其意を誠にせんと欲する者は、先づ其知を致す。知を致すは物に格るに在り。
　註　1. 推し極む。　2. 格は至と同義にして事物の理を窮至して其極まる處到らざる無きを欲するをいふ。

　五　物格而后知至。知至而后意誠。意誠而后心正。心正而后身修。身修而后家齊。家齊而后國治。國治而后天下平。——物格りて而して后に知至る。知至りて而して后に意誠なり。意誠にして而して后に心正し。心正しくして而して后に身修まる。身修まりて而して后に家齊ふ。家齊うて而して后に國治まる。國治まりて而して后に天下平なり。

will be followed by the attainment *of the desired end.*

3. Things have their root and their completion. Affairs have their end and their beginning. To know what is first and what is last will lead near to what is taught *in the Great Learning.*

4. The ancients who wished to illustrate illustrious virtue throughout the empire, first ordered well their own States. Wishing to order well their States, they first regulated their families. Wishing to regulate their families, they first cultivated their persons. Wishing to cultivate their persons, they first rectified their hearts. Wishing to rectify their hearts, they first sought to be sincere in their thoughts. Wishing to be sincere in their thoughts, they first extended to the utmost their knowledge. Such extenison of knowledge lay in the investigation of things.[1]

5. Things being investigated, knowledge became complete. Their knowledge being complete, their thoughts were sincere. Their thoughts being sincere, their hearts were then rectified. Their hearts being rectified, their persons were cultivated. Their persons being cultivated, their families were regulated. Their families beieg regulated, their States were rightly governed. Their States being rightly governed, the whole empire was made tranquil and happy.

---

1. 格, sometimes＝至, 'to come or extend to,' means 窮究 'to examine exhaustively.'

六　自天子以至於庶人¹。壹是、皆以脩身爲本。――天子より以て庶人に至るまで壹に是れ皆身を脩むるを以て本と爲す。

　註　1. 普通一般の人民に同じ。

七　其本¹亂而末²治者、否矣。其所厚³者薄⁴。而其所薄⁵者厚⁶。未之有也。――其の本亂れて末治まるものはあらず。其の厚き所薄くして其の薄き所厚きものは未だ之れ有らざるなり。

　註　1. 身を脩むること。　2. 治國平天下を指す。　3. 厚き所とは大切な所故では我が身又は我が家。　4. 忽にされる意。　5. 大切でない所故では國又は天下。　6. 大いに注意留心される意。

右經一章。蓋孔子之言。而曾子¹述之。其傳十章。則曾子之意而門人記之也。舊本頗有錯簡²。今因程子所定。而更考經文。別爲序次、如左。――右經一章は、蓋孔子の言にして、曾子之を述ぶ。其傳十章は則ち曾子の意にして、門人之を記す。舊本頗る錯簡有り。今程子の定むる所に因つて更に經文を考へ、別に序次を爲すこと、左の如し。

　註　1. 孔子の弟子にして實踐躬行家、特に孝行を以て有名。　2. 入りちがへ。

6. From the emperor down to the mass of the people, all must consider the cultivation of the person the root of *every thing besides.*

7. It cannot be, when the root is neglected, that what should spring from it will be well ordered. It never has been the case that what was of great importance has been slightly cared for, and, at the same time, that what was of slight importance has been greatly cared for.[1]

The preceding chapter of classical text is in the words of Confucius, handed down by the philosopher Tsăng. The ten chapters of explanation which follow contain the views of Tsăng, and were recorded by his disciples. In the old copies of the work, there appeared considerable confusion in these, from the disarrangement of the tablets. But now, availing myself of the decisions of the philosopher Ch'ing, and having examined anew the classical text, I have arranged it in order, as follows:—

---

1. 所厚 means 'the family,' and 所薄, the state and the empire.

第一章 一 康誥[1]曰。克[2]明德[3]。──康誥に曰く、克(よ)く德を明にす。

註 1. 周書の篇名。 2. ＝能。 3. 克明德は武王が弟を衞の君に封ぜし時文王に則るべく文王を禮讃して云へる語。

二 大甲[1]曰。顧諟天之明命[2]。──大甲(たいかふ)に曰く諟(これ)の天の明命を顧みる。

註 1. 商書の篇名。 2. 宰相伊尹が其君王季に父君大王を讃稱して言へる語。顧の主語は大王。諟は是に同じ。明命は天が大王に與(あた)へせし所以を云ふ。

三 帝典[1]曰。克明峻德[2]。──帝典に曰く、克く峻德を明にす。

註 1. 堯典に同じ。 2. 堯の德を稱へた言葉。峻＝大。

四 皆自明也[1]。──皆自ら明にするなり。

註 1. 上の三句は皆王者(文王、大王、堯帝)が王者の德を彰はしたことを述べるものであるの意。

右傳之首章。釋明明德。──右傳の首章は明德を明にすることを釋く。

第二章 一 湯之盤銘[1]曰。苟日新。日日新。又日新[2]。──湯(たう)の盤(はん)の銘に曰く、苟(いやし)も日に新(あらた)なれば、日日新にして、又日に新なれと。

註 1. 古の聖賢の格言を家財什器に刻めることは支那人古來の習慣。 2. 在來の訓み方は「まことに日に新に、日日に新にして、又日に新なり」。

COMMENTARY OF THE PHILOSOPHER TSANG

CHAPTER I. 1. In the Announcement to K'ang it is said, "He was able to make his virtue illustrious."[1]

2. In the T'ae Këě, it is said, "He contemplated and studied the illustrious decrees of Heaven."[2]

3. In the Canon of the emperor Yaou, it is said, "He was able to make illustrious his lofty virtue."[3]

4. These *passages* all *show how those sovereigns* made themselves illustrious.

The above first chapter of commentary explains the illustration of illustrious virtue.

CHAPTER II. 1. On the bathing-tub of T'ang, the following words were engraved:[4]—"If you can one day renovate yourself, do so from day to day. Yea, let there be daily renovation."

---

1. The words are part of the address of King Woo to his brother K'ang, on appointing him to the masquisate of 衞. The subject of 克 is king Wăn, to whose example K'ang is referred.

2. The sentence is part of the address of the premier, E-yin, to T'ae Këě, the 2d emperor of the Shang dynasty, B. C. 1752—1718. The subject of 顧 is T'ae-Kea's father, the great T'ang.

3. It is of the emperor Yaou that this is said.

4. It was customary among the ancients, as it is in China at the present day, to engrave, all about them, on the articles of their furniture, such moral aphorisms and lessons. But this fact about T'ang's bathing tub had come down by tradition. At least, we do not now find the mention of it anywhere but here.

二　康誥曰。作新民[1]。──康誥に曰く、新民を作すと。

註　1. 殷の不良民を義民にする又は周の新附の民を振興する意。

三　詩[1]曰、周雖舊邦。其命維新[2]。──詩に曰く、周は舊邦と雖も其命維れ新なりと。

註　1. 詩經大雅の篇。　2. 周をして千有餘年天下を保たしめし文王の德を禮讚す。

四　是故君子無所不用其極[1]。──是の故に君子は其極を用ひざる所無し。

註　1. 何事にも全力を竭さずといふことなし。

右傳之二章。釋新民。──右傳の二章は民を新にすることを釋く。

第三章　一　詩[1]云。邦畿千里[2]。維民所止[3]。──詩に云ふ、邦畿千里、維れ民の止まる所と。

註　1. 詩經商頌の篇。　2. 王者の都にして周圍一千里。　3. 此の詩は殷の盛代を謳つたもの。

二　詩[1]云。緡蠻[2]黄鳥。止于丘隅。子[3]曰。於止、知其所止、可以人而不如鳥乎[4]。──詩に云ふ、緡蠻(めんばん)たる黄鳥(くわうてう)は丘(をか)の隅(すみ)に止まると。子曰く、止まるに於いて其の止まる所を知る、人を以てして鳥に如かざる可けんやと。

註　1. 詩經小雅の篇。　2. 鳥の囀る聲。　3. 孔子。　4. その境遇の鳥にだも如かざるまでに虐げられたる人に代つての怨言。

三　詩[1]云。穆穆[2]文王。於[3]緝[4]熙[5]敬止[6]。爲人君。止於仁[7]。爲人臣。止於敬。爲人子。止於孝。爲人父。止於慈。與國人交。止

2. In the Announcement to K'ang, it is said, "To stir up the new people."¹

3. In the Book of Poetry, it is said, "Although Chow was an ancient state, the ordinance which lighted on it was new."²

4. Therefore, the superior man in everything uses his utmost endeavours.

The above second chapter of commentary explains the renovating of the people.

CHAPTER III. 1. In the Book of Poetry, it is said, "The imperial domain of a thousand le is where the people rest."³

2. In the Book of Poetry, it is said, "The twittering yellow bird rests on a corner of the mound."⁴ The Master said, "When it rests, it knows where to rest. Is it possible that a man should not be equal to this bird?"

3. In the Book of Poetry, it is said, "Profound was King Wăn. With how bright and unceasing a feeling of reverence did he regard his resting

---

1. 作新民 may mean to make the bad people of Yin into good people, or to stir up the new people, *i. e., new,* as recently subjected to Chow.

2. The subject of the ode is the praise of king Wăn, whose virtue led to the possession of the empire by his house, more than a thousand years after its first rise.

3. The ode celebrates the rise and establishment of the Shang or Yin dynasty. 畿 is the 1000 *le* around the capital, and constituting the imperial demesne.

4. Here we have the complaint of a down-trodden man, contrasting his position with that of a bird.

於信。――詩に云ふ、穆穆たる文王は於緝熙にして敬止すと。人君と爲りては仁に止まり、人臣と爲りては敬に止まり、人子と爲りては孝に止まり、人父となりては慈に止まり、國人と交はりては信に止まる。

註 1. 詩經文王の篇。 2. 深遠の意。 3. 歎美の辭。 4. 繼續の意。 5. 光明の意。 6. 敬崇の念を以て居る所に安んずるをいふ。 7. 文王の人君となつては仁に安んぜしをいふ。

四 詩[1]云。瞻彼淇[2]澳[3]。菉竹猗猗[4]。有[5]斐[6]君子。如切如磋。如琢如磨。瑟[7]兮僩[8]兮。赫[9]兮喧[10]兮。有斐君子。終不可諠[11]兮。如切如磋者。道學也。如琢如磨者。自修也。瑟兮僩兮者。恂慄[12]也。赫兮喧兮者。威儀也。有斐君子。終不可諠兮者。道盛德至善民之不能忘也[13]。――詩に云ふ、彼の淇澳を瞻れば菉竹猗猗たり。斐たる君子有り、切するが如く磋するが如く琢するが如く磨するが如し。瑟たり僩たり、赫たり喧たり、斐たる君子有り、終に諠る可からずと。切するが如く磋するが如しとは學を道ふなり。琢するが如く磨するが如しとは自ら修むるなり。瑟たり僩たりとは恂慄なり。赫たり喧たりとは威儀なり。斐たる君子有り、終に諠る可からずとは、盛德至善、民の忘るゝ能はざるを道ふなり。

註 1. 詩經衞風の篇。 2. 河の名。 3. 河水の曲り入りたる岸邊。 4. 美盛の貌。 5. 此の岸邊に居る。 6. 文雅な貌。 7. 嚴密の貌。 8. 武毅の貌。 9. 盛大の貌。 10. 宣著の貌。 11. ＝忘。 12. 戰懼。 13. 民は盛德至善を忘るゝ能はず。此の詩は衞の武公が身を修むるに切磋琢磨したのを謳つたもの。

五 詩[1]云。於戲。前王[2]不忘。君子賢其賢[3]而親其親。小人樂其樂[4]而利其利[5]。此以沒世不忘也[6]。――詩に云ふ、於戲、前王

places!" As a sovereign, he rested in benevolence. As a minister, he rested in reverence. As a son, he rested in filial piety. As a father, he rested in kindness. In communication with his subjects, he rested in good faith.

4. In the Book of Poetry, it is said, "Look at that winding course of the K'e, with the green bamboos so luxuriant! Here is our elegant and accomplished prince! As we cut and then file; as we chisel and then grind: *so has he cultivated himself.* How grave is he and dignified! How majestic and distinguished! Our elegant and accomplished prince never can be forgotten." *That expression*—"as we cut and then file,"[1] indicates the work of learning. "As we chisel, and then grind," indicates that of self culture. "How grave is he and dignified!" indicates the feeling of cautious reverence. "How commanding and distinguished," indicates an awe—inspiring deportment. "Our elegant and accomplished prince never can be forgotten," indicates how, when virtue is complete and excellence extreme, the people cannot forget them.

5. In the Book of Poetry, it is said, "Ah! the former kings[2] are not forgotten." *Future* princes deem worthy what they deemed worthy, and love

---

1. The ode celebrates the virtue of the duke Woo (武) of Wei (衛), in his laborious endevours to cultivate his person.
2. The former kings are Wăn and Woo, the founders of the Chow dynasty.

忘れられずと。君子は其賢を賢とし其親を親とす。小人は其樂を
樂みて、其利を利とす、此を以て世を没へて忘れられざるなり。

註　1. 詩經周頌烈文の篇。　2. 周の文王と武王。　3. 將來も君子は
文王武王の賢としたることを賢とする。　4. 小人も文王武王の樂を樂
む。　5. 文王武王の恩澤に浴する。　6. 文王武王は世を去つても忘れら
れぬ。

右傳之三章。釋止於至善。——右傳の三章は至善に止まること
を釋く。

第四章　子曰、聽訟吾猶人也。必也使無訟乎。無情者、不得盡
其辭。大畏民志[1]。此謂知本。——子曰く、訟を聽くは吾猶ほ人
の如きなり。必ずや訟無からしめんかと。情なき者は其辭を盡
すを得ず、大に民志を畏れしむ。此を本を知ると謂ふ。

註　1 それ故(孔子が斯く誓言したから)心に實の無い者は敢て其の
虚誕の説を言ひ盡すことが出來ず竟に人々が畏服せしめられた。

右傳之四章。釋本末。——右傳の四章は本末を釋く。

第五章　此謂知本。此謂知之至也。——此れを本を知ると謂
ふ。此れを知の至ると謂ふ。

右傳之五章。蓋釋格物致知之義。而今亡矣。閒嘗竊取程子之意
以補之。曰所謂致知在格物者。言欲致吾之知、在卽物而窮其
理也。蓋人心之靈。莫不有知。而天下之物。莫不有理。惟於理
有未窮。故其致有不盡也。是以大學始教。必使學者、既凡天

what they loved. The common people delight in what they delighted, and are benefited by their beneficial arrangements. It is on this account that the former kings, after they have quitted the world, are not forgotten.

The above third chapter of commentary explains resting in the highest excellence.

CHAPTER IV. The Master said, "In hearing litigations, I am like any other body. What is necessary is to cause the people to have no litigations?"[1] *So, those who are devoid of principle find it impossible to carry out their speeches, and a great awe would be struck into men's minds;—this is called knowing the root.*

The above fourth chapter of commentary explains the root and the issue.

CHAPTER V. This is called knowing the root. This is called the perfecting of knowledge.

The above fifth chapter of the commentary explained the meaning of "investigating things and carrying knowledge to the utmost extent," but it is now lost. I have ventured to take the views of the scholar Ch'ing to supply it, as

---

1. See the Analects XII. xiii, from which we understand that the words of Confucius terminate at 訟乎, and that what follows is from the compiler. Accorrding to the old commentors, this is the conclusion of the chapter on having the thoughts made sincere.

下之物。莫不因其已知之理。而益窮之。以求至乎其極。至於用力之久。而一旦豁然貫通焉。則衆物之表裏精粗無不到。而吾心之全體大用無不明矣。此謂物格。此謂知之至也。――右傳の五章は、蓋し格物致知の義を釋く。而るに今は亡びたり。間嘗て竊に程子の意を取つて以て之を補ふ。曰く、所謂知を致すは物に格るに在りとは、言は吾の知を致さんと欲するは、物に即きて其理を窮むるに在るなり。蓋し人心の靈、知有らざる莫し。而して天下の物理有らざる莫し。唯理に於て未だ窮めざる有り。故に其知盡さざる有るなり。是を以て大學の始めの敎は、必ず學者をして凡そ天下の物に即き、其の已に知るの理に因つて益々之を窮めて以て其の極に至るを求めざる莫からしむ。力を用ひるの久しく、一旦豁然として貫通するに至つては、則ち衆物の表裏精粗、到らざる無く、吾が心の全體大用明ならざるは莫し。此を物の格ると謂ひ、此を知の至ると謂ふなり。

第六章 一 所謂誠其意者。毋自欺也。如惡惡臭[1]。如好好色。此之謂自謙[2]。故君子必愼其獨也。――所謂其意を誠にすとは自ら欺く毋きこと、惡臭を惡むが如く、好色を好むが如し。此を之れ自ら謙すと謂ふ。故に君子は必ず其の獨りを愼むなり。

註 1. 惡臭を惡臭として惡む時のやうに自らを欺かぬ。 2. 心にこころよきこと。

follows:—The meaning of the expression, "The perfecting of knowledge depends on the investigation of things," is this:—If we wish to carry our knowledge to the utmost, we must investigate the principles of all things we come into contact with, for the intelligent mind of man is certainly formed to know, and there is not a single thing in which its principles do not inhere. But so long as all principles are not investigated, man's knowledge is incomplete. On this account, the Learning for Adults, at the outset of its lessons, instructs the learner, in regard to all things in the world, to proceed from what knowledge he has of their principles, and pursue his investigation of them, till he reaches the extreme point. After exerting himself in this way for a long time, he will suddenly find himself possessed of a wide and far-reaching penetration. Then, the qualities of all things, whether external or internal, the subtle or the coarse, will all be apprehended, and the mind, in its entire substance and its relations to things, will be perfectly intelligent. This is called the investigation of things. This is called the perfection of knowledge.

CHAPTER VI. 1. What is meant by "making the thoughts sincere," is the allowing no self-deception, as *when* we hate a bad smell, and as *when* we love what is beautiful. This is called self-enjoyment. Therefore, the superior man must

二　小人閒居爲不善。無所不至。見君子而后厭然。揜其不善。而著其善。人¹之視已。如見其肺肝然。則何益矣¹。此謂誠於中。形於外。故君子必愼其獨也。――小人閒居して不善を爲し、至らざる所無し。君子を見て而る后厭然（えんぜん）として其不善を揜（おほ）ひて、其善を著はす。人の已を視ること其肺肝を見るが如く然り。則ち何んぞ益あらん。此を中に誠なれば外に形（あらは）はると謂ふ。故に君子は必ず其の獨りを愼むなり。

註　1. 君子は小人の心中を見破るから猫を被つても駄目。

三　曾子曰。十目所視。十手所指。其嚴乎。――曾子曰く、十目の視る所、十手の指す所、其れ嚴なるかなと。

四　富潤屋。德潤身。心廣體胖。故君子必誠其意。――富は屋を潤（うるほ）す、德は身を潤し、心廣く體胖（ゆたか）なり。故に君子は必ず其意を誠にす。

右傳之六章。釋誠意。――右傳の六章は意を誠にすることを釋く。

第七章　一　所謂脩身在正其心者。身有所忿懥、則不得其正。有所恐懼、則不得其正。有所好樂。則不得其正。有所憂患。則不得其正。――所謂身を脩むるは其心を正しうするに在りとは、忿懥（こころあんず）する所有れば、則ち其正を得ず、恐懼する所有れば、則ち其正を得ず、好樂する所有れば、則ち其正を得ず、憂

be watchful over himself when he is alone.

2. There is no evil to which the mean man, dwelling retired, will not proceed, but when he sees a superior man, he instantly tries to disguise himself, concealing his evil, and displaying what is good. The other beholds him, as if he saw his heart and reins;[1]—of what use *is his disguise?* This is an instance of the saying—"What truly is within will be manifested without." Therefore, the superior man must be watchful over himself when he is alone.

3. The disciple Tsăng said, "What ten[2] eyes behold, what ten hands point to, is to be regarded with reverence!"

4. Riches adorn a house, and virtue adorns the person. The mind is expanded, and the body is at ease. Therefore, the superior man must make his thoughts sincere.

The above sixth chapter of commentary explains making the thoughts sincere.

CHAPTER VII. 1. What is meant by, "The cultivation of the person depends on rectifying the mind," *may be thus illustrated:*—If a man be under the influence of passion, he will be incorrect in his conduct. He will be the same, if he is under the influence of terror, or under the influ-

---

1. The Chinese make the lungs the seat of righteousness, and the liver the seat of benevolence.
2. 'Ten' is a round number, put for *many.*

患する所有れば、則ち其正を得ず。

　二　心不在焉[1]。視而不見。聽而不聞。食而不知其味。——心焉に在らざれば、視れども見えず、聽けども聞えず、食へども其味を知らず。

　註　1. 心が在るべき所に在らねばの意。

　三　此謂修身。在正其心。——此れを身を修むるは其心を正しうするに在りと謂ふ。

右傳之七章。釋正心修身。——右傳の七章は心を正し身を修むることを釋く。

　第八章　一　所謂齊其家。在修其身者。人之其所親愛而辟[1]焉。之其所賤惡而辟焉。之其所畏敬而辟焉。之其所哀矜[2]而辟焉。之其所敖惰[3]而辟焉。故好而知其惡。惡而知其美者。天下鮮矣[4]。——所謂其家を齊ふるは、其身を修むるに在りとは、人其の親愛する所に之て辟す、其の賤惡する所に之て辟す、其の畏敬する所に之て辟す、其の哀矜する所に之て辟す、其の敖惰する所に之て辟す。故に好みて其惡を知り、惡みて其美を知る者は、天下に鮮し。

　註　1. かたよる。2. あはれみあはれむ。3. 輕んじ疎んず。4. 惚れゝばあばたもえくぼ、坊主憎くけりや袈裟まで憎いの意。

　二　故諺有之曰。人莫知其子之惡。莫知其苗之碩[1]。——故に諺に之れ有り、曰く人其子の惡を知る莫く、其苗の碩なるを知る莫しと。

　註　1. 自分の田の苗の大いに發育したのを知らぬ。

　三　此謂身不修。不可以齊其家。——此れを身修まらざれば、以て其家を齊ふ可からずと謂ふ。

ence of fond regard, or under that of sorrow and distress.

2. When the mind is not present, we look and do not see; we hear and do not understand; we eat and do not know the taste of what we eat.

3. This is what is meant by saying that the cultivation of the person depends on the rectiflying of the mind.

The above seventh chapter of commentary explains rectifying the mind and cultivating the person.

CHAPTER VIII. 1. What is meant by, "The regulation of one's family depends on the cultivation of his person," is this:—Men are partial where they feel affection and love; partial where they despise and dislike; partial where they stand in awe and reverence; partial where they feel sorrow and compassion; partial where they are arrogant and rude. Thus it is that there are few men in the world, who love, and at the same time know the bad qualities of *the object of their love,* or who hate, and yet know the excellences of *the object of their hatred.*

2. Hence it is said, in the common adage, "A man does not know the wickedness of his son; he does not know the richness of his growing corn."[1]

3. This is what is meant by saying that if the person be not cultivated, a man cannot regulate his family.

---

[1]. Farmers were noted, it would appear, in China so long ago, for grumbling about their crops.

右傳之八章。釋脩身齊家。——右傳の八章は身を脩め家を齊ふることを釋く。

第九章 一 所謂治國。必先齊其家者。其家不可敎。而能敎人者無之。故君子不出家。而成敎於國。孝者、所以事君也。弟者、所以事長也。慈者、所以使衆也。——所謂國を治むるには、必ず先づ其家を齊ふとは、其家敎ふ可からずして、而して能く人を敎ふる者は之れ無し。故に君子は家を出でずして、敎を國に成す。孝は君に事ふる所以なり、弟は長に事ふる所以なり、慈は衆を使ふ所以なり。

二 康誥曰。如保赤子[1]。心誠求之。雖不中[2]。不遠矣。未有學養子。而后嫁者也。——康誥に曰く、赤子を保んずるが如くせよと。心誠に之を求むれば、中らずと雖も遠からず。未だ子を養ふことを學びて而して后に嫁ぐ者は有らざるなり。

註 1. 赤子を保んずるが如くあれの意。 2. 母が心から子のために心配すれば子の欲する事は略ぼ解る。

三 一家仁。一國興仁。一家讓。一國興讓。一人[1]貪戾。一國作亂。其機如此。此謂一言僨事。[2]一人定國。—— 一家仁なれば、一國仁に興り、一家讓なれば、一國讓に興る。一人貪戾なれば、一國亂を作す。其の機此の如し。此を一言事を僨り、一人國を定むと謂ふ。

註 1. 國君を云ふ。 2. 大事も一言のために破れる。

The above eighth chapter of commentary explains cultivating the person and regulating the family.

CHAPTER IX. 1. What is meant by, "In order rightly to govern his State, it is necessary first to regulate his family," is this:—It is not possible for one to teach others, while he cannot teach his own family. Therefore, the ruler, without going beyond his family, completes the lessons for the State. There is filial piety:—therewith the sovereign should be served. There is fraternal submission:—therewith elders and superiors should be served. There is kindness:—therewith the multitude should be treated.

2. In the Announcement to K'ang, it is said, "*Act*[1] as if you were watching over an infant." If a mother is really auxious about it, though she may not hit *exactly the wants of her infant*, she will not be far from doing so. There never has been *a girl* who learned to bring up a child, that she might afterwards marry.

3. From the loving *example* of one family, a whole State becomes loving, and from its courtesies, the whole State becomes courteous, while, from the ambition and perverseness of the one man, the whole State may be led to rebellious disorder; —such is the nature of the influence. This verifies the saying, "Affairs may be ruined by a single

---

1. Both in the Shoo-king (書經) and here, some verb, like *act*, must be supplied.

四　堯舜[1]帥天下以仁。而民從之。桀紂[2]帥天下以暴。而民從之。其所令反其所好。而民不從[3]。是故君子。有諸已而后求諸人。無諸已而后非諸人。所藏乎身不恕[4]。而能喩諸人者。未之有也。——堯舜天下を帥ゐるに仁を以てして、民之れに從ひ、桀紂天下を帥ゐるに暴を以てして、民之れに從ふ。其の令する所其の好む所に反しては民從はず。是の故に君子は諸(これ)を已に有りて、而して后諸を人に求め、諸を已に無くして、而して后諸を人に非とす。身に藏する所恕ならずして、而して能く諸を人に喩す者は、未だ之れ有らざるなり。

註　1. 孰れも仁君として有名。 2. 孰れも暴君として有名。 3. 君の命令する所が民の好む所に反しては民は從はぬ。 4. 思ひ遣る心。

五　故治國。在齊其家。——故に國を治むるは其の家を齊ふるに在り。

六　詩[1]云。桃之夭夭[2]。其葉蓁蓁[3]。之子[4]于歸[5]。宜其家人[6]。宜其家人。而后可以教國人。——詩に云ふ、桃の夭夭(えうえう)たる、其の葉蓁蓁(しんしん)たり。之の子于(こゝ)に歸(とつ)ぐ、其の家人に宜(よろ)しと。其の家人に宜しくして而して后に以て國人を教ふ可し。

註　1. 詩經周南の篇。 2. 少好の貌。 3. 美盛の貌。 4. 是の子（古は女子を云ひたり）。 5. こゝにとつぐは嫁に行く意。歸は女の嫁するをいふ。 6. 家を善く治むるをいふ。此の詩は文王の妃を禮讚したもの。

sentence; a kingdom may be settled by its one man."

4. Yaou and Shun led on the empire with benevolence, and the people followed them. Këĕ and Chow led on the empire with violence, and the people followed them. The orders which these issued were contrary to the practices which they loved, and so the people did not follow them.¹ On this account, the ruler must himself be possessed of the *good* qualities, and then he may require them in the people. He must not have *the bad qualities* in himself, and then he may require that they shall not be in the people. Never has there been a man, who, not having reference to his own character and wishes in dealing with others, was able effectually to instruck them.

5. Thus we see how the government of the State depends on the regulation of the family.

6. In the Book of Poetry, it is said, "That peach tree, so delicate and elegant! How luxuriant is its foliage! This girl is going to her husband's house. She will rightly order her household."² Let the household be rightly ordered, and then the people of the State may be taught.

---

1. In 其所令 and 其所好, 其 must be understood as refering to the tyrants, Këĕ and Chow. Their orders were good, but unavailing, in consequence of their own contrary example.

2. The ode celebrates the wife of king Wăn (文), and the happy influence of their family government. 之子=处子. Obs. 子 is feminine. 歸, 'going home,' a term for marriage, used by women.

七 詩云。宜兄宜弟。宜兄宜弟。而后可以敎國人。――詩に云ふ、兄に宜しく弟に宜しと。兄に宜しく弟に宜しくして、而して后以て國人を敎ふ可し。

註　1. 詩經小雅の篇。

八 詩云。其儀不忒[2]。正是四國[3]。其爲父子兄弟足法。而后民法之也。――詩に云ふ、其の儀忒はず、是の四國を正すと。其の父子兄弟たる法るに足つて、而して后民之に法るなり。

註　1. 詩經曹風の篇。　2. 行動が道に差はない。　3. 國民全般。此の詩も或る國君を禮讃したもの。

九 此謂治國。在齊其家。――此れを國を治むるは其家を齊ふるに在りと謂ふ。

右傳之九章。釋齊家治國。――右傳の九章は家を齊へ國を治むることを釋く。

第十章　一 所謂平天下。在治其國者。上老老、而民興孝。上長長、而民興弟。上恤孤[1]、而民不倍。是以君子有絜矩之道[2]也。――所謂天下を平にするは其の國を治むるに在りとは、上老を老として民孝に興り、上長を長として民弟に興り、上孤を恤みて民倍かず。是を以て君子は絜矩の道有るなり。

註　1. 幼にして父無きもの。　2. 我が心を人の心を規矩として律する方法、卽ち治國平天下の要訣。

7. In the Book of Poetry, it is said, "They can discharge their duties to their elder brothers. They can discharge their duties to their younger brothers."[1] Let the ruler discharge his duties to his elder and younger brothers, and then he may teach the people of the State.

8. In the Book of Poetry, it is said, "In his deportment there is nothing wrong; he rectifies all the people of the State."[2] *Yes;* when the ruler, as a father, a son, and a brother, is a model, then the people imitate him.

9. This is what is meant by saying, "The government of his kingdom depends on his regulation of his family."

The above ninth chapter of commentary explains regulating the family and governing the kingdom.

CHAPTER X. 1. What is meant by, "The making the whole empire peaceful and happy depends on the government of his State," is this:— When the sovereign behaves to his aged, as the aged should be behaved to, the people become filial; when the sovereign behaves to his elders, as elders should be behaved to, the people learn brotherly submission; when the sovereign treats compassionately the young and helpless, the people do the same. Thus the ruler has a principle with

---

1. The ode was sung, at entertainments, when the emperor feasted the princes.
2. The ode celebrates the praises of some ruler.

二　所惡於上。毋以使下。所惡於下。毋以事上。所惡於前。毋以先後。所惡於後。毋以從前。所惡於右。毋以交於左。所惡於左。毋以交於右。此之謂絜矩之道。――上に惡む所は以て下を使ふ毋れ。下に惡む所は以て上に事ふ毋れ。前に惡む所は以て後に先んずる毋れ。後に惡む所は以て前に從ふ毋れ。右に惡む所は以て左に交はる毋れ。左に惡む所は以て右に交はる毋れ。此れを之れ絜矩の道と謂ふ。

三　詩[1]云。樂只君子。民之父母[2]。民之所好。好之。民之所惡。惡之。此之謂民之父母。――詩に云ふ、樂只の君子は民の父母と。民の好む所は之れを好み、民の惡む所は之れを惡む。此れを民の父母と謂ふ。

註　1. 詩經小雅の篇。　2. 民の父母たる是等の君子は如何に愛好すべきぞの意。只は助辭。

四　詩[1]云。節[2]彼南山。維石巖巖。赫赫師尹[3]。民具爾瞻[4]。有國者。不可以不愼。辟[5]、則爲天下僇[6]矣。――詩に云ふ、節た

which, as with a measuring square, he may regulate his conduct.¹

2. What a man dislike in his superiors, let him not display in the treatment of his inferiors; what he dislikes in inferiors, let him not display in the service of his superiors; what he hates in those who are before him, let him not therewith precede those who are behind him; what he hates in those who are behind him, let him not therewith follow those who are before him; what he hates to receive on the right, let him not bestow on the left; what he hates to receive on the left, let him not bestow on the right:—this is what is called "The principle, with which, as with a measuring square, to regulate one's conduct."²

3. In the Book of Poetry, it is said, "How much to be rejoiced in are these princes, the parents of the people!" When *a prince* loves what the people love, and hates what the people hate, then is he what is called the parent of the people.

4. In the Book of Poetry, it is said, "Lofty is that southern hill, with its rugged masses of

---

1. It having been seen that the ruler's example is so influential, it follows that the minds of all men are the same in sympathy and tendency. He has then only to take his own mind, and measure therewith the minds of others. It he act accordingly, the grand result—the empire tranquil and happy—will ensue.

2. =the principle of reciprocity, the doing to others as we would that they should do to us, though here, as elsewhere, it is put forth negatively.

る彼の南山、維れ石巖巖。赫赫たる師尹、民具に爾を瞻ると。國を有つ者以て愼まずんばある可からず。辟すれば則ち天下の僇と爲る。

註　1. 詩經小雅の篇。　2. 巍然高大の貌。　3. 周の大師尹氏。　4. この詩は無爲無能の臣を重用した幽王を慨ち大體人尹氏を敬憚したもの。　5. 國君が卑むべき利己主義に偏すればの意。　6. 戮と同義卽ち身弑せられ國亡びるをいふ。

五　詩云。殷之未喪師。克配上帝。儀監于殷。峻命不易。道得衆則得國。失衆則失國。――詩に云ふ、殷の未だ師を喪はさるや克く上帝に配す。儀しく殷に監みるべし。峻命易からずと。衆を得れば則ち國を得、衆を失へば則ち國を失ふを謂ふ。

註　1. 詩經文王の篇。　2. ＝衆（＝民の心）。　3. 天意に背かず。　4. 天意に遵ふは易からず。

六　是故君子先愼乎德。有德此有人。有人此有土。有土此有財。有財此有用。――是の故に君子は先づ德を愼む。德有れば此れ人有り、人有れば此れ土有り、土有れば此れ財有り、財有れば此れ用有り。

註　1. ＝費用。

七　德者本也。財者末也。――德は本なり、財は末なり。

八　外本內末。爭民施奪。――本を外にして末を內にすれば、民を爭はしめ奪ふことを施す。

註　1. 輕んずる。　2. 重んずる。　3. 貪ぼることを敎へる。

九　是故財聚則民散。財散則民聚。――是の故に財聚まれば則ち民散じ、財散すれば則ち民聚る。

rocks! Greatly distinguished are you, O *grand-teacher* Yin, the people all look up to you."[1] Rulers of kingdoms may not neglect to be careful. If they deviate *to a mean selfishness*, they will be a disgrace in the empire.

5. In the Book of Poetry, it is said, "Before the sovereigns of the Yin *dynasty* had lost the *hearts of the* people, they could appear before God. Take warning from *the house of* Yin. The great decree is not easily *preserved*."[2] This shows that, by gaining the people, the kingdom is gained, and, by losing the people, the kingdom is lost.

6. On this account, the ruler will first take pains about *his own* virtue. Possessing virtue will give him the people. Possessing the people will give him the territory. Possessing the territory will give him its wealth. Possesing the wealth, he will have resources for expenditure.

7. Virtue is the root; wealth is the result.

8. If he make the root his secondary object, and the result his primary,[3] he will *only* wrangle with his people, and teach them rapine.

9. Hence, the accumulation of wealth is the way to scatter the people; and the letting it be

---

1. The ode complains of the emperor Yeu (幽), for his employing unworthy ministers.

2. The ode is supposed to be addressed to king Shing (成), to stimulate him to imitate the virtues of his grandfather Wăn (文).

3. 外 and 内 are used as verbs, = 輕, 重, 'to consider slight,' 'to consider important.'

十 是故言悖而出[1]者。亦悖而入。貨悖而入者。亦悖而出。——是の故に言悖つて出づれば亦悖つて入り、貨悖つて入れば亦悖つて出づ。

註　1. 國君が道理にもとつた言を出す。

十一 康誥曰、惟命不于常[1]。道善。則得之。不善。則失之矣。——康誥に曰く、惟れ命常に于てせずと。善なれば則ち之を得、不善なれば則ち之を失ふを道ふ。

註　1. 天命は時として我々を祐け時として我々を祐けざるをいふ。

十二 楚書[1]曰。楚國無以爲寶。惟善以爲寶[2]。——楚書に曰く、楚國は以て寶と爲す無し、惟善以て寶と爲すと。

註　1. 魯の春秋に相當する楚の歴史。　2. 楚の使が晉に行つた時彼に應接した晉の宰相が楚國には大層高價な璧が有るだらうと云つた時その使が答へて自分等の國ではそんなものは寶とは考へぬ、良臣を至寶と考へると言つたと。

十三 舅犯[1]曰。亡人無以爲寶。仁親以爲寶[2]。——舅犯が曰く、亡人は以て寶と爲す無し、仁親以て寶と爲すと。

註　1. 文王の叔父。2. 文王が若い時父に國を逐はれて秦に亡命した際秦公が彼を授けて遣らうと申出ると叔父の犯が自分の甥は國に歸ることなぞを希望してはをらぬ、只死んだ父への孝養が出來なかつたことを憾いてゐると言つた。

scattered among them is the way to collect the people.

10. And hence, the ruler's words going forth contrary to right, will come back to him in the same way, and wealth, gotten by improper ways, will take its departure by the same.¹

11. In the Announcement to K'ang, it is said, "The decree indeed may not always rest on *us;*" that is, goodness obtains the decree, and the want of goodness loses it.

12. In the Book of Ts'oo,² it is said, "The kingdom of Ts'oo does not consider that to be valuable. It values, *instead*, its good men."³

13. *Duke Wăn's* uncle, Fan, said, "Our fugitive does not account that to be precious. What he considers precious, is the affection due to his parent."⁴

---

1. Our proverb—'goods ill-gotten go ill-spent' might be translated by 貨悖而入者, 亦悖而出, but those words have a different meaning in the text.
2. The Book of Ts'oo is found in the 國語, 'National records' a collection purporting what Confucius' 'Spring and Autumn' is to Loo.
3. An officer of Ts'oo beeing sent on an embassy to Tsin (晉), the minister who received him asked about a famous girdle of Ts'oo, how much it was worth. The officer replied that his country did not look on such things as its treasures, but on its able and virtuous ministers.
4. The 亡人, or, 'fugitive', is Wăn. In the early part of his life, he was a fugitive, and suffered many vicissitudes of fortuue. Once, the duke of Ts'in (秦) having offered to help him, when he was in mourning for his father who had expelled him, to recover Tsin, his uncle Fan gave the reply in the text. The *that* in the translation refers to 得國, 'getting the kingdom.'

十四　秦誓¹曰。若有一个²臣。斷斷兮³。無他技。其心休休⁴焉。其如有容焉。人之有技。若己有之。人之彦⁵聖。其心好之。不啻若自其口出⁶。寔能容之。以能保我子孫黎民。尚亦有利哉⁷。人之有技。媢疾以惡之。人之彦聖。而違之俾不通⁸。寔不能容。以不能保我子孫黎民。亦曰殆哉。――秦誓に曰く、若し一个の臣あらんに、斷斷として他技無く、其の心休休として其れ容るゝ有るが如し。人の技有る、己之れ有るが若く、人の彦聖なる、其の心に之れを好し、啻に其の口より出すが若きのみならず、寔に能く之れを容る、以て能く我が子孫黎民を保んぜん。尚はくば亦利有らん。人の技有る、媢疾して以て之れを惡くみ、人の彦聖なる而も之れに違ひて通ぜざら俾む。寔に容るゝ能はず、以て我が子孫黎民を保んずる能はず、亦殆しと曰はんかな。

註　1. 舊經の篇名。自分の忠臣の諫言を斥けて大災厄に逢つた秦の一卿が書いたもの。 2. ＝一介＝一人。 3. 誠一の貌。 4. 寛容の貌 5. 美士を彦といふ。 6. 口に出して云ふ以上にの意。 7. 斯かる偉大な人物は亦我が國を利するならん。 8. 反抗して榮達を妨げる。

十五　唯仁人。放流之¹迸諸四夷。不與同中國。此謂唯仁人。爲能愛人。能惡人。――唯だ仁人のみ之を放流し、諸を四夷に迸け、與に中國を同じうせず。此れを唯だ仁人のみ能く人を愛し能く人を惡むことを爲すと謂ふ。

註　1. 前節後半の說く如き人を放逐することをいふ。

14. In the Declaration *of the duke of* Ts'in,[1] it is said, "Let me have but one minister, plain and sincere, not *pretending to* other abilities, but with a simple, upright, mind; and possessed of generosity, *regarding* the talents of others as though he himself possessed them, and, where he finds accomplished and perspicacious men, loving them in his heart more than his mouth expresses, and really showing himself able to bear them *and employ them:*—such a minister will be able to preserve my sons and grandsons, and black-haired people, and benefits likewise to the kingdom may well be looked for from him. But if *it be his character*, when he finds men of ability, to be jealous and hate them; and, when he finds accomplished and perspicacious men, to oppose them and not allow their advancement, showing himself really not able to bear them:—such a minister will not be able to protect my sons and grandsons and black-haired people; and may he not also be pronounced dangerous *to the State* ?"

15. It is only the truly virtuous man, who can send away such a man and banish him, driving him out among the barbarous tribes around, determined not to dwell along with him in the Middle kingdom. This is in accordance with the saying,

---

1. 桊誓 was made by one of the dukes of Ts'in to his officers, after he had sustained a great disaster, in consequence of neglecting the advice of his most faithful minister.

十六　見賢而不能舉。舉而不能先¹。命²也。見不善而不能退。退而不能遠。過也。――賢を見て舉ぐる能はず、舉げて先んづる能はざるは命なり。不善を見て退くる能はず、退けて遠ざくる能はざるは過なり。

　註　1. 直ぐに舉げられぬ意。2. 慢又は怠の誤字ならんと。

十七　好人之所惡。惡人之所好。是謂拂人之性¹。菑必逮夫身。――人の惡む所を好み、人の好む所を惡む。是を人の性に拂ふと謂ふ。菑（わざはひ）必ず夫の身に逮（およ）ばん。

　註　1. 善を好み惡を惡くむが人の性。

十八　是故君子有大道。必忠信以得之¹。驕泰²以失之。――是の故に君子には大道有り、必ず忠信以て之を得、驕泰（けうたい）以て之を失ふ。

　註　1. 之とは君子茲では君主たること。2. 茲では驕と同義（論語第十三篇第二十六章の驕泰は互に相反する意）。

十九　生財有大道。生之者衆¹。食之²者寡。爲之者疾³。用之者舒⁴。則財恆足矣。――財を生むにも大道あり。之を生むは衆く、之を食むは寡く、之を爲るは疾く、之を用ひるは舒なれば、則ち財は恆に足る。

　註　1. 國に遊民が少いこと。2. 朝臣の徒に高祿を食むこと。3. 時を逸せず動くこと。4. 入るを量り出づるを制すること。

二十　仁者。以財發身。不仁者¹。以身發財²。――仁者は財を以て身を發し、不仁者は身を以て財を發す。

　註　1. 仁君は財を散じて民を得る。2. 不仁の君は貨殖の爲に身を亡ぼす。

二十一　未有上好仁。而下不好義者也。未有好義。其事不終者也¹。未有府庫財。非其財者也²。――未だ上仁を好み下義を

"It is only the truly virtuous man who can love or who can hate others."

16. To see men of worth and not be able to raise them to office; to raise them to office, but not to do so quickly:—this is disrespectful. To see bad men and not be able to remove them; to remove them, but not to do so to a distance:—this is weakness.

17. To love those whom men hate, and to hate those whom men love;—this is to outrage the natural feeling of men. Calamities cannot fail to come down on him who does so.

18. Thus *we see that* the sovereign has a great course *to pursue*. He must show entire self-devotion and sincerity to attain it, and by pride and extravagance[1] he will fail of it.

19. There is a great course *also* for the production of wealth. Let the producers be many and the consumers few. Let there be activity in the production, and economy in the expenditure. Then the wealth will always be sufficient.

20. The virtuous *ruler*, by means of his wealth, makes himself more distinguished. The vicious ruler accumulates wealth, at the expense of his life.

21. Never has there been a case of the sovereign loving benevolence, and the people not loving righteousness. Never has there been a case where

---

1. 驕 and 泰 are here qualities of the same nature. They are not contrasted as in Ana. XIII, xxvi.

好まざるは有らず。未だ義を好み其の事終へざるは有らず。未だ府庫の財其の財に非らざるは有らず。

註 1. 下が義を為すことを好み而も上の命ずる事を為し遂げぬといふことは無い。 2. 上が仁を好み下が義を好む國の府庫に貯へられてゐる富が長く其の上の所有する所でないことは無い。

二十二 孟獻子[1]曰。畜馬乘[2]。不察於雞豚[3]。伐冰之家[4]。不畜牛羊。百乘之家[5]。不畜聚歛臣[6]。與[7]其有聚歛之臣。寧有盜臣。此謂國。不以利爲利。以義爲利也。——孟獻子曰く、馬乘を畜へば雞豚を察みず。伐冰の家は牛羊を畜はず。百乘の家は聚歛の臣を畜はず。其の聚歛の臣有らんよりは寧ろ盜臣有れと。此れを國は利を以て利と爲さず、義を以て利と爲すと謂ふ。

註 1. 魯の賢大夫。 2. 初めて任官すれば俸祿は勿論馬車一輌馬四頭を賜はり内顧の憂無し。 3. 貨殖に汲々たらず。 4. 喪祭（葬式と天神地祇に犠牲を供へる祭）用の冰を切りて貯藏する家の意にして卿大夫以上を指す。 5. 采邑を有つ家。 6. 人民に税金を賦課することばかり考へる役人を使つてはならぬ。 7. 與の前ではよりと訓む。

二十三 長國家而務財用者。必自[1]小人矣。彼爲善之[2]。小人彼之使爲國家。菑[3]害竝至。雖有善者。亦無如之何矣。此謂國不以利爲利。以義爲利也。——國家に長として財用を務むる者は必ず小人に自る。彼は之を善と爲す。小人に之れ國家を爲め

the people have loved righteousness, and the affairs of the sovereign have not been carried to completion. And never has there been a case where the wealth in such a State, collected in the treasuries and arsenals, did not continue in the sovereign's possession.

22. The officer Mäng Heen said, "He who keeps horses and a carriage[1] does not look after fowls and pigs. The family which keeps its stores of ice[2] does not rear cattle or sheep. *So, the house which possesses a hundred chariots should not keep a minister to look out for imposts that he may lay them on the people. Than to have such a minister, it were better for that house to have one who should rob it *of its revenues*." This is in accordance with the saying:—"In a State, *pecuniary* gain is not to be considered to be prosperity, but its prosperity *will* be found in righteousness."

23. When he who presides over a State or a family makes his revenues his chief business, he must be under the influence of some small, mean, man. He may consider this man to be good; but when such a person is employed in the administra-

---

1. On a scholar's being first called to office, he was gifted by his prince with a carriage, and four horses. He was then supposed to withdraw from petty ways of getting wealth.

2. The 鄉, or high officers of a State, kept ice for use in their funeral rites and sacrifices. 伐水,—with reference to the cutting the ice to store it.

しめは𦾔害(さいがいなが)ら並び至らん。善者有りと雖も亦之を如何ともする無けん。此れを國は利を以て利と爲さず、義を以て利と爲すと謂ふ。

註　1. 自（小人のそゝのかす所に由る）。　2. 彼或は此の小人を以て善人と爲さん。　3. 天の降す殃(わざはひ)にして人爲的の禍たる害に對す。詩經大雅――無菑無害。

右傳之十章。釋治國平天下。凡傳十章。前四章。統論綱領指趣。後六章。細論條目工夫。其第五章。乃明善之要。第六章。乃誠身之本。在初學。尤爲當務之急。讀者不可以其近而忽之也。――右傳の十章は國を治め天下を平かにすることを釋く。凡そ傳は十章にして、前の四章は綱領の指趣(しゝゅ)を統論し、後の六章は條目の工夫を細論す。其の第五章は乃ち善を明かにするの要、第六章は乃ち身に誠なるの本、初學に在りては、尤も當に務むべき急と爲す。讀者其の近きを以て之を忽にす可からず。

tion of a State or family, calamities *from Heaven*, and injuries *from men*, will befal it together, and, though a good man may take his place, he will not be able to remedy the evil. This illustrates *again* the saying, "In a State, gain is not to be considered prosperity, but its prosperity will be found in righteousness."

The above tenth chapter of commentary explains the government of the State, and the making the empire peaceful and happy. There are thus, in all, ten chapters of commentary, the first four of which discuss, in a general manner, the scope of the principal topic of the Work; while the other six go particularly into an exhibition of the work required in its subordinate branches. The fifth chapter contains the important subject of comprehending true excellence, and the six, what is the foundation of the attainment of true sincerity. Those two chapters demand the especial attention of the learner. Let not the reader despise them because of their simplicity.

中　庸

子程子[1]曰。不偏之謂中。不易之謂庸。中者、天下之正道。庸者、天下之定理。此篇乃孔門傳授[2]心法。子思[3]恐其久而差也。故筆之於書。以授孟子。其書始言一理。中散爲萬事。末復合爲一理。放[4]之則彌六合。[5] 卷之則退藏於密。[6] 其味無窮。皆實學也。善讀者、玩索而有得焉。則終身用之。[7] 有不能盡者矣。
――子程子曰く、偏よらざる之れを中と謂ひ、易らざる之れを庸と謂ふ。中は天下の正道、庸は天下の定理、此篇は乃ち孔門傳授の心法。子思其久しくして差はんことを恐る。故に之を書に筆して以て孟子に授く。其書始めは一理を言ひ、中は散じて萬事と爲り、末復た合して一理と爲る。之れを放てば則ち六合に彌り、之れを卷けば則ち密に退藏す。其の味窮り無し。皆實學なり。善讀者の玩索して得る有らば、則ち終身之れを用ひて、盡す能はざる者あらん。

註　1. 子程子の最初の子は編者が自己の師に對して用ひた尊稱。
　　2. 孔子の門人等が口傳にした。 3. 孔子の孫。 4. 卷くの反。
　　5. 天地東西南北即ち宇宙。 6. 秘密裡にかくれる。 7. 玩味詮索して得たもの。

THE DOCTRINE OF THE MEAN.

My master, the philosopher Ch'ing, says," Being without inclination to either side is called CHUNG; *admitting of no change is called* YUNG. *By* CHUNG *is denoted the correct course to be pursued by all under heaven; by* YUNG *is denoted the fixed principle regulating all under heaven. This work contains the law of the mind, which was handed down from one to another, in the Confucian school, till Tsze-sze, fearing lest in the course of time errors should arise about it, committed it to writing, and delivered it to Mencius. The book first speaks of one principle; it next spreads this out, and embraces all things; finally, it returns and gathers them all up under the one principle. Unroll it, and it fills the universe;*[1] *roll it up, and it retires and lies hid in mysteriousness. The relish of it is inexhaustible. The whole of it is solid learning. When the skilful reader*[2] *has explored it with delight till he has apprehended it, he may carry it into practice all his life, and will find that it cannot be exhausted.*

1. 六合 = 'heaven, earth, and the four cardinal points.'
2. 善讀者,—not our 'good reader.'

第一章 一 天命之謂性。率性之謂道。修道之謂敎。――天の命ずる之れを性と謂ひ、性に率ふ之れを道と謂ひ、道を修むる之れを敎と謂ふ。

二 道也者。不可須臾[1]離也。可離。非道也。是故君子戒愼乎其所不睹。[2] 恐懼乎其所不聞。――道なる者は、須臾も離る可からざるなり。離る可きは道に非ざるなり。是の故に君子は其の睹ざる所に戒愼し、其の聞かざる所に恐懼す。

註 1. 一刻片時（原義は二十四時間の三十分の一の時間）。 2. 未だ見ざるに早くも戒愼するの意、人に見られぬ所にゐても戒愼するが從來普通の意味。次句も同斷。

三 莫見乎隱。莫顯乎微。故君子愼其獨也。――隱れたるより覺はるゝは莫く、微なるより顯なるは莫し。故に君子は其の獨を愼む。

四 喜怒哀樂之未發。謂之中。發而皆中節。謂之和。中也者。天下之大本也。和也者。天下之達道也。――喜怒哀樂の未だ發せざる之れを中と謂ひ、發して皆な節に中る之れを和と謂ふ。中なる者は、天下の大本なり。和なる者は、天下の達道なり。

五 致中和。天地位焉。萬物育焉。――中和を致して、天地位し、萬物育せらる。

右第一章。子思述所傳之意[1]以立言。首明道之本原出於天、而不可易。其實體備於己、而不可離。次言存養省察之要。終言聖神功化之極。蓋欲學者於此。反求諸身而自得之。以去夫外誘

CHAPTER I. 1. What Heaven has conferred is called THE NATURE; an accordance with this nature is called THE PATH *of duty;* the regulation of this path is called INSTRUCTION.

2. The path may not be left for an instant. If it could be left, it would not be the path. On this account, the superior man does not wait till he sees things, to be cautious, nor till he hears things, to be apprehensive.

3. There is nothing more visible than what is secret, and nothing more manifest than what is minute. Therefore the superior man is watchful over himself, when he is alone.

4. While there are no stirrings of pleasure, anger, sorrow, or joy, the mind may be said[1] to be in the state of EQUILIBRIUM. When those feelings have been stirred, and they act in their due degree, there ensues what may be called the state of HARMONY. This EQUILIBRIUM is the great root *from which grow all the human actings* in the world, and this HARMONY is the universal path *which they all should pursue.*

5. Let the states of equilibrium and harmony exist in perfection, and a happy order will prevail throughout heaven and earth, and all things will be nourished and flourish.

In the first chapter which is given above Tsze-sze states the views which had been handed down

---

1. 謂之 is different from 謂之 in par. 1. That defines; this describes.

之私。而充其本然之善。楊氏所謂一篇[2]之體要是也。其下十章。蓋子思引夫子之言。以終此章之義。——右第一章は、子思傅ふる所の意を述べて以て言を立つ。首めには道の本原は天に出でて而して易ふ可からず、其實體已に備へて、而して離る可からさるを明にす。次には存養省察の要を言ひ、終には聖神功化の極を言ふ。蓋し學者此に於し、諸を身に反求して、而して之れを自得し、以て夫の外誘の私を去つて、而して其の本然の善を充さんことを欲す。楊氏の所謂一篇の體要是れなり、其の下十章は、蓋し子思夫子の言を引き、以て此章の義を終ふ。

註　1. 傅へ聞いた教の意。 2. 楊氏の所謂此の一篇（楊氏は八百餘年前即ち英宗皇帝時代の學者）。

第二章　一　仲尼曰。[1]君子中庸。小人反中庸。——仲尼曰く、君子は中庸し、小人は中庸に反す。

註　1. 子曰と云はぬ理由今猶は判明せぬ。

二　君子之中庸也。君子而時中。[1] 小人之中庸也。小人而無忌憚也。[2]——君子の中庸や、君子にして時に中す。小人の中庸に反するや、小人にして忌憚無きなり。

註　1. 君子が中庸なのは君子故常に中庸を得るからである。 2. 小人

to him, as the basis of his discourse. First, it shows clearly how the path of duty is to be traced to its origin in Heaven, and is unchangeable, while the substance of it is provided in ourselves, and may not be departed from. Next, it speaks of the importance of preserving and nourishing this, and of exercising a watchful self-scrutiny with reference to it. Finally, it speaks of the meritorious achievements and transforming influence of sage and spiritual men in their highest extent. The wish of Tsze-sze was that hereby the learner should direct his thoughts inwards, and by searching in himself, there find these truths, so that he might put aside all outward temptations appealing to his selfishness, and fill up the measure of the goodness which is natural to him. This chapter is what the writer Yang called it,—"The sum[1] of the whole work." In the ten chapters which follow, Tsze-sze quotes the words of the Master to complete the meaning of this.

CHAPTER II. 1. Chung-ne said, "The superior man *embodies*[2] the course of the Mean; the mean man acts contrary to the course of the Mean.

2. "The superior man's embodying the course of the Mean is because he is a superior man, and so always maintains the Mean. The mean man's

---

1. 體要, 'the substance and the abstract.'
2. Some verb must be understood between 君子 and 中庸, and I have supposed it to be 體, with most of the paraphrasts.

が中庸でないのは小人故何事をも忌み憚らぬからである。

第三章　子曰。中庸其至矣乎[1]。民鮮能久矣。——子曰く、中庸は其れ至れるかな。民能くする鮮なきこと久し。

註　1. 中庸の德は完全至極なるかな。

第四章　一　子曰。道[1]之不行也。我知之矣。知者過之。愚者不及也。道之不明[2]也。我知之矣。賢者過之。不肖者不及也。——子曰く、道の行はれざるや、我れ之れを知る。知者は之れに過ぎ、愚者は及ばざるなり。道の明ならざるや、我れ之れを知る。賢者は之れに過ぎ、不肖者は及ばざるなり。

註　1. 中庸の道。　2. 明かに理解する。

二　人莫不飲食也。鮮能知味也。[1]——人飲食せざる莫きも、能く味を知るは鮮し。

註　1. 此の一節は前節の説明で比喩ではない。而も大いに解し難い。我々は物を飲食するがその物の眞の味を知らぬやうに、中庸の道も我々の平常の行爲のすべてに附き纏つてゐながら慈々特殊の行爲の裡に中庸の道を求め常住座臥之を認識實行することが出來ぬ。

第五章　子曰。道其不行矣夫。[1]——子曰く、道は其れ行はれざるか。

註　1. 何んと中庸の道の世間に行はれぬことよ、噫！

第六章　子曰。舜其大知也與。舜好問、而好察邇言。[1]隱惡而揚善。執其兩端。用其中於民。[2]其斯以爲舜乎。——子曰く、舜は其れ大知なるか、舜問を好んで而して好みて邇言を察す。惡を隱して而して善を揚げ其兩端を執つて、其中を民に用ふ。其れ斯れ以て舜たるか。

註　1. 他人に質問を發し淺薄でも他人の言を研究することを好んだ。　2. 民の善惡の兩極端を捉へてその中庸なものを認定し之を用ひて民を治めた。

acting contrary to the course of the Mean is because he is a mean man, and has no caution."

CHAPTER III. The Master said, "Perfect is the virtue which is according to the Mean! Rare have they long been among the people, who could practise it!"

CHAPTER IV. 1. The Master said, "I know how it is that the path *of the Mean* is not walked in:—The knowing[1] go beyond it, and the stupid do not come up to it. I know how it is that the path of the Mean is not understood:—The men of talents and virtue[1] go beyond it, and the worthless do not come up to it.

2. "There is no body but eats and drinks. But they are few who can distinguish flavours."

CHAPTER V. The Master said, "Alas! How is the path of the Mean untrodden!"[2]

CHAPTER VI. The Master said, "There was Shun:—He indeed was greatly wise! Shun loved to question *others*, and to study their words, though they might be shallow. He concealed what was bad *in them*, and displayed what was good. He took hold of their two extremes, *determined*

---

1. 知者 and 賢者 are not to be understood as meaning the truly wise and the truly worthy, but only those who in the degenerate times of Confucius deemed themselves to be such.

2. One commentator says:—'From not being understood, therefore it is not practised.' According to another, the remark is a lament that there was no intelligent sovereign to teach the path. But the two views are reconcileable.

第七章 子曰。人皆曰予知。驅而納諸罟[1]擭[2]陷阱[3]之中。而莫之知辟也。人皆曰予知。擇乎中庸而不能期月守也。[4]――子曰く、人皆予知ありと曰ふ。驅つて諸を罟擭陷阱の中に納れて、而して之を辟くるを知る莫きなり。人皆予知ありと曰ふ。中庸を擇んで、而して期月を守る能はざるなり。

註 1. 魚を捕る具。 2. 獸を捕る具。 3. 落し穴。 4. 丸一ケ月と中庸の道を踏むことは出來ぬ。

第八章 子曰。回[1]之爲人也。擇乎中庸。得一善。則拳拳服膺。而弗失之矣。――子曰く、回の人たるや、中庸を擇び、一善を得れば則ち拳拳服膺して、而して之れを失はず。

註 1. 孔子の最も愛した門弟顏回。

第九章 子曰。天下國家可均也。[1] 爵祿可辭也。[2] 白刃可蹈也。[3] 中庸不可能也。[4]――子曰く、天下國家は均しくす可きなり、爵祿は辭す可きなり、白刃は蹈む可きなり、中庸は能くす可からざるなり。

註 1. 天下とその侯國とその家庭とは立派に治めることが出來る。 2. 爵位俸祿は辭退することが出來る。 3. 白刃は蹈むことが出來る。 4. 中庸の道は能く踏むことが出來ぬ。

第十章 一 子路問強。[1]――子路強を問ふ。

註 1. 孔子の高弟ながら勇を好みこの問を爲した。

二 子曰。南方之強與。北方之強與。抑而強[1]與。――子曰く、南方の強か、北方の強か。抑も而の強か。

註 1. 汝の修養すべき強。

三 寬柔以敎。[1] 不服無道。[2] 南方之強也。君子居之。[3]――寬柔以て敎へ、無道に服ぜざるは、南方の強なり。君子之れに居る。

註 1. 人を敎へるに寬柔を以てする。 2. 亂暴な行爲に服響しない。 3. 君子は之を擧ぶ。敎ふるに只寬柔を以てするは未だ中庸の道

the Mean, and employed it in *his government of the people*. It was by this that he was Shun!"

CHAPTER VII. The Master said, "Men all say, 'We are wise;' but being driven forward and taken in a net, a trap, or a pitfall, they know not how to escape. Men all say, 'We are wise;' but happening to choose the course of the Mean, they are not able to keep it for a round month."

CHAPTER VIII. The Master said, "This was the manner of Hwuy:—he made choice of the Mean, and whenever he got hold of what was good,[1] he clasped it firmly,[2] as if wearing it on his breast, and did not lose it."

CHAPTER IX. The Master said, "The empire, its States, and its families, may be perfectly ruled; dignities and emoluments may be declined; naked weapons may be trampled under the feet;—but the course of the Mean cannot be attained to."

CHAPTER X. 1. Tsze-loo asked about energy.

2. The Master said, "Do you mean the energy of the South, the energy of the North, or the energy which you should cultivate yourself?'

3. "To show forbearance and gentleness in teaching others; and not to revenge unreasonable conduct:—this is the energy of Southern regions,

---

1. 一善 is not 'one good point,' so much as any one.

2. 拳 is 'the closed fist;' 拳拳,—'the appearance of holding firm.'

3. 而 (=汝)彊 must be — 'the energy which you should cultivate,' not 'which you have.'

に及ばざること遠し、故に茲の君子は只善人の如き意で本章第五節の君子とは大いに異る。

四　衽金革。¹　死而不厭。北方之強也。而強者居之。——金革を衽として死して厭はざるは、北方の強なり。強者之れに居る。

註　1. 刄や鎧甲をしとねとして野に伏す。

五　故君子和不流¹。強哉矯²。中立而不倚。強哉矯。國有道不變塞焉³。強哉矯。國無道。至死不變⁴。強哉矯。——故に君子は和すれども流れず、強なるかな矯。中立して而して倚らず、強なるかな矯。國道あらば塞を變せず、強なるかな矯。國道無ければ死に至るも變ぜず、強なるかな矯。

註　1. 友情味に富む和氣を奘つて而も弱に流れぬ。　2. 強の貌。　3. 晴耕雨讀の隱遯生活を變へぬ。塞=實。　4. 死ぬまで主義の爲に盡す。

第十一章

一　子曰。素隱行怪。後世有述焉。吾弗爲之矣¹。——子曰く、隱れたるを索め怪しきを行ふ。後世述ぶる有らんも、吾れは之れを爲さず。

註　1. 深く隱僻の理を求むるために生き過つて詭異の行を爲れば後世に傳はるかも知れぬが自分はそんな事はしない。

二　君子遵道而行¹。半塗而廢。吾弗能已矣。——君子は道に遵ひて行ひ半途にして而して廢す。吾は已む能はず。

註　1. 道に遵つて行ふには努力を要し自然に之に依るとは異る故茲の君子も前章第三節のそれの如く只善人位の意。

三　君子依乎中庸。遯世¹不見知而不悔。唯聖者能之。——君子は中庸に依り、世を遯れ知られずして悔いず、唯聖者のみ之れを能くす。

註　1. 隱士の爲す所をいふ、避世ならば俗界に在つて俗化せぬ高士の爲す所をいふ。

and the good man[1] makes it his study.

4. "To lie under arms;[2] and meet death without regret:—this is the energy of Northern regions, and the forceful make it their study.

5. "Therefore, the superior man cultivates *a friendly* harmony, without being weak.—How firm is he in his energy! He stands erect in the middle, without inclining to either side. — How firm is he in his energy! When good principles prevail in the government of his country, he does not change from what he was in retirement.— How firm is he in his energy! When bad principles prevail in the country, he maintains his course to death without changing.—How firm is he in his energy!"

CHAPTER XI. 1. The Master said, "To live in obscurity, and yet practise wonders, in order to be mentioned with honour in future ages;—this is what I do not do.

2. "The good man[3] tries to proceed according to the right path, but when he has gone half way, he abandons it;—I am not able *so* to stop.

3. "The superior man[4] accords with the course of the Mean. Though he may be all unknown,

---

1. 君子 is taken with a low and light meaning, far short of what it has in par. 5.
2. 袵金革, 'to make a mat of the leather dress (革) and weapons (金).'
3. 君子 is here the same as in last ch. par. 3.
4. 君子 here has its very highest signification, and=聖者 in the last clause.

第十二章　一　君子之道。費而隱[1]。――君子の道は費にして隱。

註　1. 君子の踏む道は津々浦々に達し而も隱れて顯はれぬ。

二　夫婦之愚。可以與知焉[1]。及其至也[2]。雖聖人亦有所不知焉。夫婦之不肖。可以能行焉[3]。及其至也。雖聖人亦有所不能焉。天地之大也。人猶有所憾[4]。故君子語大。天下莫能載焉[5]。語小。天下莫能破[6]焉。――夫婦の愚も、以て與り知る可し。其の至れるに及びてや、聖人と雖も亦知らざる所あり。夫婦の不肖も以て能く行ふ可し。其の至れるに及びてや、聖人と雖も亦能くせざる所有り。天地の大なる、人猶ほ憾むる所有り。故に君子大を語れば、天下能く載する莫く、小を語れば、天下能く破る莫きなり。

註　1. 匹夫匹婦如何に愚ならんも或は君子の道を與り知ることあらんの意。　2. 君子の道その至大至高を極むればの意。　3. 匹夫匹婦如何に不肖ならんも或は君子の道を行ふことあらんの意。　4. 天地また如何に大ならんも人猶ほ之を小となさむことあらん。　5. 故に君子その道の大なるを語らば之を容るゝ者天下になきは怪むに足らず。　6. 割くと同義。

三　詩云。鳶飛戾天。魚躍于淵。言其上下察也[1]。――詩に云ふ。鳶飛んで天に戻り、魚淵に躍ると。其の上下に察（あきらか）なるを言ふ。

註　1. これこそ君子の道の俯仰天地に顯然たるを形容した詩句である。

四　君子之道。造端乎夫婦。及其至也。察乎天地[1]。――君子の道は端を夫婦に造（な）す。其の至れるに及びてや、天地に察（あきらか）なり。

註　1. 君子の道はこれを小にしては匹夫匹婦の交際に見れこれを大にしては天地の間に昭々たりの意。

unregarded by the world, he feels no regret. — It is only the sage who is able for this."

CHAPTER XII. 1. The way which the superior man pursues, reaches wide and far, and yet is secret.

2. Common men and women,[1] however ignorant, may intermeddle with the knowledge of it; yet in its utmost reaches, there is that which even the sage does not know. Common men and women, however much below the ordinary standard of character, can carry it into practice; yet in its utmost reaches, there is that which even the sage is not able to carry into practice. Great as heaven and earth are, men still find some things in them with which to be dissatisfied. Thus it is, that were the superior man to speak of his way in all its greatness, nothing in the world would be found able to embrace it, and were he to speak of it in its minuteness, nothing in the world would be found able to split it.

3. It is said in the Book of Poetry, "The hawk flies up to heaven; the fishes leap in the deep."[2] This expresses how this *way* is seen[3] above and below.

4. The way of the superior man may be found, in its simple elements, in the intercourse of com-

---

1, 夫婦＝匹夫, 匹婦.

2. The ode is in praise of the virtue of king Wăn.

3. 察 is in the sense of 昭著, 'brightly displayed.' The application of the words of the ode does appear strange.

右第十二章。子思之言。蓋以申明[1]首章道不可離之意也。其下八章。雜引孔子之言以明之。――右第十二章は、子思の言、蓋し以て首章の道は離る可からざるの意を申明するなり。其の下八章は、孔子の言を雜引して以て之を明にす。

註 1. 說明に同じ。

第十三章 一 子曰。道不遠人。人之爲道而遠人[1]。不可以爲道。――子曰く、道は人に遠からず、人の道を爲して人に遠ければ以て道と爲す可からず。

註 1. 若しも人が自分の良心の命ずる所と遠く異なる道を追ひ求めようとするならばの意。

二 詩云。伐柯伐柯。其則不遠[1]。執柯以伐柯。睨而視之。猶以爲遠[2]。故君子以人治人。改而止[3]。――詩に云ふ、柯を伐り柯を伐る。其の則遠からず、と。柯を執り以て柯を伐る、睨んで之れを視る、猶ほ以て遠しと爲す。故に君子は人を以て人を治め、改めて止む。

註 1. 斧で斧の柄を伐りつゝある時には其のお手本は手近に有る。 2. しかし手斧を振ふ我々が自分の手に握つてゐる斧の柄を睨んだその目で今將に伐り取らうとしてゐる斧の柄となるべき枝を見渡して大分其間には距離があると想ふのは間違である。 3. それ故君子は民を治めるに民の本質を以てし而もその民が善い方に改め始めれば直ぐに手を引いてしまふ（治める君子と治められる凡人との間に素質の距りの無いことを悟つてゐるから）。

mon men and women; but in its utmost reaches, it shines brightly through heaven and earth.

The twelfth chapter above contains the words of Tsze-sze, and is designed to illustrate what is said in the first chapter, that "The path may not be left." In the eight chapters which follow, he quotes, in a miscellaneous way, the words of Confucius to illustrate it.

CHAPTER XIII. 1. The Master said, "The path is not far from man. When men try to pursue a course, which is far from the common indications of consciousness, this course cannot be considered THE PATH.[1]

2. "In the Book of Poetry, it is said, 'In hewing an axe-handle, in hewing an axe-handle, the pattern is not far off.' We grasp one axe-handle to hew the other, and yet, if we look askance from the one to the other, we may consider them as apart. Therefore, the superior man governs men, according to their nature, with what is proper to them, and as soon as they change *what is wrong*, he stops.[2]

---

1. 人之爲道而遠人,—'When men practise a course, and *wish to be* far from men.' The meaning is as in the translation.
2. The object of the par. seems to be to show that the rule for dealing with men, according to the principles of the Mean, is nearer to us than the axe in the hand is to the one which is to be cut down with, and fashioned after, it. The branch is hewn, and its form altered from its natural one. Not so with man. The change in him only brings him to his proper state.

三 忠恕[1]違道不遠。施諸已而不願。亦勿施於人。——忠恕は道を違ること遠からず。諸を己に施して願はずんば、亦人に施すこと勿れ。

註 1. 自己の衷情を修め之を互助の主旨に則つて人に施すことをいふ。忠恕が同情の意味であることは忠は心の中を示し恕は他人の如き心を示す文字であることから推して知らるゝと。論語里仁第十五章參照。

四 君子之道四。丘[1]未能一焉。所求乎子、以事父、未能也。所求乎臣、以事君、未能也。所求乎弟、以事兄、未能也。所求乎朋友、先施之、未能也。庸德之行[2]、庸言之謹[3]、有所不足[4]、不敢不勉、有餘、不敢盡[5]。言顧行[6]。行顧言。君子胡不慥慥爾[7]。——君子の道四、丘未だ一を能くせず。子に求むる所、以て父に事ふるは、未だ能はざるなり。臣に求むる所、以て君に事ふるは、未だ能はざるなり。弟に求むる所、以て兄に事ふるは、未だ能はざるなり。朋友に求むる所、先づ之れを施すは、未だ能はざるなり。庸德を之れ行ひ庸言を之れ愼みつゝ、足らざる所有らば、敢て勉めずんばあらず、餘り有らば敢て盡さず。言は行を顧み、行は言を顧みる。君子胡ぞ慥慥爾たらざらん。

註 1. ＝孔子。 2. 是の四つの平常の德を行ふことに努めつゝ。 3. 是の四つの平常の德を口にすることを愼みつゝ。 4. 苟も斯等の德を行ふて足らぬ所があれば。 5. 苟も斯等の德を口にして誇張の嫌があれば決して言ひ盡すことはしない。 6. 言は行に一致するように行を顧みる。 7. 篤實の貌。

第十四章 一 君子素其位而行[1]。不願乎其外。——君子は其の位に素して行ひ、其の外を願はず。

註 1. 其の位に基いて行ふ意。

3. "When one cultivates to the utmost the principles of his nature, and exercises them on the principle of reciprocity, he is not far from the path. What you do not like, when done to yourself, do not do to others.

4. "In the way of the superior man there are four things, to not one of which have I as yet attained.—To serve my father, as I would require my son to serve me: to this I have not attained; to serve my prince, as I would require my minister to serve me: to this I have not attained; to serve my elder brother, as I would require my younger brother to serve me: to this I have not attained; to set the example in behaving to a friend, as I would require him to behave to me: to this I have not attained. Earnest in practising the ordinary virtues, and careful in speaking about them,[1] if, in his practice, he has anything defective, the superior man dares not but exert himself; and if, in his words, he has any excess, he dares not allow himself such license. Thus his words have respect to his actions, and his actions have respect to his words; is it not just an entire sincerity which marks the superior man?"

CHAPTER XIV. 1. The superior man does

---

1. 庸德之行, 庸言之謹,—'in the practice of ordinary virtues,' *i. e.*, the duties of a son, minister, &c., mentioned above, and 'in the carefulness of ordinary speech,' *i. e.*, speaking about those virtues. To the practice belong the clauses 有所不足, 不敢不勉, and to the speaking, the two next clauses.

二　素¹富貴。行乎富貴。素貧賤。行乎貧賤。素夷狄。行乎夷狄。素患難。行乎患難。君子無入²而不自得焉。――富貴に素しては富貴に行ひ、貧賤に素しては貧賤に行ひ、夷狄に素しては夷狄に行ひ、患難に素しては患難に行ふ。君子入るとして自得せざる無し。

註　1. 在るべき所に在る。　2. 境遇に入るの意。

三　在上位。不陵¹下。在下位。不援²上。正己而不求於人。則無怨。上不怨天。下不尤人。――上位に在りて下を陵がず、下位に在りて上を援かず、已を正しくして人に求めずんば則ち怨む無し。上天を怨みず、下人を尤めず。

註　1. 輕蔑する。　2. 御機嫌を取ってすがる。

四　故君子居易以俟命。小人行險以徼幸。――故に君子は易に居て以て命を俟ち、小人は險を行ひて以て幸を徼む。

五　子曰。射有似乎君子。失諸正鵠¹。反求諸其身²。――子曰く射は君子に似たる有り、諸を正鵠に失すれば、反つて諸を其の身に求む。

註　1. 金的を射損ふ。　2. 失敗の原因を自分に歸する。

what is proper to the station in which he is; he does not desire to go beyond this.

2. In a position of wealth and honour, he does what is proper to a position of wealth and honour. In a poor and low position, he does what is proper to a poor and low position. Situated among barbarous tribes, he does what is proper to a situation among barbarous tribes. In a position of sorrow and difficulty, he does what is proper to a position of sorrow and difficulty. The superior man can find himself in no situation in which he is not himself.

3. In a high situation, he does not treat with contempt his inferiors. In a low situation, he does not court the favour of his superiors. He rectifies himself, and seeks for nothing from others, so that he has no dissatisfactions. He does not murmur against heaven, nor grumble against men.

4. Thus it is that the superior man is quiet and calm, waiting for the appointments *of Heaven,* while the mean man walks in dangerous paths, looking for lucky occurences.

5. The Master said, "In archery we have something like the way of the superior man. When the archer misses the centre of the target,[1] he

---

1. 正 and 鵠 are both names of birds, small and alert, and dfficult to be hit on this account, a picture of the former was painted on the middle of the target and a figure of the latter was attached to it in leather. It is not meant, however, by this, that they were both used in the same target, at the same time.

第十五章 一 君子之道。辟如行遠。必自邇。辟如登高。必自卑。――君子の道は辟へば遠きに行くに必ず邇き自りするが如く、辟へば高きに登るに必ず卑き自りするが如し。

二 詩曰。妻子好合[1]。如鼓瑟琴。兄弟既翕。和樂且耽[2]。宜爾室家[3]。樂爾妻孥[4]。――詩に曰く、妻子好合して、瑟琴を鼓するが如し、兄弟既に翕ひ、和樂し且つ耽しむ。爾の室家に宜しく爾の妻孥を樂まむと。

註　1. 妻子と折合良く暮すこと。 2. 兄弟と仲良く暮せばいつも樂しい。 3. 斯く和合して暮せば一家を齊へることが出來る。 4. 妻子と暮すのを幸福に思ふ。

三 子曰。父母其順矣乎[1]。――子曰く、父母は其れ順なるか。

註　1. 斯う云ふ境遇にあれば父母はさぞ滿足するだらう。

第十六章 一 子曰。鬼神之爲德。其盛矣乎[1]。――子曰く、鬼神の德たる、其れ盛なるか。

註　1. 此の一章は鬼神の怪力を讚へるのではない、鬼神の怪力を例に引いて中庸の德の盛んなることを述べる。

二 視之[1]而弗見。聽之而弗聞。體物而不可遺[2]。――之れを視れども見えず、之れを聽けども聞えず、物に體となりて遺る可からず。

註　1. 鬼神（實は中庸の德）。 2. 鬼神（實は中庸の德）は萬物の中に遣入つてゐる、遣入つてをらぬものは天下に一つもない。即ち中庸の德は鬼神と同じく萬物の精である。

三 使天下之人。齊明盛服[1]。以承祭祀。洋洋乎[2]。如在其上。如在其左右。――天下の人をして齊明盛服せしめ、以て祭祀を承く。洋洋乎として、其の上に在るが如く、其の左右に在るが如し。

註　1. 齊戒沐浴して美服を着る。 2. 流動充滿の貌。

turns round and seeks for the cause of his failure in himself."

CHAPTER XV. 1. The way of the superior man may be compared to what takes place in travelling, when to go to a distance we must first traverse the space that is near, and in ascending a height, when we must begin from the lower ground.

2. It is said in the Book of Poetry, "Happy union with wife and children, is like the music of lutes and harps. When there is concord among brethren, the harmony is delightful and enduring. *Thus* may you regulate your family, and enjoy the pleasure of your wife and children."

3. The Master said, "In such a state of things, parents have entire complacence!"

CHAPTER XVI. 1. The Master said, "How abundantly do spiritual beings display the powers that belong to them!

2. "We look for them, but do not see them; we listen to, but do not hear them; yet they enter into all things, and there is nothing without them.

3. "They cause all the people in the empire to fast and purify themselves, and array themselves in their richest dresses, in order to attend at their sacrifices. Then, like overflowing water, they seem to be over the heads, and on the right and left *of their worshippers.*

四　詩曰。神之格思[1]。不可度[2]思。矧可射[3]思。――詩に曰く、神の格る、度る可からず、矧んや射ふ可けんやと。

註　1. 助辭。　2. ＝豫知。　3. ＝厭＝不敬。

五　夫微之顯。誠之不可揜[1]。如此夫。――夫れ微の顯なる、誠の揜ふ可からざる此の如きか。

註　1. ＝掩。

第十七章　一　子曰。舜其大孝也與。德爲聖人。尊爲天子。富有四海之內、宗廟饗之[1]、子孫保之[2]。――子曰く、舜は其れ大孝なるか。德聖人たり、尊きこと天子たり、富四海の內を有ち、宗廟之れを饗け、子孫之れを保つ。

註　1. 祖先の靈を祀るために犧牲を供へた。　2. 舜の子孫は舜の靈を祀るために犧牲を供へた。

二　故大德[1]。必得其位[2]。必得其祿。必得其名。必得其壽[3]。――故に大德あれば必ず其の位を得、必ず其の祿を得、必ず其の名を得、必ず其の壽を得。

註　1. 斯のやうな大德、故では大孝（舜を指す故）。　2. 帝位（其は大德を指す）。　3. 舜は百歲の天壽を全ふした。

三　故天之生物。必因其材而篤焉[1]。故栽[2]者培之。傾者覆之。――故に天の物を生ずる、必ず其の材に因りて篤くす、故に栽つ者は之れを培ひ、傾く者は之れを覆へす。

註　1. 天の物を生ずる其の質に從つて或は厚く或は薄くこれを遇す。　2. ＝築植。

4. "It is said in the Book of Poetry, 'The approaches of the spirits, you cannot surmise;—and can you treat them with indifference?'¹

5. "Such is the manifestness of what is minute! Such is the impossibility of repressing the outgoings of sincerity!"

CHAPTER XVII. 1. The Master said, "How greatly filial was Shun! His virtue was that of a sage; his dignity was the imperial throne; his riches were all within the four seas. He offered his sacrifices² in his ancestral temple, and his descendants preserved the sacrifices to himself.

2. "Therefore having such great virtue, it could not but be that he should obtain the throne, that he should obtain those riches, that he should obtain his fame, that he should attain to his long life.³

3. "Thus it is that Heaven, in the production

---

1. The ode is said to have been composed by one of the dukes of Wei, and was repeated daily in his hearing for his adomonition. In the context of the quotation, he is warned to be careful of his conduct, when alone as when in company. 'Millions of spiritual beings walk the earth,' and can take note of us. 思 is a final particle here, without meaning. It is often used so in the She-king. 度 (入聲)=to conjecture. 射 (入聲)=to dislike.

2. 饗之 here may be taken,—'enjoyed him;' that is, his sacrifices. As Shun resigned the throne to Yu (禹), and it did not run in the line of his family, we must take 保之 as in the translation. In the time of the Chow dynasty, there were descendants of Shun, possessed of the state of Ch'in (陳), and of course sacrificing to him.

3. He died at the age of 100 years.

四　詩曰。嘉樂君子[1]。憲憲令德。宜民宜人。受祿于天。保佑命之[2]。自天申之[3]。——詩に曰く、嘉樂の君子は、憲憲たる令德あり、民に宜しく人に宜しく、祿を天に受く、保佑して之れに命じ、天より之れを申さぬと。

註　1. 賞讃すべく愛慕すべき君子即ち文王。　2. 天は文王を保ち、文王を佑け、文王を帝位に即けと命じた。　3. 幾度となく天より文王に是うした恩惠を授けた。

五　故大德[1]者。必受命[2]。——故に大德ある者は、必ず命を受く。

註　1. 茲でも第二節の場合のやうに大學と同義。　2. 天より帝位に即くべき命を受ける。

第十八章　一　子曰。無憂者。其惟文王乎。以王季爲父[1]。以武王爲子[2]。父作之[3]。子述之[4]。——子曰く、憂無き者は、其れ惟だ文王か。王季を以て父と爲し、武王を以て子と爲す。父之れを作して子之れを述ぶ。

註　1. 文王の父は王季といふ偉い人であつた（舜の父は惡人、堯や禹の父は凡人であつた）。　2. 文王の子武王は賢君（堯舜の子は惡人禹の子は無名）。　3. 基業を創めた。　4. 武王は基業を成した。

of things, is surely bountiful to them, according to their qualities. Hence the tree that is flourishing, it nourishes, while that which is ready to fall, it overthrows."

4. "In the Book of Poetry, it is said, 'The admirable, amiable, prince, displayed conspicuously his excelling virtue, adjusting his people and adjusting his officers. *Therefore*, he received from Heaven the emoluments of dignity. It protected him, assisted him, decreed him the throne; sending from heaven these favours, *as it were*, repeatedly.'"[1]

5. "*We may say* therefore that he who is greatly virtuous will be sure to receive the appointment of Heaven."

CHAPTER XVIII. 1. The Master said, "It is only king Wăn of whom it can be said that he had no cause for grief! His father was king Ke, and his son was king Woo. His father laid the foundations of his dignity, and his son transmitted it."[2]

---

1. The prince spoken of is king Wăn, who is thus brought forward to confirm the lesson taken from Shun. That lesson, however, is stated much too broadly in the last paragraph. It is well to say that only virtue is a solid title to eminence, but to hold forth the certain attainment of wealth and position as an inducement to virtue is not favourable to morality. The case of Confucius himself, who attained neither to power nor to long life may be adduced as inconsistent with these teachings.

2. Shun's father was bad and the fathers of Yaou (尭) and Yu (禹) were undistinguished. Yaou and Shun's sons were both bad, and Yu's not remarkable. But to Wăn neither father nor

二　武王纘大王[1]王季文王之緒。壹戎衣。而有天下[2]。身不失天下之顯名[3]。尊爲天子。富有四海之內。宗廟饗之[4]。子孫保之[5]。——武王は大王、王季、文王の緒を纘ぎ、壹たび戎衣して天下を有ち、身天下の顯名を失はず、尊きことは天子たり、富は四海の內を有ち、宗廟は之れを饗け、子孫は之れを保つ。

註　1. 王季の父で殷の衰へるに乘じ能く民望を收めた。 2. 一度戰爭したゞけで天下を取つた(殷を滅ぼして周の天下とした)。戎衣＝甲冑 3. 武王は殷の紂王といふ正天子を征伐したが民望を失はなかつた。 4. 宗廟に犧牲を供へて祖先の靈を祀つた。 5. 子孫も彼の靈を祀つた。

三　武王末受命[1]。周公成文武之德[2]。追王[3]大王王季。上祀先公以天子之禮。斯禮[4]也。達乎諸侯大夫。及士庶人。父爲大夫。子爲士。葬以大夫。祭以士。父爲士。子爲大夫。葬以士。祭以大夫。期之喪。達乎大夫[5]。三年之喪。達乎天子。父母之喪。無貴賤一也[6]。——武王末に命を受け、周公文武の德を成し、大王、王季を追王す。上先公を祀るに天子の禮を以てす。斯の禮や諸侯大夫に達し士庶人に及ぶ。父大夫たり、子士たれば、葬むるには大夫を以てし、祭るには士を以てす。父士たり、子大夫たれば、葬るには士を以てし、祭るには大夫を以てす。期の喪は大夫に達し、三年の喪は天子に達す。父母の喪は貴賤と無く一なり。

註　1. 武王が天子になつたのは八十の老人になつた後で在位僅に七年で崩じた。末＝老。 2. 周公(武王の弟にしてその宰相)は文武二王の德政を輔佐完成した。 3. 王號を追稱した。 4. 葬には死者の爵を

2. "King Woo continued the enterprise of king T'ae,[1] king Ke, and king Wăn. He once buckled on his armour,[2] and got possession of the empire. He did not lose the distinguished personal reputation which he had throughout the empire. His dignity was the imperial throne. His riches were the possession of all within the four seas. He offered his sacrifices in his ancestral temple, and his descendants maintained the sacrifices to himself.

3. "It was in his old age[3] that king Woo received the appointment *to the throne*, and the duke of Chow[4] completed the virtuous course of Wăn and Woo. He carried up the title of king to T'ae and Ke, and sacrificed to all the former dukes above them with the imperial ceremonies. And this rule he extended to the princes of the empire, the great officers, the scholars, and the common people. Was the father a great officer and the son a scholar, then the burial was that due to a great officer, and the sacrifice that due

---

son gave occasion but for satisfaction and happiness. King Ke was the duke Ke-lik (季歷), the most distinguished by his virtues and prowess, of all the princes of his time.

1. 大王,—this was the duke T'an-foo (亶父), the father of Ke-lik, a prince of great eminence, and who, in the decline of the Yin dynasty, drew to his family the thoughts of the people.

2. He distroyed the great Yin.

3. 末=老, 'when old.' Woo was 87 when he became emperor, and he only reigned 7 years.

4. Woo's brother Tan (旦), the duke of Chow, acted as his chief minister.

用ひ祭には生者の祿を用ひる禮法。　5. 親の死に對し一年の喪に服するは大夫に限る。　6. 大夫以下は貴賤親の喪を一にす。

第十九章　一　子曰。武王周公。其達孝矣乎。——子曰く、武王、周公は其れ達孝なるか。

二　夫孝者。善繼人[1]之志。善述人之事[2]者也。——夫れ孝は善く人の志を繼ぎ、善く人の事を述ぶる者なり。

註　1. 祖先。　2. 祖先の事業を成就させる。

三　春秋。修其宗廟。陳其宗器[1]。設其裳衣[2]。薦其時食[3]。——春秋に、其の宗廟を修め、其の宗器を陳ね、其の裳衣を設け、其の時食を薦む。

註　1. 祖先の器物を陳列する。　2. 祖先の衣裳を展覽する。　3. 其季節の食物を供へる。

四　宗廟之禮。所以序昭穆[1]也。序爵[2]。所以辨貴賤也。序事[3]。所以辨賢也。旅酬下爲上。所以逮賤[4]也。燕毛。所以序齒也[5]。

to a scholar. Was the father a scholar, and the son a great officer, then the burial was that due to a scholar, and the sacrifice that due to a great officer. The one year's mourning was made to extend *only* to the great officers, but the three years' mourning extended to the emperor. In the mourning for a father or mother, he allowed no difference between the noble and the mean."

CHAPTER XIX. 1. The Master said, "How far extending was the filial piety of king Woo and the duke of Chow!

2. "Now filial piety is seen in the skilful carrying out of the wishes of our fore-fathers,[1] and the skilful carrying forward of their undertakings.

3. "In spring and autumn, they repaired and beautified the temple-halls of their fathers, set forth their ancestral vessels, displayed their various robes,[2] and presented the offerings of the several seasons.

4. "By means of the ceremonies of the ancestral temple, they distinguished the imperial kindred according to their order of descent.[3] By ordering

---

1. 人＝前人, 'antecedent men,' but English idiom seems to require the addition of *our*.
2. 裳衣,—'lower and upper garments.
3. The emperor had seven 祖廟,—'halls or temples of ancestors, all included in the name of 宗廟. One belonged to the remote ancestor to whom the dynasty traced its origin. At the great sacrifices, his spirit-tablet was placed fronting the east, and on each side were arranged, three in a row, tablets belonging to the six others, those of them which fronted the south

——宗廟の禮は昭穆を序する所以なり。爵を序するは貴賤を辨ずる所以なり。事を序するは賢を辨ずる所以なり。旅酬に下上の爲めにするは賤(いやしき)に逮(およぶ)す所以なり。燕毛(えんもう)は齒(よはひ)を序する所以なり。

註 1.皇族の親等を順序立てる(祭日の座次によつて)。 2.爵位を區分すること。 3.職務に上役下役の等級を附けること。 4.上下合同の宴會に各自が酒杯を獻酬することは然らずんば全然事にあづからぬ下賤の者を手持無沙汰に苦ましめぬためである。旅＝衆。 5.宗廟の祭の畢りに頭髪の黒白で皇族の席次を定めて燕樂することは長幼の區別を立てるためである。燕＝宴。

五 踐其位。行其禮。奏其樂。敬其所尊。愛其所親。事死如事生。事亡如事存。孝之至也。——其の位を踐み、其の禮を行ひ、其の樂を奏し、其の尊ぶ所を敬し、其の親む所を愛し、死に事ふること生に事ふるが如くし、亡に事ふること存に事ふるが如くするは孝の至りなり。

the parties present according to their rank, they distinguished the more noble and the less. By the arrangement of the services, they made a distinction of talents and worth. In the ceremony of general pledging,[1] the inferiors presented the cup to their superiors, and thus something was given the lowest to do. At the *concluding* feast,[2] places were given according to the hair, and thus was made the distinction of years.

5. "They occupied the places of their forefathers, practised their ceremonies, and performed their music. They reverenced those whom they honoured, and loved those whom they regarded with affection. Thus they served the dead as they would have served them alive; they served the

---

being, in the genealogical line, the fathers of those who fronted the north. As fronting the sounth, the region of *brilliancy*, the former were called 昭 ; the latter, from the north, *sombre* region, were called 穆. As the dynasty was prolonged, and successive emperors died, the older tablets were removed, and transferred to what was called the 祧廟, yet so as that one in the 昭 line displaced the topmost 昭, and so with the 穆. At the sacrifices, the imperial kindred arranged themselves as they were descended from a 昭, on the left, and from a 穆, on the right, and thus a genealogical correctness of place was maintained among them.

1. The ceremony of 'general (旅＝衆) pledging' occurred towards the end of the sacrifice. To have anything to do at those services was accounted honourable, and after the emperor had commenced the ceremony by taking 'a cup of blessing,' all the juniors presented a similar cup to the seniors, and thus were called into employment.

2. The 燕 was a concluding feast confined to the imperial kindred.

六　郊社[1]之禮。所以事上帝也。宗廟之禮。所以祀乎其先也。明乎郊社之禮。禘[2]嘗[3]之義。治國其如示諸掌乎[4]。――郊社の禮は上帝に事ふる所以なり。宗廟の禮は其の先を祀る所以なり。郊社の禮、禘嘗（ていしょう）の義を明にせば、國を治むること、其れ諸を掌（たなごころ）に示（み）るが如きか。

註　1. 天子が郊外に出て天神を祭る儀式。　2. みそぎ卽ち夏の祭。3. 秋の祭。　4. 此の一節は治國平天下の秘訣は上帝祖先に敬事するに限ることを述ぶ。

第二十章

一　哀公[1]問政。――哀公政を問ふ。

註　1. 孔子の生國魯の君。

二　子曰。文武之政。布在方策[1]。其人[2]存。則其政擧。其人亡。則其政息。――子曰く、文武の政は布きて方策に在り。其の人存すれば則ち其の政擧り、其の人亡ずれば則ち其の政息む。

註　1. 記錄に載せてある。方は木の札策は竹の札。　2. 文王や武王のやうな人々。

三　人道敏政[1]。地道敏樹[2]。夫政也者。蒲盧也[3]。――人道は政に敏し、地道は樹するに敏し。夫れ政なる者は蒲盧（ほろ）なり。

註　1. その人を得た政治は駸々として進步する。　2. その地を得た植物がズンズン大きくなるやうに。　3. その人を得た政治は蒲や盧のやうにグングン進步發達する。

四　故爲政在人[1]。取人以身[2]。修身以道。修道以仁。――故に政を爲すは人に在り。人を取るには身を以てし、身を修むるには道を以てし、道を修むるには仁を以てす。

departed as they would have served them had they been continued among them.

6. "By the ceremonies of the sacrifices to Heaven and Earth[1] they served God, and by the ceremonies of the ancestral temple they sacrificed to their ancestors. He who understands the ceremonies of the sacrifices to Heaven and Earth, and the meaning of the several sacrifices to ancestors,[2] would find the government of a kingdom as easy as to look into his palm!"

CHAPTER XX. 1. The duke Gae asked about government.

2. The Master said, "The government of Wăn and Woo is displayed in *the records,*—the tablets of wood and bamboo. Let there be the men[3] and the government will flourish; but without the men, their government decays and ceases.

3. "With the *right* men the growth of government is rapid,[4] just as vegitation[5] is rapid in the earth; and moreover *their* government *might be called* an easily growing rush.

4. "Therefore the administration of government lies in *getting proper* men. Such men are

---

1. 郊 is the sacrifice to Heaven, offered, at the winter solstice, in the southern suburb (郊) of the imperial city; and 社 that offered to the Earth, at the summer solstice, in the northern.
2. The Emperors of China sacrificed, as they still do, to their ancestors every season. Reckoning from the spring, the names of the sacrifices appear to have been--礿, 禘. 嘗, and 烝.
3. Rulers like Wăn and Woo, and ministers such as they had.
4. 人道敏政 = 'man's way hastens government.'
5. 樹 = 殖.

註　1. 人を得るに在り。　2. 人を得るには國君その人の爲人を以てするより他に方法はない。

五　仁者、人也[1]。親親爲大[2]。義者、宜也[3]。尊賢爲大。親親之殺[4]。尊賢之等。禮所生也。――仁は人なり、親を親むを大と爲す。義は宜きなり、賢を尊ぶを大と爲す。親を親むの殺、賢を尊ぶの等は禮の生ずる所なり。

註　1. 仁は人の人たる特性である。　2. 親類と親しむことは仁の働の最も大なるものである。　3. 義とは行ひの宜しきにかなふことである。　4. 殺聲の時は隆の反對で漸々に低減することの意。

六　在下位。不獲乎上。民不可得而治矣[1]。――下位に在りて上に獲られずんば民得て治む可からず。

註　1. 國君の下に大臣宰相となりながら國君に信用されぬやうでは民を治めることは不可能だ。

七　故君子不可以不修身。思修身。不可以不事親。思事親。不可以不知人。思知人。不可以不知天。――故に君子は以て身を修めざる可からず。身を修めんと思はば以て親に事へざる可からず。親に事へんと思はば以て人を知らざる可からず。人を知らんと思はば以て天を知らざる可からず。

八　天下之達道[1]五。所以行之者三。曰。君臣也[2]。父子也。夫婦也。昆弟也。朋友之交也。五者、天下之達道也。知、仁、勇、三者。天下之達德也[3]。所以行之者一也[4]。――天下の達道五つ、之れを行ふ所以のもの三つ。曰く、君臣なり、父子なり、夫婦なり、昆弟なり、朋友の交なり。五つのものは天下の達道なり。

to be got by means of *the ruler's own* character. That character is to be cultivated by his treading in the ways *of duty*. And the treading those ways of duty is to be cultivated by the cherishing of benevolence.

5. "Benevolence is *the characteristic element of* humanity, and the great exercise of it is in loving relatives. Righteousness is *the accordance of actions with what is* right, and the great exercise of it is in honouring the worthy. The decreasing measures[1] of the love due to relatives, and the steps in the honour due to the worthy, are produced by *the principle of* propriety.

6. "When those in inferior situations do not possess the confidence of their superiors, they cannot retain the government of the people.

7. "Hence the sovereign may not neglect the cultivation of his own character. Wishing to cultivate his character, he may not neglect to serve his parents. In order to serve his parents, he may not neglect to acquire a knowledge of men. In order to know men, he may not dispense with a knowledge of Heaven.

8. "The duties of universal obligation are five, and the virtues wherewith they are practised are three. The duties are those between sovereign and minister, between father and son, between husband and wife, between elder brother and younger, and those belonging to the intercourse of

---

1. 殺 is opposed to 隆.

智仁勇の三者は天下の達德なり。之れを行ふ所以のもの一つなり。

註　1. 天下萬民の盡すべき義務本分。2. 君臣間の義務本分。以下同斷。3. 天下萬人の行ふべき德行。4. 是等の義務本分を實行する手段方法は單一である。

九　或生而知之[1]。或學而知之。或困而知之。及其知之、一也。或安而行之。或利而行之。或勉强而行之。及其成功。一也。——或は生れながらにして之れを知り、或は學びて之れを知り、或は困みて之れを知る。其の之れを知るに及びては一つなり。或は安んじて之れを行ひ、或は利せんとして之れを行ひ、或は勉强して之れを行ふ。其の功を成すに及びては一つなり。

註　1. 前節に述べた五つの達道卽ち義務本分。

十　子曰。好學近乎知。力行近乎仁。知恥近乎勇。——子曰く、學を好むは知に近く、力(つと)め行ふは仁に近く、恥を知るは勇に近し。

十一　知斯三者。則知所以脩身。知所以脩身。則知所以治人。知所以治人。則知所以治天下國家矣。——斯の三者を知れば、則ち身を脩むる所以を知る。身を脩むる所以を知れば、則ち人を治むる所以を知る。人を治むる所以を知れば、則ち天下國家を治むる所以を知る。

十二　凡爲天下國家有九經[1]。曰。脩身也。尊賢也。親親也。敬大臣也。體[2]群臣也。子庶民也。來百工也。柔遠人也。懷諸侯也。——凡そ天下國家を爲(を)むるに九經(けい)有り。曰く、身を脩むるなり、賢を尊ぶなり、親を親(したし)むなり、大臣を敬するなり、羣臣

friends. Those five are the duties of universal obligation. Knowledge, magnanimity, and energy, these three, are the virtues universally binding. And the means by which they carry *the duties* into practice is singleness.

9. "Some are born with the knowledge *of those duties;* some know them by study; and some acquire the knowledge after a painful feeling of their ignorance. But the knowledge being possessed, it comes to the same thing. Some practise them with a natural ease; some from a desire for their advantages; and some by strenuous effort. But the achievement being made, it comes to the same thing."

10. The Master said, "To be fond of learning is to be near to knowledge. To practise with vigour is to be near to magnanimity. To possess the feeling of shame is to be near to energy.

11. "He who knows these three things, knows how to cultivate his own character. Knowing how to cultivate his own character, he knows how to govern other men. Knowing how to govern other men, he knows how to govern the empire with all its States and families.

12. "All who have the government[1] of the empire with its States and families have nine standard rules to follow;—viz., the cultivation of their own characters; the honouring of men of virtue and

---

1. 為 = 治, 'to govern.'

を體するなり、庶民を子とするなり、百工を來たすなり、遠人を柔ぐるなり、諸侯を懷(なつ)くるなり。

註　1. 遵守すべき規則。　2. いたはること。

十三　脩身、則道立。尊賢、則不惑。親親、則諸父昆弟不怨。敬大臣、則不眩¹。體群臣、則士之報禮重。子庶民、則百姓勸。來百工、則財用足。柔遠人、則四方歸之。懷諸侯、則天下畏之。
——身を脩むれば則ち道立つ。賢を尊べば則ち惑はず。親を親めば則ち諸父昆弟怨みず。大臣を敬すれば則ち眩せず。群臣を體すれば則ち士の報禮重し。庶民を子とすれば則ち百姓勸(つと)む。百工を來たせば則ち財用足る。遠人を柔ぐれば則ち四方之れに歸す。諸侯を懷(なつ)くれば則ち天下之れを畏る。

註　1. 行政上過失を犯さぬ。

十四　齊明盛服。非禮不動。所以脩身也。去讒遠色。賤貨而貴德。所以勸賢也。尊其位。重其祿。同其好惡。所以勸親親也。官盛任使¹。所以勸大臣也。忠信重祿²。所以勸士也。時使薄

talents; affection towards their relatives; respect towards the great ministers; kind and considerate treatment[1] of the whole body of officers; dealing with the mass of the people as children; encouraging the resort of all classes of artizans; indulgent treatment of men from a distance; and the kindly cherishing of the princes of the States.

13. "By the ruler's cultivation of his own character, the duties *of universal obligation* are set forth. By honouring men of virtue and talents, he is preserved from errors of judgment. By showing affection to his relatives, there is no grumbling nor resentment among his uncles and brethren. By respecting the great ministers, he is kept from errors in the practice of government. By kind and considerate treatment of the whole body of officers, they are led to make the most grateful return for his courtesies. By dealing with the mass of the people as his children, they are led to exhort one another to what is good. By encouraging the resort of all classes of artizans, his resources for expenditure are rendered ample. By indulgent treatment of men from a distance, they are brought to resort to him from all quarters. And by kindly cherishing the princes of the States, the whole empire is brought to revere him.

14. "Self-adjustment and purification, with careful regulation of his dress, and the not making a movement contrary to the rules of pro-

---

1. 體＝與之同體, 'being of the same body with them.'

斂³。所以勸百姓也。日省月試⁴。既廩稱事。所以勸百工也。送往迎來。嘉善而矜不能。所以柔遠人⁵也。繼絕世、舉廢國。治亂持危⁶。朝聘以時⁷。厚往而薄來、所以懷諸侯也。——齊明盛服し、禮に非れば動かざるは、身を脩むる所以なり。讒を去り、色を遠ざけ、貨を賤みて德を貴ぶは賢を勸むる所以なり。其の位を尊くし、其の祿を重くし、其の好惡を同じくするは、親を親しむを勸むる所以なり。官を盛んにして任使せしむるは、大臣を勸むる所以なり。忠信祿を重くするは、士を勸むる所以なり。時に使ひて薄く斂するは、百姓を勸むる所以なり。日に省み月に試み、既廩事に稱ふは、百工を勸むる所以なり。往を送り來を迎へ、善を嘉し不能を矜むは遠人を柔ぐる所以なり。絕世を繼ぎ廢國を擧げ亂を治め危きを持し、朝聘は時を以てし、往に厚くし來に薄くするは、諸侯を懷くる所以なり。

註　1. 多勢の下役人を使はせること。2. 充分信任し俸祿を重くすること。3. 使う可き時にのみ使ひ税金を輕くすること。4. 毎日試驗して給與を勞力に相當させること。5. 遠國から來た人。6. 危い國を授けること。7. 時を定めて諸侯の大夫を朝廷に來獻さすること。

priety :—this is the way for the ruler to cultivate his person. Discarding slanderers, and keeping himself from *the seductions of* beauty; making light of riches, and giving honour to virtue :—this is the way for him to encourage men of worth and talents. Giving them places *of honour* and large emolument, and sharing with them in their likes and dislikes:—this is the way for him to encourage his relatives to love him. Giving them numerous officers to discharge their orders and commissions :—this is the way for him to encourage the great ministers. According to them a generous confidence, and making their emoluments large:—this is the way to encourage the body of officers. Employing them only at the proper times, and making the imposts light :—this is the way to encourage the people. By daily examinations and monthly trials, and by making their rations in accordance with their labours':—this is the way to encourage the classes of artizans. To escort them on their departure and meet them on their coming; to commend the good among them, and show compassion to the imcompetent :—this is the way to treat indulgently men from a distance. To restore families whose line of succession has been broken, and to revive States that have been extinguished; to reduce to order States that are in confusion, and support those which are in

---

1. 餼 is to be substituted here for 既. 稱, 'to weigh,' 'to be according to.'

十五 凡爲天下國家有九經。所以行之者[1]一也。——凡そ天下國家を爲むるに九經有り。之を行ふ所以は一なり。

註　1. 此の九經を實行する方法。

十六 凡事豫則立。不豫則廢[1]。言前定。則不跆。事前定。則不困。行前定。則不疚。道前定。則不窮。——凡そ事は豫(あらかじめ)すれば則ち立ち、豫せざれば則ち廢る。言は前に定まれば則ち跆(つまづ)かず。事は前に定まれば則ち困(くるし)まず。行は前に定まれば則ち疚(やま)しからず。道は前に定まれば則ち窮せず。

註　1. 事の成否は準備の如何に由つて決まる意。

十七 在下位。不獲乎上[1]。民不可得而治矣。獲乎上有道。不信乎朋友。不獲乎上矣。信乎朋友有道。不順乎親。不信乎朋友矣。順乎親有道。反諸身不誠。不順乎親矣。誠身有道。不明乎善。不誠乎身矣。——下位に在りて上に獲られざれば民得て治む可からず。上に獲らるゝに道有り。朋友に信ぜられざれば上に獲られず。朋友に信ぜらるゝに道有り。親に順ならざれば朋友に信ぜられず。親に順なるに道有り。諸(これ)を身に反して誠あらざれば親に順ならず。身を誠にするに道有り。善に明ならざれば身に誠あらず。

peril; to have fixed times for their own reception at court, and the reception of their envoys; to send them away after liberal treatment, and welcome their coming with small contributions:—this is the way to cherish the princes of the States.

15. "All who have the government of the empire with its States and families have the above nine standard rules. And the means by which they are carried into practice is singleness.

16. "In all things[1] success depends on previous preparation, and without such previous preparation there is sure to be failure. If what is to be spoken be previously determined, there will be no stumbling. If affairs be previously determined, there will be no difficulty with them. If one's actions have been previously determined, there will be no sorrow in connection with them. If principles of conduct have been previously determined, the practice of them will be inexhaustible.

17. "When those in inferior situations do not obtain the confidence of the sovereign, they cannot succeed in governing the people. There is a way to obtain the confidence of the sovereign;—if one is not trusted by his friends, he will not get the confidence of his sovereign. There is a way to being trusted by one's friends;—if one is not obedient to his parents, he will not be true to friends. There is a way to being obedient to one's

---

1. The 'all things' is to be understood with reference to the universal duties, universal virtues, and the nine standard rules.

註　大臣になつて國君に信用されねば。

十八　誠者天之道也。誠之者[1]、人之道也。誠者[2]、不勉而中[3]。不思而得[4]。從容中道。聖人也。誠之者、擇善而固執之者也。——誠は天の道なり。之れを誠にするは人の道なり。誠なる者は勉めずして中り、思はずして得。從容として道に中るは聖人なり。之れを誠にする者は善を擇んで固く之れを執る者なり。

註　1. 誠を得るのはの意。　2. 誠を體得してゐる者。　3. 勉めずして行ひ正中を得る意。　4. 考えずに解る意。

十九　博學之[1]。審問之。愼思之。明辨之。篤行之。——博く之れを學び、審に之れを問ひ、愼んで之れを思ひ、明に之れを辨じ、篤く之れを行ふ。

註　1. 誠を得るために必要な事は博く之(養)を學ぶことである……。

parents;—if one, on turning his thoughts in upon himself, finds a want of sincerity, he will not be obedient to his parents. There is a way to the attainment of sincerity in one's-self;—if a man do not understand what is good, he will not attain sincerity in himself.[1]

18. "Sincerity is the way of Heaven. The attainment of sincerity is the way of men. He who possesses sincerity, is he who, without an effort, hits what is right, and apprehends, without the exercise of thought;—he is the sage who naturally and easily embodies the *right* way. He who attains to sincerity, is he who chooses what is good, and firmly holds it fast.

19. "To this attainment there are requisite the extensive study of what is good, accurate inquiry about it, careful reflection on it, the clear discrimination of it, and the earnest practice of it.[2]

---

1. The object of this par. seems to be to show that the singleness, or sincerity, lies at the basis of that previous preparation, which is essential to success in any and every thing. The steps of the climax conduct us to it as the mental state, neccessary to all virtues, and this sincerity is again made dependent on the understanding of what is good, upon which point see the next chapter. 不獲乎上 = 不得於君上之意, 'do not get the mind—pleased feeling—of the sovereign.' We use 'to gain,' and 'to win,' sometimes in a similar way.

2. There are here described the different processes which lead to the attainment of sincerity. 備旨 says that 'the five 之 all refer to the *what is good* in the last chapter, the five universal duties, and the nine standard rules being included therein.' Rather it seems to me, that the 之, according to the idiom pointed out several times in the Confucian Analects, simply intensifies the meaning of the different verbs, whose regimen it is.

二十 有弗學。學之弗能。弗措也[1]。有弗問。問之弗知。弗措也。有弗思。思之弗得。弗措也。有弗辨。辨之弗明。弗措也。有弗行。行之弗篤。弗措也。人一能之。己百之。人十能之。己千之。――學ばず、之れを學んで能くせざる有れば措かざるなり。問はず、之れを問ひて知らざる有れば措かざるなり。思はず、之れを思ひて得ざる有れば措かざるなり。辨ぜず、之れを辨じて明ならざる有れば措かざるなり。行はず、之れを行ひて篤からざる有れば措かざるなり。人一たびにして之れを能くせば、己は之れを百たびにす。人十たびにして之れを能くせば、己は之れを千たびにす。

註 1. 聖人は未だ學ばざるものがあれば、或は學んで未だ理解せざるものがあれば、中途で之を學ぶことを止めることはない。以下類推を要す。

二十一 果能此道矣[1]。雖愚必明。雖柔必強。――果して此の道を能くすれば愚と雖も必ず明に、柔と雖も必ず強し。

註 1. 若し人にして斯の方法に由り進まばの意。

第二十一章 自誠明。謂之性[1]。自明誠。謂之教[2]。誠則明矣。明則誠矣。[3]――誠なるより明なる、之れを性と謂ひ、明なるより誠なる、之れを教と謂ふ。誠なれば則ち明に、明なれば則ち誠なり。

註 1. 誠實の結果明敏ならばそは性の然らしむる所であるといふべきである。 2. 明敏の結果誠實ならばそは教の然らしむる所とすべきだ。 2. しかし誠であれば明になる、また明であれば誠になる。

右第二十一章。子思承上章夫子天道人道之意。而立言也。自此

20. "The superior man, while there is any thing he has not studied, or while in what he has studied there is any thing he can not understand, will not intermit his labour. While there is any thing he has not inquired about, or any thing in what he has inquired about which he does not know, he will not intermit his labour. While there is any thing which he has not reflected on, or any thing in what he has reflected on which he does not apprehend, he will not intermit his labour. While there is any thing which he has not discriminated, or his discrimination is not clear, he will not intermit his labour. If there be any thing which he has not practised, or his practice fails in earnestness, he will not intermit his labour. If another man succeed by one effort, he will use a hundred efforts. If another man succeed by ten efforts, he will use a thousand.

21. "Let a man proceed in this way, and, though dull, he will surely become intelligent; though weak, he will surely become strong."

CHAPTER XXI. When we have intelligence resulting from sincerity, this condition is to be ascribed to nature; when we have sincerity resulting from intelligence, this condition is to be ascribed to instruction. But given the sincerity, and there shall be the intelligence; given the intelligence, and there shall be the sincerity.

The above is the twenty-first chapter. Tsze-sze

以下十二章。皆子思之言。以反覆推明此章之意。——右第二十一章、子思上章夫子天道人道の意を承けて言を立つるなり。此れより以下十二章は皆子思の言にして、以て此の章の意を反覆推明せり。

第二十二章 唯天下至誠。爲能盡其性[1]。能盡其性。則能盡人之性[2]。能盡人之性。則能盡物之性[3]。能盡物之性。則可以贊天地之化育[4]。可以贊天地之化育。則可以與天地參矣。――唯天下の至誠は、能く其の性を盡くすを爲す。能く其の性を盡くせば、則ち能く人の性を盡くす。能く人の性を盡くせば、則ち能く物の性を盡くす。能く物の性を盡くせば、則ち以て天地の化育を贊す可し。以て天地の化育を贊す可ければ、則ち以て天地と參たる可し。

註 1. 自分の性質を充分に發達せしめ得る者は獨り至誠の人あるのみである。 2. 自分の性質を充分に發達させ得る者は他人の性質をも充分に發達させることが出來る。 3. 動物其他のものゝ性質をも充分發達させることが出來る。 4. 天地の化育をも助けることが出來る。 5. さう出來る人は天地と共に三位一體となることが出來る。

第二十三章 其次致曲[1]。曲能有誠[2]。誠則形。形則著。著則明。明則動。動則變[3]。變則化。唯天下至誠爲能化[4]。――其の次は曲を致す。曲なれば能く誠有り。誠あれば則ち形る。形るれば則ち著し。著しければ則ち明なり。明なれば則ち動かす。動かせば則ち變ぜらる。變ぜらるれば則ち化せらる。唯天下の至誠は、能く化することを爲す。

註 1. 生れながら誠有る人の次に位する者は心中の善の傾向を極力

takes up in it, and discourses from, the subjects of "the way of Heaven" and "the way of men," mentioned in the preceding chapter. The twelve chapters that follow are all from Tsze-sze, repeating and illustrating the meaning of this one.

CHAPTER XXII. It is only he who is possessed of the most complete sincerity that can exist under heaven, who can give its full development to his nature. Able to give its full development to his own nature, he can do the same to the nature of other men. Able to give its full development to the nature of other men, he can give their full development to the natures of animals and things. Able to give their full development to the natures of creatures and things, he can assist the transforming and nourishing powers of Heaven and Earth. Able to assist the transforming and nourishing powers of Heaven and Earth, he may with Heaven and Earth form a ternion.[1]

CHAPTER XXIII. Next to the above is he who cultivates to the utmost the shoots *of goodness* in him. From those he can attain to the possession of sincerity. This sincerity becomes apparent. From being apparent, it becomes manifest. From

---

1. 參 is 'a file of three,' and I employ, 'ternion,' to express the idea, just as we use 'quaternion,' for a file of four. What is it but blasphemy, thus to file man with the supreme power?

發達せしむる人である。　2. 善の傾向を發達せしむれば誠の持主となれる。　3. 他人の心を動かすことさへ出來ればまたそれは變ぜしめられる。　4. 初から能動的に他人を化する者は至誠の人のみである。

第二十四章　至誠之道。可以前知[1]。國家將興。必有禎祥[2]。國家將亡。必有妖孽[3]。見乎蓍龜[4]。動乎四體[5]。禍福將至。善[6]、必先知之。不善、必先知之。故至誠[7]如神。——至誠の道は以て前知す可し。國家將に興らんとすれば必ず禎祥有り。國家將に亡びんとすれば必ず妖孽あり、蓍龜に見はれ、四體に動く。禍福將に至らんとすれば、善も必ず先づ之れを知る、不善も必ず先づ之れを知る。故に至誠は神の如し。

　註　1. 至誠の力には將來を前知することが出來る。　2. ＝吉兆。3. ＝凶兆。　4. 「めとぎ」と龜の甲、孰も昔の占に用ひたもの。　5. 至誠の人の四體。　6. ＝扇。　7. 至誠は至誠の人、至誠之道は抽象的の至誠。

第二十五章　一　誠者、自成也[1]。而道、自道也[2]。——誠は自ら成すなり。而して道は自ら道なり。

　註　1. 誠は自己完成の由つて來る根源である。　2. 誠の道は人間が自己を導くに必要缺くべからざる道である。

　二　誠者。物之終始。不誠無物。是故君子誠之[1]爲貴。——誠は物の終始なり、誠ならざれば物無し。是の故に君子は之を誠にするを貴しとなす。

　註　1. 誠を得ること。

being manifest, it becomes brilliant. Brilliant, it affects others. Affecting others, they are changed by it. Changed by it, they are transformed. It is only he who is possessed of the most complete sincerity that can exist under heaven, who can transform.

CHAPTER XXIV. It is characteristic of the most entire sincerity[1] to be able to foreknow. When a nation or family is about to flourish, there are sure to be happy omens; and when it is about to perish, there are sure to be unlucky omens. *Such events are* seen[2] in milfoil[3] and tortoise,[3] and affect[2] the movements of the four limbs.[4] When calamity or happiness is about to come, the good shall certainly be foreknown by him, and the evil also. Therefore the individual possessed of the most complete sincerity is like a spirit.

CHAPTER XXV. 1. Sincerity is that whereby self completion is effected, and *its* way is that by which man must direct himself.

2. Sincerity is the end and beginning of things; without sincerity there would be nothing. On this

---

1. 至誠之道 is the quality in the abstract, while 至誠 at the end, is the entirely sincere individual,—the sage, by nature, or by attainment.

2. The subject of the verbs 見 and 動 is the events, not the omens.

3. Divination by the milfoil was called 筮; that by the tortoise was called 卜.

4. 四體 are interpreted of the feet of the tortoise or of the four limbs of the human body.

三　誠者。非自成已而已也。所以成物¹也。成已。仁也²。成物。知也³。性之德也⁴。合外內之道也。故時措之宜也⁵。──誠は自ら已を成すのみに非ざるなり、物を成す所以なり。已を成すは仁なり、物を成すは知なり。性の德なり、外內を合するの道なり。故に時に之れを措きて宜しきなり。

註　1.誠を以て他の人他の物をも完成する。 2.誠の所有者が已を完全にするのは彼の德の完全なるを示すものである。 3.他人他物を完全にするのは彼の知を示すものである。 4.斯の兩者は誠てふ性質の固有する德である、また外と內とを合一せしむるものである。 5.故に誠の所有者が斯の兩者を用ひる時はいつも兩者の作用はその宜しきを得るのである。故の措は用と同義。

第二十六章　一　故至誠無息¹。──故に至誠よ息む無し。

註　1.至誠には不休不息の性質がある。

二　不息則久¹。久則徵²。──息まざれば則ち久し。久しければ則ち徵あり。

註　1.息まぬから誠は永續する。 2.それ自體を現はす。

三　徵則悠遠¹。悠遠則博厚²。博厚則高明³。──徵あれば則ち悠遠なり。悠遠なれば則ち博厚なり。博厚なれば則ち高明なり。

註　1.それ自體を現はすから誠は遠きに達する。 2.大きく且頑丈。 3.輝かしい。

四　博厚。所以載物也。高明。所以覆物也。悠久。所以成物也。──博厚は物を載する所以なり。高明は物を覆ふ所以なり。悠久は物を成す所以なり。

五　博厚配地。高明配天。悠久無疆¹。──博厚は地に配し、高明は天に配し、悠久は疆無し。

註　1.悠久は總ての物を完全にする所以である。

六　如此者。不見而章¹。不動而變。無爲而成。──此の如け

account, the superior man regards the attainment of sincerity as the most excellent thing.

3. The possessor of sincerity does not merely accomplish the self completion of himself. With this quality he completes *other men and* things *also*. The completing himself *shows his* perfect virtue. The completing *other men and* things *shows his* knowledge. *Both these are* virtues belonging to the nature, and *this is* the way by which a union is effected of the external and internal. Therefore, wherever he—*the entirely sincere man*—employs them,—*that is, these virtues,—their action will be* right.

CHAPTER XXVI. 1. Hence to entire sincerity there belongs ceaselessness.

2. Not ceasing, it continues long. Continuing long, it evidences itself.

3. Evidencing itself, it reaches far. Reaching far, it becomes large and substantial. Large and substantial, it becomes high and brilliant.

4. Large and substantial;—this is how it contains *all* things. High and brilliant;—this is how it overspreads *all* things. Reaching far and continuing long;—this is how it perfects *all* things.

5. So large and substantial, *the individual possessing it* is the coequal of Earth. So high and brilliant, it makes him the coequal of Heaven. So far-reaching and long-continuing, it makes him infinite.

6. Such being its nature, without any display,

れば見さずして章はれ、動かずして變じ、爲すこと無くして成る。

註　1. 斯様な譯であるから誠は示さずして顯はれる。

七　天地之道。可一言而盡也¹。其爲物不貳、則其生物不測²。——天地の道は一言にして盡す可きなり。其の物たる貳ならず則ち其の物を生ずる測られず。

註　1. 一言にして説き盡すことが出來る。　2. 天地は一元であるから測り知る可からざる方法を以て萬物を造る。

八　天地之道¹。博也。厚也。高也。明也。悠也。久也。——天地の道は博なり、厚なり、高なり、明なり、悠なり、久なり。

註　1. 天地の物を造る方法。

九　今夫¹天。斯昭昭²之多³。及其無窮也。日月星辰繋焉。萬物覆焉。今夫地。一撮土⁴之多。及其廣厚。載華嶽而不重。振河海而不洩。萬物載焉。今夫山。一卷石⁵之多。及其廣大。草木生之、禽獸居之。寶藏興焉。今夫水。一勺之多。及其不測。黿鼉蛟龍魚鼈生焉、貨財殖焉。——今夫れ天は斯の昭昭の多きなり。其の窮りなきに及んでや、日月星辰繋り、萬物覆はる。今夫れ地は一撮土の多きなり。其の廣厚なるに及んでや、華嶽を載せて而して重しとせず、河海を振めて洩らさず、萬物載せらる。今夫れ山は一卷石の多きなり。其の廣大なるに及んでや、草木これに生じ、禽獸これに居り、寶藏興る。今夫れ水は一勺の多きなり。其の測られざるに及んでや、黿鼉蛟龍魚鼈生じ、貨財殖す。

註　1. 今我々の眼前に見える。　2. 斯のきらきら光るもの。　3. ＝少許耳。　4. 一撮の土。　5. 一塊の石。

it becomes manifested; without any movement, it produces changes; and without any effort, it accomplishes its ends.

7. The way of Heaven and Earth may be completely declared in one sentence.—They are without any doubleness, and so they produce things in a manner that is unfathomable.

8. The way of Heaven and Earth is large and substantial, high and brilliant, far-reaching and long-enduring.

9. The heaven now before us is only this bright shining spot; but when viewed in its inexhaustible extent, the sun, moon, stars, and constellations of the zodiac, are suspended in it, and all things are overspread by it. The earth before us is but a handful of soil; but when regarded in its breadth and thickness, it sustains mountains like the Hwa and the Yoh, without feeling their weight, and contains the rivers and seas, without their leaking away. The mountain now before us appears only a stone; but when contemplated in all the vastness of its size, we see how the grass and trees are produced on it, and birds and beasts dwell on it, and precious things which men treasure up are found on it. The water now before us appears but a ladleful; yet extending our view to its unfathomable depths, the largest tortoises, iguanas, iguanadons, dragons, fishes, and turtles, are produced in them, articles of value and sources of wealth abound in them.

十　詩云。維天之命。於穆不已[1]。蓋曰。天之所以爲天也。於乎不顯。文王之德之純[2]。蓋曰。文王之所以爲文也。純亦不已[3]。——詩に云ふ、維れ天の命、於穆として已まずと。蓋し天の天たる所以を曰ふ。於乎顯ならざらんや、文王の德の純と。蓋し文王の文たる所以を曰ふ。純も亦已まざるなり。

　　註　1. あゝ天の命は深遠且つ不息なりの意。2. 文王の德の純なることは實に顯著であるの意。3. 純も誠同樣不息である。

第二十七章　一　大哉。聖人之道。——大なる哉、聖人の道。

二　洋洋乎、發育萬物、峻極于天[1]。——洋洋乎として萬物を發育し、峻として天を極む。

　　註　1. 聖人の道は九天の高きに達す。

三　優優大哉、禮儀三百、威儀三千。——優優として大なる哉、禮儀三百、威儀三千。

　　註　1. 聖人の道は至大至優禮法三百威法三千これを然らしむる乎。

四　待其人而後行[1]。——其の人を待つて而る後に行はる。

　　註　1. 聖人の道はその人を待つて始めて行はる。

五　故曰、苟不至德、至道不凝焉[1]。——故に曰く、苟も至德ならざれば、至道凝らずと。

　　註　1. 至道は至德に由つて初めて行はる。

六　故君子、尊德性[1]、而道問學[2]、致廣大、而盡精微、極高明、而道中庸、溫故、而知新、敦厚以崇禮。——故に君子は德性を尊んで問學に道る。廣大を致めて精微を盡くす。高明を極めて中庸に道る。故を溫ねて新を知り、敦厚にして禮を崇ぶ。

　　註　1. 自己の德性。2. 絕へず學問研究を續ける。

10. It is said in the Book of Poetry, "The ordinances of Heaven, how profound are they and unceasing!" The meaning is, that it is thus that Heaven is Heaven. *And again,* "How illustrious was it, the singleness of the virtue of king Wăn!" indicating that it was thus that king Wăn was what he was. Singleness likewise is unceasing.

CHAPTER XXVII. 1. How great is the path proper to the sage!

2. Like overflowing water, it sends forth and nourishes all things, and rises up to the height of heaven.

3. All complete is its greatness! It embraces the three hundred rules of ceremony, and the three thousand rules of demeanour.

4. It waits for the proper man, and then it is trodden.

5. Hence it is said, "Only by perfect virtue can the perfect path, in all its courses, be made a fact."

6. Therefore, the superior man honours his virtuous nature, and maintains[1] constant inquiry and study, seeking to carry it out to its breadth and greatness, so as to omit none of the more exquisite and minute points which it embraces, and to raise it to its greatest height and brilliancy, so as to pursue the course of the Mean. He chrishes his old knowledge, and is continually acquiring

---

1. 道 in both cases here, = 由, 'to proceed from', or 'by.'

七　是故居上不驕、爲下不倍、國有道、其言足以興[1]、國無道、其默足以容[2]、詩[3]曰、既明且哲、以保其身、其此之謂與。――是の故に上に居つて驕らず、下と爲りて倍かず、國道有れば、其の言は以て興るに足り、國道無ければ、其の默は以て容るゝに足る。詩に曰ふ、既に明且つ哲、以て其の身を保つと。其れ此れをこれ謂ふ與。

　註　1. 自分の首のために立身する。　2. 默々として我慢することが出來る。　3. 詩經大雅篇。

第二十八章　一　子曰、愚而好自用[1]、賤而好自專[2]、生乎今之世[3]、反古之道、如此者、裁及其身者也。――子曰く、愚にして自ら用ふるを好み、賤にして自ら專にするを好み、今の世に生れて、古の道に反へる。此の如き者は裁其の身に及ぶ者なり。

　註　1. 愚物の癖に自分の判斷を用ひることを好めば禍其の身に及ばん。　2. 賤しい身分の癖に自分のみ人に命令を下すことを好めば……。　3. 今の世に生れて古の道に反へれば……。

二　非天子、不議禮[1]、不制度、不考[2]文。――天子に非されば禮を議せず、度を制せず、文を考へず。

　註　1. 天子以外の者には禮を論ずる權利はない。　2. 吟味する。

三　今天下、車同軌、書同文、行同倫。――今天下車軌を同じうし、書文を同じうし、行倫を同じうす。

四　雖有其[1]位、苟無其德、不敢作禮樂[2]焉。雖有其德、苟無其位、亦不敢作禮樂焉。――其の位有りと雖も、苟も其の德無ければ、敢て禮樂を作らず。其の德有りと雖も、苟も其の位無ければ、亦敢て禮樂を作らず。

　註　1. 天子の。　2. 禮樂を作つてはならぬ。（第二節の度を制し文を考へることは略されてゐる。）

new. He exerts an honest, generous, earnestness, in the esteem and practice of all propriety.

7. Thus, when occupying a high situation, he is not proud, and in low situation, he is not insubordinate. When the kingdom is well-governed, he is sure by his words to rise; and when it is ill-governed, he is sure by his silence to command forbearance to himself. Is not this what we find in the Book of Poetry,—"Intelligent is he and prudent, and so preserves his person?"

CHAPTER XXVIII. 1. The Master said, "Let a man who is ignorant[1] be fond of using his own judgment; let a man without rank be fond of assuming a directing power to himself; let a man who is living in the present age go back to ways of antiquity;—on the persons of all who acts thus calamities will be sure to come."

2. To no one but the emperor does it belong to order ceremonies, to fix the measures, and to determine the characters.

3. Now,[2] over the empire, carriages have all wheels of the same size; all writing is with the same characters; and for conduct there are the same rules.

4. One may occupy the throne, but if he have not the proper virtue, he may not dare to make ceremonies or music. One may have the virtue,

---

1. 愚 is he who wants the virtue.
2. 今, 'now,' is said with reference to the time of Tsze-sze.

五　子曰、吾說夏禮、杞¹不足徵也、吾學殷禮、有宋存焉²、吾學周禮、今用之、吾從周。――子曰く、吾れ夏の禮を說くも、杞は徵するに足らず。吾れ殷の禮を學ぶ、宋の存するあり。吾れ周の禮を學ぶ、今之れを用ふ。吾れは周に從はん。

註　1. 夏王の天神を祀つた犧牲が杞の國に殘つてゐるが自分の說を證明することは出來ぬ（論語第三篇第九章參看）。　2. 宋にその禮式は存續してゐる。

第二十九章　一　王天下有三重¹焉、其寡過²矣乎。――天下に王とし三重を有せば、其れ過寡き乎。

註　1. 議禮、制度、考文をいふ。　2. 君主としての過。

二　上焉者¹、雖善、無徵。無徵、不信。不信、民弗從。下焉者²、雖善、不尊。不尊、不信。不信、民弗從。――上なる者は善と雖も徵なし、徵無ければ信ぜられず、信ぜられざれば民從はず。下なる者は善と雖も尊からず、尊からざれば信ぜられず、信ぜられざれば民從はず。

註　1. 古代の帝王の法令。　2. 近代の帝王のそれ。

三　故君子之道¹、本諸身²、徵諸庶民³、考諸三王而不繆⁴、建諸天地而不悖⁵、質諸鬼神而無疑⁶、百世以俟聖人而不惑⁷。――故に君子の道は、諸を身に本づけ、諸を庶民に徵し、諸を三王に考へて繆らず、諸を天地に建てゝ悖らず、諸を鬼神に質して疑無し、百世以て聖人を俟つて惑はず。

註　1. 眞乎の君主の法令。　2. 自分の爲人行動に本づいて定める。　3. 人民がその法令に誤りのないことを充分に證明する。　4. 堯舜禹の法令に比べても誤つてゐない。　5. 天地の建て前に照して悖つてゐな

but if he do not occupy the throne, he may not presume to make ceremonies or music.

5. The Master said, "I may describe the ceremonies of the Hea dynasty, but Ke cannot sufficiently attest my words. I have learned the ceremonies of the Yin dynasty, and in Sung they still continue. I have learned the ceremonies of Chow, which are now used, and I follow Chow."

CHAPTER XXIX. 1. He who attains to the sovereignty of the empire, having *those* three important things, shall be able to effect that there shall be few errors *under his government.*

2. However excellent may have been the regurations of those of former times, they cannot be attested. Not being attested, they cannot command credence, and not being credited, the people would not follow them. However excellent might be the regulations made by one in an inferior situation, he is not in a position to be honoured. Unhonoured, he cannot command credence, and not being credited, the people would not follow his rules.

3. Therefore the institutions of the Ruler are rooted in his own character and conduct, and sufficient attention of them is given by the masses of the people. He examines them *by comparison* with those of the three kings, and finds them without mistake. He sets them up before heaven and earth, and finds nothing in them contrary to their mode of operation. He presents himself

い。6. 祖先の靈に犠牲を供へ饗しても何等之れを冒瀆するかも知れぬとの疑念が起らぬ。7. 百年の後聖人が起らうとも何んともない、所謂聖人復た起るも吾が言を易へずと同義。

四　質鬼神而無疑、知天也、百世以俟聖人而不惑、知人也。――鬼神に質して疑無きは天を知ればなり。百世以て聖人を俟つて惑はざるは人を知ればなり。

五　是故君子、動而世爲天下道、行而世爲天下法、言而世爲天下則。遠之、則有望[1]。近之、則有厭[2]。――是の故に君子は動いて世々天下の道となり、行ひて世々天下の法となり、言ひて世々天下の則となる。之れを遠さくれば則ち望む有り。之れを近づくれば則ち厭はず。

註　1. 君子と東西萬里其の處を異してゐる者は遠方から彼を望見して逢ひたがる。　2. 君子の側近者は毎日彼と鼻を突き合はしてゐても厭きぬ。

六　詩曰、在彼無惡、在此無射、庶幾夙夜、以永終譽[1]。君子未有不如此、而蚤有譽於天下者也。――詩に曰く、彼に在りても惡まるゝなく、此れに在りても射るゝなし。庶幾くば夙夜以て永く譽を終へんと。君子未だ此の如くならずして蚤く天下に譽ありし者はあらざるなり。

註　1. 彼處にゐたときも惡まれたことがなく、此處にゐても厭はれぬから彼等は斯く日夜譽められることを永久に續けるだらう。此の詩は詩經周頌篇の中で周の諸侯を譽めたもの故茲のやうに眞の君子を嘆美するために引用したのは僭越である。彼は周の諸侯の昔の封土。此は周の天下。

第三十章　一　仲尼、祖述堯舜[1]、憲章文武[2]、上[3]律天時、下[4]襲水土[5]。――仲尼堯舜を祖述し、文武を憲章し、上天の時に律り、下水土に襲る。

註　1. 堯舜の政道を恰も堯舜が孔子の祖先でゝもあるかのやうに後世のために述べ傳へた。　2. 文王武王の法令を自分の法典のやうに立

with them before spiritual beings, and no doubts about them arise. He is prepared to wait for the rise of a sage, hundred ages after, and has no misgivings.

4. His presenting himself *with his institutions* before spiritual beings, without any doubts about them arising, shows that he knows Heaven. His being prepared, without any misgivings, to wait for the rise of a sage a hundred ages after, shows that he knows men.

5. Such being the case, the movements of such a ruler, *illustrating his institutions*, constitute an example to the empire for ages. His acts are for ages a law to the empire. His words are for ages a lesson to the empire. Those who are far from him, look longingly for him; and those who are near him, are never wearied with him.

6. It is said in the Book of Poetry,—" Not disliked there, not tired of here,[1] from day to day and night to night, will they perpetuate their praise." Never has there been a ruler, who did not realize this description, that obtained an early renown throughout the empire.

CHAPTER XXX. 1. Chung-ne handed down the doctrines of Yaou and Shun, as if they had been his ancestors, and elegantly displayed the regulations of Wăn and Woo, taking them as his model. Above, he harmonized with the times of

---

1. 在彼, 'there,' means their own States; and 在此, 'here,' is the imperial court of Chow.

派に譽め立てゝ書いた。 3. 仰いでは。 4. 俯しては。 5. 水土＝地。

二　辟如天地之無不持載、無不覆幬¹。辟如四時之錯行²、如日月之代明。――辟へば天地の持載せざる無く覆幬せざる無きが如く、四時の錯行するが如く、日月の代明するが如し。

註　1. 孔子は萬物を戰覆する天地にも譬へることが出來る。 2. 孔子は新陳代謝する春夏秋冬にも譬へることが出來る。

三　萬物並育、而不相害。道並行、而不相悖¹。小德²川流、大德³敦化。此天地之所以爲大也。――萬物並び育せられて相害せず。道並び行はれて相悖らず。小德は川流し大德は敦く化す。此れ天地の大たる所以なり。

註　1. 四時の循環日月の運行は年中並進して衝突を來たさない。 2. 天地の小なる力。 3. 天地の大なる力。

第三十一章　一　唯天下至聖、爲能聰明睿知足以有臨也¹、寬裕溫柔、足以有容也²、發强剛毅足以有執也³、齊莊中正足以有敬也⁴、文理密察足以有別也⁵。――唯天下の至聖は能く聰明睿知以て臨む有るに足り、寬裕溫柔以て容るゝ有るに足り、發强剛毅以て執る有るに足り、齊莊中正以て敬する有るに足り。文理密察以て別つ有るに足ると爲す。

註　1. 天下を支配することが出來る。 2. 出來ぬ堪忍をすることが出來る。 3. 主義主張を固く守ることが出來る。 4. 愛敬を博するに足る。 5. 取捨辨別することが出來る。

二　溥博淵泉、而時出之¹。――溥博淵泉にして時に之れを出だす。

註　1. 至聖の人は泉のやうに周ねく闊く深い德を有つてゐるから隨時にこれを人に施す。

heaven, and below, he was conformed to the water and land.

2. He may be compared to heaven and earth, in their supporting and containing, their overshadowing and curtaining, all things. He may be compared to the four seasons in their alternating progress, and to the sun and moon in their successive shining.

3. All things are nourished together without their injuring one another. The courses *of the seasons, and of the sun and moon*, are pursued without any collision among them. The smaller energies are like river currents; the greater energies are seen in mighty transformations. It is this which makes heaven and earth so great.

CHAPTER XXXI. 1. It is only he, possesed of all sagely qualities that can exist under heaven, who shows himself quick in apprehension, clear in discernment, of far-reaching intelligence, and, all-embracing knowledge, fitted to exercise rule; magnanimous, generous, benign, and mild, fitted to exercise forbearance; impulsive, energetic, firm, and enduring, fitted to maintain a firm hold; self-adjusted, grave, never swerving from the Mean, and correct, fitted to command reverence; accomplished, distinctive, concentrative, and searching, fitted to exercise discrimination.

2. All-embracing is he and vast, deep and active as a fountain, sending forth in their due seasons his virtues.

三　溥博如天[1]、淵泉如淵。見而民莫不敬。言而民莫不信。行而民莫不説。──溥博は天の如く、淵泉は淵の如く、見て民敬せざる莫く、言うて民信ぜざる莫く、行うて民説（よろこ）ばざる莫し。

註　1. 至聖の人の德は周ねきこと天の如しである。

四　是以聲名洋溢乎中國。施及蠻貊[1]。舟車所至。人力所通。天之所覆。地之所載。日月所照。霜露所隊。凡有血氣者。莫不尊親。故曰配天[2]。──是を以て聲名中國に洋溢し施て蠻貊（ばんぱく）に及ぶ。舟車の至る所、人力の通ずる所、天の覆ふ所、地の載する所、日月の照す所、霜露の隊（お）つる所、凡そ血氣有る者は尊親せざる莫し。故に天に配すと曰ふ。

註　1. 未開野蠻の地方。　2. 至聖の人は天に等しい。

第三十二章　一　唯天下至誠。爲能經綸天下之大經。立天下之大本。知天地之化育。夫焉有所倚[1]。──唯天下の至誠は能く天下の大經を經綸し、天下の大本を立て、天地の化育を知ると爲す。夫れ焉んぞ倚（よ）る所あらん。

註　1. 至誠者が斯くあるはその至誠に由る以外に何等由る可きものはなからう。

二　肫肫其仁[1]。淵淵其淵[2]。浩浩其天[3]。──肫肫（じゅんじゅん）として其れ仁なり。淵淵として其れ淵なり。浩浩として其れ天なり。

註　1. 理想の人とせば如何に熱心なることよ！　2. 淵の如しとせば如何に深きことよ！　3. 天の如しとせば如何に闊きことよ！

三　苟不固聰明聖知達天德者。其孰能知之[1]。──苟も固に聰明聖知天德に達せる者にあらずんば、其れ孰（たれ）か能く之れを知らん。

註　1. 至誠の人。

3. All-embracing and vast, he is like heaven. Deep and active as a fountain, he is like the abyss. He is seen, and the people all reverence him; he speaks, and the people all believe him; he acts, and the people all are pleased with him.

4. Therefore his fame overspreads the middle kingdom, and extends to all barbarous tribes.[1] Wherever ships and carriages reach; wherever the strength of man penetrates; wherever the heavens overshadow and the earth sustains; wherever the sun and moon shine; wherever frosts and dews fall:—all who have blood and breath unfeignedly honour and love him. Hence it is said,—"He is the equal of Heaven."

CHAPTER XXXII. 1. It is only the individual possessed of the most entire sincerity that can exist under heaven, who can adjust the great invariable relations of mankind, establish the great fundamental virtues of humanity, and know the transforming and nurturing operations of Heaven and Earth;—shall this individual have any being or anything beyond himself on which he depends?

2. Call him man in his ideal, how earnest is he! Call him an abyss, how deep is he! Call him Heaven, how vast is he!

3. Who can know him, but he who is indeed

---

1. 蠻 is the general name for the rude tribes south of the Middle kingdom. 貉 is another name for the 狄, or rude tribes on the north. The two stand here, like 夷狄, as representatives of all barbarous tribes.

第三十三章　一　詩曰[1]、衣錦尚絅[2]。惡其文之著也[3]。故君子之道。闇然而日章。小人之道。的然而日亡。君子之道。淡而不厭。簡而文。溫而理。知遠之近[4]。知風之自[5]。知微之顯。可與入德矣[6]。——詩に曰く、錦を衣て絅を尚ふと。其の文の著るゝを惡むなり。故に君子の道は闇然として日に章かに、小人の道は的然として日に亡ぶ。君子の道は、淡にして厭はれず、簡にして文、溫にして理。遠きの近きを知り、風の自るを知り、微の顯るゝを知る。德に入るを與す可し。

　　註　1. 詩經國風の篇にあり、衞君の妃が淑女なるも夫君に愛せられざりしを民が悼んで作つたもの。　2. 私衣をその上に重ねる。　3. 其の華麗さの目立つを惡む。　4. 遠くにあると想はれるものが實は近くにあることを即ち治むべき國家は修むべき身にあることを知る。　5. 風はどこから吹いてくるか知つてゐる。茲の風は人を感化する德、その德風が何處から出て來るかを即ち自分自身から出て來ることを知つてゐる。　6. 斯う云ふ人は屹度德に入る。

二　詩云[1]、潛雖伏矣。亦孔之昭[2]。故君子內省不疚。無惡於志。君子之所不可及者。其唯人之所不見乎[3]。——詩に云ふ、潛まりて伏すと雖も、亦孔だ之れ昭と。故に君子は內に省みて疚

quick in apprehension, clear in discernment, of far-reaching intelligence, and all-embracing knowledge, possessing all heavenly virtue?

CHAPTER XXXIII. 1. It is said in the Book of Poetry, "Over her embroidered robe she puts a plain, single garment,"[1] intimating a dislike to the display of the elegance of the former. Just so, it is the way of the superior man to prefer the concealment *of his virtue*, while it daily becomes more illustrious, and it is the way of the mean man to seek notoriety, while he daily goes more and more to ruin. It is characteristic of the superior man, appearing insipid, yet never to produce satiety; while showing a simple negligence, yet to have his accomplishments recognized; while seemingly plain, yet to be discriminating. He knows how what is distant lies in what is near.[2] He knows where the wind proceeds from.[3] He knows how what is minute becomes manifested. Such an one, we may be sure, will enter into virtue.

2. It is said in the Book of Poetry, "Although *the fish* sink and lie at the bottom, it is still quite

---

1. The ode is understood to express the condolence of the people, with the wife of the duke of Wei, worthy of, but denied, the affection of her husband.

2. 知遠之近,—what is *distant*, is the nation to be governed, or the family to be regulated; what is *near*, is the person to be cultivated.

3. 知風之自,—the *wind* is the influence exerted upon others, the *source* of which is one's own virtue.

しからず、志(こころざし)に悪(にく)む無し。君子の及ぶ可からざる所は其れ唯人の見ざる所か。

註　1. 詩經小雅の篇にあり。　2. 淺瀨の魚はいくら潛つても見られてしまうの意で暴君治下の民を憫むだ詩。對子が斯く内省するのを此詩を引いて喩へたのは不適當。　3. 凡人が君子に到底及ばぬ所は君子が人の見ざる所に愼むことである。

三　詩云[1]。相在爾室。尚不愧於屋漏[2]。故君子不動而敬[3]。不言而信[4]。――詩に云ふ、爾の室に在るを相(み)るに、尚くば屋漏(こひわかみ)に愧(はぢ)ざれと。故に君子は動かずして敬し、言はずして信ず。

註　1. 詩經大雅の篇。　2. 自分の室に在る所をいつ見られても譬へば突然屋根の隙間から差し込む日光に照されてさへ恥づる所が無いようにせよ。屋漏は古代の支那では室の北西隅(一家中最も奥まつた部分)、今は日光を洩す一枚屋根。　3. 尊敬の念を催ふす。　4. 信實を尚ぶ念を起す。

四　詩曰[1]。奏假無言[2]。時靡有爭[3]。是故君子不賞而民勸。不怒而民威於鈇鉞。――詩に曰く、奏假(そうか)して言ふなく、時に爭ふこと有る靡(な)しと。是の故に君子は賞せずして民勸(はげ)み、怒らずして民

clearly seen."[1] Therefore the superior man examines his heart, that there may be nothing wrong there, and that he may have no cause for dissatisfaction with himself. That wherein the superior man cannot be equalled is simply this,— his *work* which other men cannot see.

3. It is said in the Book of Poetry, "Looked at in your apartment, be there free from shame, where you are exposed to the light of heaven."[2] Therefore, the superior man, even when he is not moving, has *a feeling of* reverence, and while he speaks not, he has *the feeling of* truthfulness.

4. It is said in the Book of Poetry, "In silence is the offering presented, and *the spirit* approached to; there is not the slightest contention."[3] There-

---

1. The ode appears to have been written by some officer who was bewailing the disorder and misgovernment of his day. This is one of the comparisons which he uses;—the people are like fish in a shallow pond, unable to save themselves by diving to the bottom. The application of this to the superior man, dealing with himself, in the bottom of his soul, so to speak, and thereby realising what is good and right, is very far-fetched.

2. The ode is the same which is quoted in ch. xvi. 4, and the citation is from the same stanza of it. 屋漏 was the northwest corner of ancient apartments, the spot most secret and retired. The single panes, in the roofs of Chinese houses, go now by the name, the light of heaven leaking in (漏) through them. Looking at the whole stanza of the ode, we must conclude that there is reference to the light of heaven, and the inspection of spiritual beings, as especially connected with the spot intended.

3. The ode describes the imperial worship of T'ang, the founder of the Shang dynasty. The first clause belongs to the emperor's act and demeanour: the second to the effect of these on his assistants in the service. They were awed to reverence, and had no striving among themselves.

鈇鉞よりも威る。

　　註　1. 詩經商頌の篇。 2. 商王は先祖の靈に供物を薦むる時に無言であつた。 3. 其の式に列つてゐた有司百官は王の無言に畏をなし一人も口論なぞする者がなかつた。

　五　詩曰[1]。不顯惟德[2]。百辟[3]其刑[4]之。是故君子篤恭而天下平。
――詩に曰く、顯ならざらんや惟れ德、百辟其れ之れに刑ると。是の故に君子は篤恭にして天下平なり。

　　註　1. 詩經周頌の篇。 2. 見せびらかさずとも誰にもそれと知れるものは德である。 3. ＝諸侯。 4. 則る。

　六　詩云[1]。予懷明德。不大聲以色[2]。子曰。聲色之於以化民。末也[3]。詩曰。德輶如毛[4]。毛猶有倫[5]。上天之載。無聲無臭[6]。至矣[7]。――詩に云ふ、予明德を懷ふ、聲と色とを大にせじと。子曰く、聲色の以て民を化するに於けるは、末なり。詩に曰く、德の輶きこと毛の如しと。毛は猶ほ倫有り。上天の載は、聲もなく臭もなしと。至れり。

　　註　1. 詩經大雅の篇。 2. 聲と色とを以て大いに見せびらかさぬ汝の明德を予は嘉みす。こゝの予は神、汝は文王を指す。 3. 孔子は大いに聲色を用ひぬ德と云つて德を賞めたのに不滿を感じ聲色は民を化するに役に立たぬと評した。 4. そこで孔子は更に文王の德を輕い毛に喩へた詩經の句を引用した。 5. 然し此の句も毛は比較を許すものであるとして孔子には面白くなくなつた。 6. 依つて孔子は殷を殲滅した天の事業を詩經が聲も無し臭も無しと歌つた句を取つて來て始めて滿足した。 7. それこそ至德である。

右第三十三章。子思因前章極致之言。反求其本[1]。復自下學[2]為己謹獨之事。推而言之。以馴致乎篤恭而天下平之盛。又贊其妙。至於無聲無臭。而後已焉。蓋擧一篇之要而約言之。其反

fore the superior man does not use rewards, and the people are stimulated *to virtue*. He does not show anger, and the people are awed more than by hatchets and battle-axes.

5. It is said in the Book of Poetry, "What needs no display is virtue. All the princes imitate it."[1] Therefore, the superior man being sincere and reverential, the whole world is conducted to a state of happy tranquillity.

6. It is said in the Book of Poetry, "I regard with pleasure your brilliant virtue, making no great display of itself in sounds and appearances."[2] The Master said, "Among the appliances to transform the people, sounds and appearances are but trivial influences. It is said in another ode, 'His virtue is light as a hair.' Still, a hair will admit of comparison *as to its size*. 'The doings of the supreme Heaven have neither sound nor smell.'— That is perfect virtue."

The above is the thirty-third chapter. Tsze-sze having carried his descriptions to the extremest point in the preceding chapters, turns back in this, and examines the source of his subject; and then again from the work of the learner, free from all selfishness, and watchful over

---

1. In the She-king we must translate.—'There is nothing more illustrious than the virtue *of the sovereign*, all the princes will follow it'

2. The '*I*' is God, who announces to king Wăn the reasons why he had called him to execute his judgments.

復丁寧示人之意。至深切矣。學者其可不盡心乎。——右第三十三章、子思前章極致の言に因りて、其の本を反求し、復た下學己の爲に獨を愼むの事自り、推して之れを言ひ、以て篤恭にして天下平なるの盛に馴致し、又其の妙を贊して、聲無く臭無きに至りて、而して後已む。蓋し一篇の要を擧げて之れを約言す。其の反復丁寧人に示すの意、至りて深切なり。學者其れ心を盡さゞる可けんや。

註　1. 子思は前章に於て自分の所論を聖人君子の極致に進めたから本章に於ては再び其本に歸つて之を論じた。　2. 初學者と同義。

himself when he is alone, he carries out his description, till by easy steps he brings it to the consummation of the whole empire tranquillized by simple and sincere reverentialness. He farther eulogizes its mysteriousness, till he speaks of it at last as without sound or smell. He here takes up the sum of his whole Work, and speaks of it in a compendious manner. Most deep and earnest was he in thus going again over his ground, admonishing and instructing men:—shall the leraner not do his utmost in the study of the Work?

|版權所有| 英和双譯支那古典全集
第三編　老子　大學　中庸　奥附

昭和八年二月六日印刷
昭和八年二月十一日發行

【定價金貳圓】

編註者　　清　水　起　正
編註者　　廣　瀬　又　一
發行者　　清　水　正　雄
　　　　　東京市神田區錦町三丁目九番地
印刷者　　佐　久　間　修　三
印刷所　　有　朋　印　刷　社
　　　　　東京市神田區錦町三丁目九番地

發行所　　二三子堂書店
　　　　　東京市神田區錦町三丁目九番地
　　　　　振替東京五三八一二番
　　　　　電話神田(25)二四〇五番

大取次店
東京堂・東海堂・北隆館・泰文堂・有精堂
大阪屋號・富貴堂・川瀬書店・三宅書店
柳原書店・福音社・菊竹金文堂

英和雙譯支那古典全集　全五卷

オックスフォード大學教授　ジェームズ、レッグ先生英譯〔清水起正
神學博士
貴族院議員　德富蘇峰先生推獎〔廣瀨又一 編註
東日大每社 寶

論語
全一函送料共
十五册錢一圓四十錢

世界全聖の隨一たる孔子七十年の生涯を貫く仁の主張と體驗とが實に人間生活の最高峰であり、その尊い文獻「論語」が人類道德の最高展望であることは言を俟たない。此の永遠的生命を有つ原文を邦文により訓註して足れりとせず、レッグ博士の英語の譯文及び詳註を加へたる本書が現代人の要求に非ずして何ぞ。

孟子
全一函送料共
十五册錢二圓四十錢

性善の原理、愛他の人道、仁義の政道を四方に唱道して、修身齊家治國平天下の大義を東洋民族の精華たらしめ、孔門々下に出藍の譽を擅にした王道萬能主義の開山高樹の大文字を邦文により訓註して足れりとせず、レッグ博士の英語の譯文及び詳註を加へたる本書が現代人の要求に非ずして何ぞ。

老子
大學
中庸
全二册料
一册錢二十圓

無爲主義の革命的大旆を道德界に押し立てゝ、絶對藥智廢學無愛を高調した氣宇雄大思想幽玄の老子、道德と政治の相對性的原理を說いて人倫の大本を闡明した大學、理想に偏せず俗に落ちずその中庸を力說した中庸を邦文により訓註して足れりとせず、レッグ博士の英語の譯文及び詳註を加へたる本の要求に非ずして何ぞ。

莊子
上下　各二
卷卷
錢十五圓
（未刊）

宇宙の不可解、人生の謎を解くに奇想天外より落つる底の比喩寓話を以てし、厭世的否定の人生觀から出發して超絕的人生觀に到達したる經緯を悲觀見るが如く說き去って何人をも愉絕快絕措く能はざらしむる莊子全卷を邦文により訓註して足れりとせず、レッグ博士の英語の譯文及び詳註を加へたる本書が現代人の要求に非ずして何ぞ。

www.ingramcontent.com/pod-product-compliance
Lightning Source LLC
Chambersburg PA
CBHW032102230426
43672CB00009B/1616